The Politics of Drug Control

Mandy Bentham

First published in Great Britain 1998 by
MACMILLAN PRESS LTD
Houndmills, Basingstoke, Hampshire RG21 6XS and London
Companies and representatives throughout the world

A catalogue record for this book is available from the British Library.

ISBN 0–333–72546–8

First published in the United States of America 1998 by
ST. MARTIN'S PRESS, INC.,
Scholarly and Reference Division,
175 Fifth Avenue, New York, N.Y. 10010

ISBN 0–312–21188–0

Library of Congress Cataloging-in-Publication Data
Bentham, Mandy.
The politics of drug control / Mandy Bentham.
p.   cm.
Includes bibliographical references and index.
ISBN 0–312–21188–0 (cloth)
1. Narcotics, Control of—International cooperation.
2. Narcotics, Control of—Government policy.   3. Drug abuse–
–Prevention—International cooperation.   4. Money laundering–
–Government policy—International cooperation.   I. Title.
HV5801.B427 1997
363.45—dc21   97–40095
                                                         CIP

This book is printed on paper suitable for recycling and made from fully managed and
sustained forest sources.

10   9   8   7   6   5   4   3   2   1
07   06   05   04   03   02   01   00   99   98

Printed and bound in Great Britain by
Antony Rowe Ltd, Chippenham, Wiltshire

To My Mother and Husband
with Love and Thanks

Contents

List of Figures

Acknowledgements

I would like to thank everyone who has helped and supported me throughout the research for this book. In particular, many thanks are owed to my PhD supervisor, Dr Peter Willetts, for his endless enthusiasm and encouragement. I would also like to thank my colleagues, David Humphreys, Peter Hough and Lewis Clifton of the Transgovernmental Relations Research Group at City University for their willingness to discuss and debate this work.

List of Abbreviations

AIDS	Acquired Immune Deficiency Syndrome
BCCI	Bank of Credit and Commerce International
BSA	Bank Secrecy Act 1971 (US)
BCP	Burmese Communist Party
CATF	Chemical Action Task Force of the Group of Seven
CCC	Customs Cooperation Council
CIA	Central Intelligence Agency
CMO	Comprehensive Multidisciplinary Outline of Future Activities in Drug Abuse Control (see Appendix A)
CND	Commission on Narcotic Drugs of ECOSOC
CORA	Coordinamento Radicale Antiproibizionista
CTR	Currency Transaction Report
DEA	Drug Enforcement Administration (US)
DIU	Drugs Intelligence Unit of Europol
DND	Division of Narcotic Drugs of the UN Secretariat
DPF	Drug Policy Foundation
DTOA	Drug Trafficking Offences Act 1986 (UK)
ECOSOC	Economic and Social Council of the United Nations
EDU	European Drugs Unit
EMNDP	European Movement for the Normalization of Drug Policy
FAO	Food and Agriculture Organization of the United Nations
FATF	Financial Action Task Force of the Group of Seven
FOPAC	Fonds provenant des activités criminelles
GATT	General Agreement on Tariffs and Trade
HIV	Human immune deficiency virus
HONLEA	Heads of National Drug Law Enforcement Agencies
ICDAIT	UN Conference on Drug Abuse and Illicit Trafficking 1987
ICAO	International Civil Aviation Organization

ICPO/Interpol	International Criminal Police Organization
ILO	International Labour Organization
IMO	International Maritime Organization
INCB	International Narcotics Control Board (UN)
MAG	Mutual Assistance Group of the European Community
MLAT	Mutual Legal Assistance Treaty
NATO	North Atlantic Treaty Organization
NORML	National Organisation for the Reform of Marijuana Laws
OECD	Organization for Economic Cooperation and Development
Pompidou Group	Co-operation Group to Combat Drug Abuse and Illicit Trafficking in Drugs
Swift	Society for Worldwide Interbank Financial Telecommunications
UNDCP	UN International Drug Control Programme
UNDP	UN Development Programme
UNFDAC	UN Fund for Drug Abuse Control
UNICEF	UN Children's Fund
UNIDO	UN Industrial Development Organization
UNITAR	UN Institute for Training and Research
UPU	Universal Postal Union
WFP	World Food Programme
WHO	World Health Organization (UN)

1 The Global Politics of Drug Control

INTRODUCTION

Unprecedented developments in world politics since the 1980s (the dismantling of the Berlin Wall, the ending of the Cold War, the dissolution of the Soviet Union, the ending of apartheid in South Africa and the signing of a Middle East peace agreement), have led to a growing number of other concerns emerging at the forefront of the international political agenda which demonstrate the complexity and interdependence of world politics. Environmental concerns such as global warming, rainforest depletion and pollution; human rights concerns such as increasing numbers of displaced peoples; and the control of disease such as Acquired Immune Deficiency Syndrome (AIDS), have led to increased international action across state boundaries and increased attention to international organisations that handle these concerns. The significance of this for the student of International Relations has been a re-evaluation of the orthodox view of international politics, exemplified by Hans Morgenthau, that the nation-state is the sole, principal actor in the international arena and that the dominant issue in international relations is the struggle for power.[1] This has led to an increasing interest in emerging alternative forms of transnational co-operation by International Relations scholars.

The concept of *international regimes* as 'sets of governing arrangements that affect relationships of *interdependence*'[2] has been developed predominately by the traditional Realist school of International Relations, to combat the challenge of interdependence and to explain the growth in new forms of co-ordination and organisation. However, in this approach, international regimes are created by states to further the state's interests, and are not expected to survive the demise of the hegemon under which they were created.[3] States are viewed as the dominant actors in the international system, but co-operation in the form of international regimes may be necessary to secure the optimal outcome under conditions of interdependence in some situations.[4] This writer believes that international regimes can and do influence behaviour and outcomes in the international arena independently of the wishes or needs of state actors. As Keohane says, 'If international regimes did not exist they would have to be invented',[5] but in order for the concept to be analytically useful we need to see regimes as having an independent impact on world politics through a synthesis of regime literature with the literature on issues, developed by writers such as Rosenau, Mansbach and Vasquez, and Keohane and Nye, from a more thorough use of the concept of interdependence. As James Rosenau states in *The Study of Global Interdependence*: 'Four characteristics seem salient as central features of all the diverse issues of interdependence.' They are highly complex and technical phenomena, involve non-governmental actors, have fragmented governmental decision-making, and necessitate multi-lateral co-operation for their management.[6]

The response to the drug phenomenon by those involved at the international, national and grass-roots level has been as if it were a single issue, with constant references to the 'drug problem' by policy-makers, the judiciary, the media, educationalists, and health organisations alike. The 'drug problem' clearly demonstrates the characteristics of interdependence as outlined above. This work attempts to set the 'drug problem', as it has become known, into a theoretical framework which aids our understanding of the phenomenon, by further developing theories of regime creation. In so doing, basic concepts used in regime literature need to be clarified. The literature on international regimes implicitly suggests that a regime must have an issue that it seeks to regulate. The concept of an issue, however, suffers from lack of clarification in current International Relations literature. This book will show that the 'drug problem' is too multi-faceted and multi-dimensional to be viewed as a single issue, as an analysis of the values and the stakes evoked will demonstrate.

How and why issues come on to the agenda, and how and why regimes are created from certain issues and not others, will be shown as different stages in the same process of agenda-building. A clearer understanding of values and norms, their evolution and role in international decision-making, is needed to give international regimes an independent impact in international relations and is also central for an alternative understanding of change in world politics. For the traditional Realist school, change in world politics is defined in terms of changes in state power, and the emergence of

regimes is similarly defined. An alternative approach to the emergence and role of international regimes challenges this established
belief by asserting that agendas are determined by the attempts of
actors to allocate values authoritatively on specific issues. Therefore new actors can be considered from both above and below the
state, and we do not just need to consider the state.

This chapter will attempt to set the drug phenomenon into an
initial theoretical framework within International Relations theory.
The usefulness of what are viewed as the two major competing
paradigms to explore the complexity of the multi-faceted and multi-
dimensional phenomenon will be examined. The presumption will
be that a regime analysis which emphasises the role of norms and
values in agenda-formation, rather than concentrating on rules and
decision-making procedures, is necessary for an understanding of
the drug phenomenon. The rigidity of the Cold War gave the discipline of International Relations an excuse for not taking into account
the advances, concepts and methods from alternative disciplines,
such as sociology, philosophy, anthropology, and history, with their
concepts of identity, values and community. In the study of drug
control, these disciplines have obviously a great deal to offer. The
connections between these disciplines and the discipline of
International Relations needs to be explored in order to understand and respond to the current changes in world politics.

INTERDEPENDENCE: ROSENAU'S FOUR CHARACTERISTICS

The technological and economic changes that took place during
the 1970s saw a swift response from International Relations theorists with the work on the concept of 'interdependence', credited to
Robert Keohane and Joseph Nye.[7] However, 'complex interdependence' as described in their book *Power and Interdependence,* consisting of multiple channels of communication, the absence of
hierarchy among issues, with military force playing a minor role,
did not so much rock the foundations of Realist orthodoxy as knock
politely on the door. Keohane and Nye restricted the use of the
concept by applying their work to economic issues, only offering
'complex interdependence' as an alternative to Realism when it
provides greater understanding of the nature of the issue in a particular situation, an area where Realist writers were willing to concede

to a development of their ideas to encompass the changing economic realities.

However, as Rosenau suggested in *The Study of Global Inter-dependence,* the restriction of the concept to economic issues and thereby merely adapting the Realist paradigm to changes in the real-world limits the usefulness of the concept. The concept of inter-dependence, when followed to its logical theoretical conclusions, giving non-state actors influence in world affairs, is a direct chal-lenge to the Realist paradigm. Furthermore a focus on issues and the interactions between actors, rather than the units themselves, and the idea of multiple issue-based systems rather than a single international system with each system featuring a unique cast of governmental, inter-governmental and non-governmental actors gives a more useful framework for an analysis of regime creation.

Global action on drug control clearly demonstrates the immedi-ate and increasing interdependence of world politics as understood by Rosenau, with the inclusion of non-state actors giving the term interdependence a greater meaning. As stated in the *United Nations Comprehensive Multidisciplinary Outline of Future Activities in Drug Abuse Control*:

> The value of NGOs and governmental agencies working together on complex national and international problems is nowhere more apparent than in the comprehensive long term effort to reduce illicit demand for narcotic drugs and psychotropic substances.[8]

The Geneva International Opium Convention of 1925 created the first international non-governmental body concerned with drug control: the Permanent Central Board.[9]

The drug phenomenon involves the participation of not only health, welfare and education groups on a domestic, national and inter-national level, but also private banks and insurance companies (con-cerned with drug-money laundering), the church, the mafia, and the drug barons. An indication of the extent of the influence that can be exercised by the drug barons is illustrated by the events following the assassination of the Colombian Justice Minister, Rodrigo Lara Bonilla, in 1984. The Colombian government's determination to end the drug-related violence and enforce the 1979 extradition treaty with the United States, forced several important traffickers to move with their financial assets from Colombia to Panama. As a result, the value of the dollar on the black market rose (to 140 pesos compared to the official rate of 100 pesos). In an attempt to negotiate their return to Colombia the traffickers released some of their funds back into the economy, and the dollar value on the black market stabilised.[10] Indeed the wealth and influence of the drug barons, particularly in South America, makes them dominant actors in any analysis of the drug phenomenon.

The drug phenomenon is multi-faceted and multi-dimensional. It is the concern of educationalists, sociologists, anthropologists, health workers, social workers, policy-makers, economists, the police and the judiciary. It also involves numerous departments of government, and challenges the orthodox view of the state as a unified and autonomous rational actor. Clashes in France between the Health Ministry, supporting improved public health care for French drug addicts, including a needle-exchange programme to reduce the risk of HIV infection, and the Ministry for the Interior pledging to crack down on drugs and apply systematic pressure on street traders and users, have seen addicts collect needles from the needle-exchange programme only to be picked up by the police and have the needles destroyed.[11] A similar complexity exists at the international level, as this study will demonstrate.

The drug phenomenon also challenges the orthodox view of the separation of domestic and foreign policy by International Relations scholars. On a recent drugs fact-finding mission to Colombia, it was the British Home Secretary, rather than a minister from the Foreign Office, who travelled to Colombia. The domestic effects of international drug trafficking can be seen to blur the artificial divide between what have been seen as two separate fields of study.

The drug phenomenon necessitates multi-lateral co-operation among governments. As with environmental concerns such as air and marine pollution, drug trafficking does not conform to political boundaries and cannot be controlled by a single state acting in isolation. Drug trafficking is now a problem which 'most governments can thus neither dismiss nor handle on their own' and is an example of the fourth characteristic of interdependence as described by Rosenau.[12] The Global Programme of Action, which was the product of the seventeenth Special Session of the General Assembly of the United Nations on 20 February 1990, stressed the need for collective action in combatting both drug abuse and illicit trafficking, stating that governments were not in a position to deal with this problem individually. The Secretary-General's opening statement to the Special Session said:

Drug abuse is now right at the top of the list of priorities requiring urgent attention from the international community. It is by
its nature truly international; and it demands a co-ordinated international response.[13]

With the collapse of international communism, the end of the Cold
War and the opening up of the former Soviet Union and the Eastern bloc countries, new markets and transit routes have been exploited by drug traffickers. The previously denied problem of drug
use in communist societies has been recognised, with a steady expansion in drug use in recent years.[14] No one country can hope to
isolate itself from such a transnational phenomenon, or hope to
solve its domestic 'drug problem' independently.

In his work on the structure of interdependence issues, Rosenau
states: 'Perhaps the most pervasive characteristic of all such issues
is the large degree to which they encompass highly complex and
technical phenomena.'[15] Furthermore, as Rosenau explains, most
of the issues 'overlap so thoroughly that proposed solutions to any
one of them have important ramifications for the others.'[16] The
drug phenomenon clearly illustrates these two points. As has already been stated, the drug phenomenon is a multi-faceted and
multi-dimensional problem and is too complex to be viewed as a
single issue. In order to understand the nature of international
regimes and the nature of issues, the linkages with other wider
issues need to be understood.

ISSUE-LINKAGE

The complexity of the drug phenomenon is illustrated by the diversity of the issues linked to drug production and usage. The drug
phenomenon is linked to environmental concerns such as deforestation, pollution, the destruction of ecosystems and the issues of
pesticide control. The destruction of the environment caused by
modern day coca-growing has earned the plant the title, the 'Attila
of Tropical Agriculture'.[17] In Bolivia the previously sparsely populated Chapare region saw an influx of coca-growers during the 1980s
which has led to huge environmental degradation. President Paz-
Estenssoro's Under-Secretary for crop substitution said that it constituted the greatest devastation in Bolivian history.[18] In Peru,
President Alberto Fujimori has described the drug trade as the
'number one enemy' of the Amazon rainforest.[19] The International

Narcotics Control Board Report of 1990 stated that: 'Coca bush cultivation threatens to alter the whole ecological balance of vast areas of the country.'[20] Deforestation has occurred from the slash-and-burn agriculture of the coca-producing peasants for actual coca plantations and also from the planting of subsistence crops such as cassava, bananas and corn for the workers. The estimated amount of land calculated to have been deforested, directly or indirectly, in Peru due to coca production is 700,000 hectares – about 10 per cent of the total deforestation in the Peruvian Amazon region during the twentieth century.[21] The recent expansion of opium poppy cultivation in Latin America and Colombia in particular, has led to the cutting and burning of large areas of virgin cloud forest to plant opium poppies.[22] It has been recently reported that, in Colombia, the area under illicit poppy cultivation has expanded to an estimated 18,000 hectares, thereby equalling the size of the area under illicit coca bush cultivation.[23]

Coca-growers use large quantities of pesticides and herbicides, which drain into rivers and cause pollution. However, it is the manufacture of cocaine that utilises the most harmful chemicals. Producers of cocaine in the Upper Huallaga Valley in Peru have polluted the valley's rivers with the kerosene, sulphuric acid, quicklime, carbide, acetone and other dangerous substances used in cocaine processing.[24] These rivers now exceed the pollution standards for fresh and inland water established by the World Health Organization (WHO).[25] The pollution of the rivers poses a threat to many species of fish, amphibians, aquatic reptiles, and crustaceans.[26]

Attempts to eradicate coca crops by law-enforcement agencies have led to the controversial use of herbicides such as paraquat (used extensively in Mexico and Colombia in the 1970s to eradicate marijuana) and gliphosate (used in Colombia in the 1980s). Both paraquat and gliphosate were found to destroy not only coca but other crops, and to cause numerous health problems, such as liver damage, to those living in the drug-producing regions. Fears concerning the danger to health of paraquat spraying in Mexico in the 1970s (and particularly its association with birth defects) led to the adoption by the United States Congress of the Percy Amendment, which made it illegal to support fumigation programmes in other countries.[27] It has been suggested, however, that the real reason for the temporary ruling (which was annulled in 1981) was concern over the amount of paraquat being ingested by smokers of marijuana in the United States, and not the environmental and health risks to those living in the drug-producing regions in Mexico. Despite reports of medical and environmental dangers, the United States government has continued to apply pressure on governments in Latin America to permit aerial spraying in crop-eradication programmes[28] and during the early 1990s increased the drug-budget proposal for the Agricultural Research Service.[29]

In 1988, environmental groups were successful in disrupting the Reagan administration's plans to implement coca-eradication programmes in Peru, using the herbicide tebuthurion (more commonly known as 'Spike'). Eli Lilly, the company responsible for Spike, refused to sell it to the Peruvian government for planned eradication programmes. Environmental groups stressed Spike's effects on the fragile tropical ecosystem in Peru: the destruction of endangered plant species, and the draining of chemicals into the Amazon, as well as the dangers to the health of farmers. The long-term significance of the use of environmentally unsafe chemicals to fight the drug war is especially serious since the regions which are targeted are often populated by the poorest segments of the population, often totally dependent on the land. According to Fagan, the intensive use of herbicides to eradicate illicit drug production in Latin America in the 1960s and 1970s caused high levels of herbicide poisoning with the accumulation of toxins such as DDT in humans, as well as in livestock and the entire food chain.[30]

The link between environmental issues and drug control is reflected in the participation of the United Nations International Drug Control Programme (UNDCP) in the United Nations Conference on Environment and Development, held at Rio de Janeiro, Brazil, from 3 to 14 June 1992. At the Conference, the UNDCP submitted a paper on the linkages between drug issues and environmental concerns, highlighting the cultivation of illicit drugs and the release into water sources of chemical products from cocaine and heroin processing, and pledging its support for Agenda 21.[31]

The failure of countries to comply with the United States administration's crop-eradication programmes has often resulted in a suspension of US aid to the country concerned. In July 1989, aid was suspended to Bolivia and US troops were sent to 'assist' anti-narcotics forces after the Bolivian government objected to chemical spraying. The relationship between the use of chemicals in the war on drugs, development and debt is a close one. As Andreas and Bertram note, 'US economic aid to the Andean nations is conditioned on co-operation in counter-narcotics efforts; US trade policy and loan approval through multi-lateral lending institutions are similarly linked to anti-drug objectives.'[32]

The drug phenomenon has been linked with questions of debt, development and the support for a New International Economic Order for countries whose economies are suffocated by the present economic order and who depend on the cultivation of coca and opium for economic survival. Heroin is reportedly funding Afghanistan's reconstruction after the destruction caused by the war, as refugees returning to their devastated villages need money to rebuild their farms and homes, and no crop is as financially rewarding as opium.[33] In many developing countries, the production and distribution of illicit drugs are major sources of employment and export earnings, as we will see in the next chapter. Latin American leaders have always seen the 'drug problem' as fundamentally an economic problem. The Peruvian President Alberto Fujimori, shortly after taking up office in 1990, rejected massive military aid packages from the United States, emphasising the need for an analysis of the 'global context' of the drug problem, alternative economic strategies and a political system permitting peasant participation.[34]

The revenue from drug production has led to increased incomes for peasants in countries such as Bolivia and Peru, and in some cases a strengthening of the position of peasant associations and workers' unions. In many cases the peasant unions are closely tied to the national labour movement. The increasing influence of the peasant agrarian unions (in which coca-growers have taken a prominent role) was reflected in the decision of Peru's then President, Alan Garcia, to attempt to introduce a peasant leader to President George Bush at the Drug Summit in Cartagena in February 1992.[35] As LaMond Tullis speculates, this may lead to increasing demand for social restructuring: 'illicit drugs may, where other avenues have failed, force the issue of such change before the close of the century'.[36]

The lack of economic development has been described as a core element of the Andean cocaine trade, and one possible anti-narcotic option would be to combine debt reduction and drug enforcement. An alternative anti-narcotic strategy would be for the United States to purchase portions of a country's debt on the secondary market and give it to them as a form of anti-narcotics assistance. MacDonald uses the example of Mexico as an illustration. If the United States brought $10 million of Mexican debt on the secondary market, where the value of the debt has an actual worth of under 50 cents for each dollar at face value, then officially $20 million could be utilised for investment in the country in a conversion of bilateral debt into local currency debt, with annual interest payments to be set aside for use in alternative development.[37]

Bolivia, approaching the problem as an economic one, is considering the industrialisation of the cultivation of the coca bush in order to export coca leaves and particularly coca tea, which they believe could become more profitable than cocaine production and would generate greater revenue than the country's gas exports to Argentina (in 1991 worth $214 million). In a formal statement at the 22nd Assembly of the Organization of American States in Nassau, Mr Ronald MacLean, the foreign minister, called for 'the legitimisation, industrialisation and commercialisation of the sub-products derived from the innocent coca leaf and its protein-rich and medicinal qualities'.[38] More recently, international attention has focused on cannabis production in Morocco, which has also been challenging the illegal status of the plant on the grounds that it is an important source of livelihood for thousands of peasants.[39]

A complex web of issues therefore exists which affects and is affected by the drug phenomenon. Questions of debt and development, the need to improve living conditions and prospects for the peasant growers are inextricably caught up in drug control policies in the Americas. As Kempe Hope describes,

> The cardinal aim of rural development is viewed not simply as agricultural and economic growth in the narrow sense, but as balanced social and economic development, including the generation of new employment; the equitable distribution of income; widespread improvement in health, nutrition, and housing; greatly broadened opportunities for all individuals to realize their full potential through education; and a strong voice for all rural people in shaping the decisions and actions that affect their lives.[40]

Concern with the displacement of peoples is also linked to the drug phenomenon and in turn is linked to environmental and developmental concerns. As has already been suggested, the migration of peasants to drug-producing regions in South-East Asia and Latin America throughout the 1980s can be seen as a challenge to the prevailing political and social structure of these countries. These migrations, often towards remote areas, frontier regions, forests and jungles, have partly replaced the earlier movements from rural to urban shanty towns and slums. This transfer of peoples has, however, resulted in damage to the environment as already described, and has also had effects on food production. The migration of labour to coca-growing areas throughout Latin America, but particularly in Bolivia and Peru, has led to a decline in food production due to increased labour costs, the result of a short-fall in labour and the lack of seasonal labour being available. In Peru, where nutrition data is available, this has led to a rise in the level of malnutrition among the poorest of the population since 1980.[41]

The war on drugs has also had the effect of encouraging large-scale militarisation in Latin America, which can be seen as threatening democratic control by fragile governments. This has led to large-scale violations of human rights and is closely connected to the growth of the infamous 'death squads'.[42] The United States administration has poured funds, training and hardware into co-operating with Latin American governments in the fight against drug trafficking. Most of the resources have been for the police and the military. The United States administration has been accused of assisting repressive right-wing regimes on the pretext of fighting the war against drugs.[43] Critics of the administration's drug policy see its main aim as the continuation of United States authority in the region, as established by the Monroe Doctrine and the 'not in my backyard' philosophy of the fight against communist encroachment during the period of the Cold War.

The Colombian military, for example, has been closely linked with right-wing death squads and assassinations, torture, disappearances, and sometimes mass murder. In September 1989, when George Bush, then President of the United States, declared an all-out war on drugs, the Andean Commission of Jurists in Lima published a critical report on the Colombian military called *Excesses in the Anti-Drug Effort*.[44] The strength of the military, due to United States resources, has also assisted other Latin American oligarchies, such as in Peru and Bolivia, in similar erosions of human rights and the repression of opposition groups, trade unions and church leaders. In November 1989, the killing of six Jesuit priests, their housekeeper and her daughter, drew attention to the human rights abuses of the Salvadoran military. Despite allegations that top military officers were responsible for the murders, United States funding for the Salvadoran military in the fight against drugs, which had been temporarily decreased by Congress, was restored by George Bush in late 1990.

The drug war has created a situation where the military can conveniently blame their own violence on the cartels. The cartels in response have claimed for themselves the role of the defenders of human rights. For example, in February 1991, the Medellin cartel claimed that the killing of the sister of a former presidential aide who had helped plan a large-scale anti-drug crackdown was in retaliation for human rights abuses against the Colombian people by the police.

The drug war has intensified anti-American sentiment in many developing countries and has undermined popular support for elected governments whose leaders are forced to co-operate with United States sponsored drug-control operations and to accept increased United States military aid. This discontent has enabled groups such as the Sendero Luminoso, or Shining Path, in Peru to gain support among the population as defenders of human rights against the abuses of the government-supported military and United States intervention.

Drug traffickers themselves are also abusers of human rights, with drug-related violence affecting the lives of millions of people throughout South-East Asia and Latin America in particular. Because of the large amounts of money involved in drug trafficking, developed and developing countries alike are suffering from the effects of the corruption of officials and institutions by drug traffickers, with the threat that this poses to the human rights of their citizens. After taking office in 1990, the Colombian President, Cesar Gaviria Trujillo, reaffirmed his government's resolve to fight drug trafficking, but emphasised that his government's highest priority was to end the drug-related violence rather than to combat international drug smuggling.[45] A United States report depicts the Peruvian dilemma:

> Peru considers drug trafficking its third priority. With a 6,000 per cent inflation, the economy is in shambles. Insurgents control portions of the country... Peruvian politicians have made statements that Peru can live with the narcotics problem for the next fifty years, but may not survive the next two years if the economic and insurgent problems are not dealt with now... The will to deal with the drug issues, when faced with problems that threaten the immediate survival of the country, remains the most difficult issue.[46]

The effect of the drug-related violence and corruption on developing and developed countries alike will be dealt with in the next chapter.

Attempts by law-enforcement agencies to control drug use in developed countries have also found themselves accused of infringing civil liberties through a broad range of measures, such as random searches based on police suspicions, aimed primarily at young ethnic minorities. In the UK there has also been a challenge that the law allowing the government to retrieve the proceeds of drug deals breaches the European Convention on Human Rights. Lawyers have argued that the Drug Trafficking Offences Act of 1986, which allows profits of crimes committed before the Act came into force to be confiscated, breaches Article 7 of the Convention: that no one convicted of a crime shall suffer a heavier penalty than was applicable at the time the offence was committed.[47]

Widely quoted in the debate over the infringement of human rights with regard to drug control is the work of the nineteenth-century philosopher John Stuart Mill. Mill believed that any attempt by the state to restrict the freedom of the individual to choose what he does was an illegitimate interference on the freedom of the individual and that

> His own good, either physical or moral, is not a sufficient warrant. He cannot rightfully be compelled to do or forbear because it will be better for him to do so, because it will make him happier, because, in the opinion of others, to do so would be wise, or even right.[48]

Many of the participants in the current debate favouring de-criminalisation of illicit drugs share Mill's philosophy, and their views will be explored in the concluding chapter to this book. Mill's work was widely quoted during the time of Prohibition in the United States. The rationale for the restriction of alcohol during Prohibition and the current restriction on certain drugs is still central to much of the current debate on drug control, as Chapter 3 on the nature of the values and the stakes involved in the drug phenomenon will demonstrate,

The drug phenomenon is also linked to a number of less obvious issues. During the 1970s and first half of the 1980s, the vast majority of cocaine and marijuana, and to a lesser extent heroin, was transported to its destinations around the world by ship. Since the transportation of the illicit drugs occurred along the same routes as legitimate trade and recreational vessels, efforts at interdiction have had a profound effect on the evolution of the law of the sea, in negotiation during the same period. As Andrew Anderson states, efforts at international drug control have had a major impact on the renewed salience of the need for consensus on the law of the sea, making it an area of the law with a 'new vitality, vibrancy and relevancy'.[49]

The above examples of the linkages of other issues with the drug phenomenon serve to illustrate the complex nature of issues and emphasise the necessity of reaching an understanding of issues by exploring the values and stakes involved, as the next two chapters will illustrate. The drug phenomenon affects different countries in different ways, since there are different stakes involved for different actors.

THE CHALLENGE TO REALISM FROM INTERDEPENDENCE

The Rosenau concept of interdependence as outlined above also challenges the traditional distinction between domestic and international politics in the Morgenthau analysis of international politics. Efforts to control drugs suggest the domestic and the international are inextricably linked. Indeed, with the case of the regulation of opium at the turn of the century, international legislation preceded national legislation, challenging another Morgenthau concept, central to the Realist understanding of agenda-building, that of the 'national interest'. Furthermore, as S. D. Stein notes, 'International considerations still impinge directly on domestic drug-control programmes.' According to Stein, the work of international bodies like the United Nations and the World Health Organization 'institutionalised the processes whereby the drug-control policies of one country are dictated by considerations that do not emanate from, or have a direct bearing upon, its own domestic situation at the time they are introduced.'[50]

The drug phenomenon challenges the Realist response to increasing interdependence and the creation of international regimes, that their concerns are of the 'low politics' type, i.e. issues that do not affect security and diplomatic prestige, do not involve the highest decision-makers in government, do not lead to crises and are not dominated by states, and that a new paradigm to understand and explain international politics is not needed. For the countries of Latin America, the problem of cocaine is intrinsically linked to their very survival:

The issues that will determine the fate of the region in the 1990s – foreign debt, economic crisis, civilian–military relations, human rights, democratization, and guerilla insurgencies – are being shaped by the politics of cocaine.[51]

As the next chapter will demonstrate, a social problem can affect security and prestige, involve the highest decision-makers in government and lead to crisis. The phenomenon can also help illustrate the irrelevance of the Realist high/low politics distinction to explain agenda-formation and change in international politics.[52]

The drug phenomenon also challenges the Realist concept of state sovereignty. As has already been stated, the drug phenomenon is such that no one country can deal with this multi-faceted and multi-dimensional phenomenon in isolation. Furthermore, the influence and organisation of the Colombian and Bolivian drug cartels have spread to a point where they are described in a United States Department of Justice Report as a state-within-a-state in Colombia and Bolivia, operating openly and with impunity.[53] The wealth of the drug barons through their illicit activities has enabled them to offer to pay their countries' national debt in exchange for immunity from prosecution, and in many cases the barons have private armies better equipped than the state's own military (see Chapter 2). Drug traffickers therefore have to be viewed as major actors in any analysis of the drug phenomenon.

THE GLOBAL POLITICS PARADIGM

An alternative approach to the traditional Realist school of thought is the paradigm variously known as pluralism, the multi-centric approach, issue-politics, or the term favoured by this writer, the Global Politics paradigm. The Global Politics approach attempts to synthesise the literature on interdependence (already introduced) and international regimes with the literature on foreign policy analysis (developed by Rosenau) and with the literature on transnationalism and international organisations (as developed by Mansbach and Vasquez). In this way the Global Politics approach or Globalism allows for a greater understanding of the dynamics of change in the ever changing area of world politics, whereas mere adaptions to an approach which emphasises anarchy and continuity cannot do so. In the Global Politics approach to International Relations, international regimes are central.

The concept of 'international regimes' was first introduced into International Relations literature by John Ruggie. In his 1975 article, 'International responses to technology: Concepts and trends', Ruggie defined a regime as 'a set of mutual expectations, rules and regulations, plans, organisational energies and financial commitments, which have been accepted by a group of states.'[54] A conference on international regimes held in 1982 led to the emergence of the now classical definition of international regimes as 'sets of implicit or explicit principles, norms, rules and decision-making procedures around which actors' expectations converge in a given area of international relations.'[55] Yet despite the almost universal acceptance of this definition, credited to Stephen Krasner, there has been little development on the conceptual ambiguity inherent in the definition, which this work has tried to clarify. Susan Strange's criticism of regime theory, a decade ago, as 'woolly' and 'imprecise', still applies to much of the current regime literature.[56] Krasner defines the four recognisable characteristics of an international regime as 'principles' – beliefs of fact, causation and rectitude; 'norms' – standards of behaviour defined in terms of rights and obligations; 'rules' – prescriptions or proscriptions for action; and 'decision-making procedures' as prevailing practices for making and implementing collective choice. These characteristics, however, are not clarified and are hard to differentiate conceptually – 'principles' blur values with facts, and 'norms' are difficult to distinguish here from 'implicit rules'. This ambiguity is not helpful in attempting to establish why international collaboration on an issue, in the form of an international regime, occurs in some areas and not others. Furthermore, the implicit linking together of rules (prescriptions or proscriptions for action) and decision-making procedures (prevailing practices for making and implementing collective choice) loses information concerning the importance of formal institutions for effective implementation of the regimes' norm-regulated rules, as Chapter 4 will demonstrate.

The Krasner definition suggests that 'values' and 'norms' are central to an understanding of the evolution of an international regime. As Krasner himself emphasises, 'Principles and norms provide the basic defining characteristics of a regime . . . Changes in rules and decision-making procedures are changes within regimes.'[57] Unfortunately, the concepts suffer from lack of clarification in the literature on regimes and the discipline of International Relations in general. This book will attempt to clarify and develop the reasons for the emergence of issues, values and norms in international politics in order to create a theoretical framework for an analysis of the drug phenomenon.

A similar confusion over terminology and use of concepts can be found within the area of drug control.

THE POLITICS OF SEMANTICS

> Words are, of course, the most powerful drug used by mankind.
>
> Kipling

The basic premise of the drug-control system is that a number of substances, decided by the World Health Organization, are harmful and dangerous and are therefore prohibited by the international system.[58] Under the Single Convention there are four schedules of controlled substances. Schedule I includes those substances having addiction-producing or addiction-sustaining properties greater than those of codeine and more or less comparable to those of morphine; those substances that constitute a risk of abuse greater than codeine or have a liability to abuse comparable to that of cannabis, cannabis resin or cocaine; and those convertible into substances having a liability to abuse comparable to that of cannabis, cannabis resin or cocaine. Schedule II includes substances having addiction-producing or addiction-sustaining properties not greater than those of codeine but at least as great as those of dextropoxyphene; or a substance convertible into a substance that constitutes a risk of abuse not greater than that of codeine. Schedule III contains those substances intended for legitimate medical use which have no, or negligible risk of abuse, and cannot easily be converted into a substance that has. Schedule IV, however, states that substances under this schedule are those which have strong addiction-producing qualities, or a liability to abuse not offset by therapeutic advantages which cannot be afforded by some other drug; and/or for which deletion from medical practice is desirable because of the risk to public health. Substances under Schedule IV are therefore also placed under Schedule I.

The categorisation of certain substances as illegal and others as legal (and some drugs as if they were not drugs at all, as in the case of alcohol – see later) is, however, not simply an objective, scientific exercise based on scientific facts, which the above implies.

Rather it varies from country to country, from culture to culture and from generation to generation. The main concern in England during the late seventeenth and early eighteenth centuries was the 'gin epidemic'. In the 1950s the problem was seen as heroin use; in the 1960s, particularly in the United States, the problem drug was LSD; in the late 1980s in the United Kingdom, glue-sniffing became a dominant concern. In the early 1990s, Ecstasy has taken over as the drug of concern in the United Kingdom and crack-cocaine is seen by many in the United States as being the dominant problem. In Russia, for the greater part of two centuries, the problem has been defined as the consumption of vodka; in Canada and Australia alcohol and solvent abuse among Native Americans and Aborigines has received widespread attention. In some cases, substances previously regarded as being perfectly harmless have been the focus for concern. A good example of this is the condition termed chatorpan, found among the Hindi-speaking people of western Uttar Pradesh in northern India. The substances of their 'addiction' are sweets and spicy snacks.[59]

Most drugs when first introduced to European society were thought of as negative and harmful to both the individual and to society as a whole, and serve to illustrate the changing values and concerns of society, as well as those of the ruling élite. Tobacco, coffee, chocolate and even the potato, when first introduced, faced opposition.[60] Tobacco was first smoked in Europe by a colleague of Christopher Columbus (nearly a century before Sir Walter Raleigh introduced tobacco from Virginia to the English Court), with the consequence that the Spaniard was tried by the Inquisition and sent to prison, since they believed that the Devil had entered him due to the exhalation of smoke. Soon after, however, tobacco became popular in the courts of Europe. But by the seventeenth century, James I of England was denouncing it,[61] as was the Chinese Emperor. In the Moghul Empire, smokers had their lips cut, and in Russia smokers faced execution. The introduction of coffee from Ethiopia to Egypt in the sixteenth century led to its ban, the burning of stocks, and the arrest of coffee drinkers. In the seventeenth century in England coffee-houses were treated with suspicion by the government as dens of sedition. Both tobacco and coffee proceeded to become well-established in European culture and yet the latter half of the twentieth century has again seen a shift in attitudes towards their consumption.

Recent changing attitudes towards alcohol consumption and

cigarette smoking in the West emphasise the changing salience of certain drugs for different generations. Thirty years ago smoking could be seen to be integral to adult social life, yet today in public places such as restaurants, cinemas and on public transport, the smoker is often now in the minority and even the outcast. In America, particularly on the West Coast, anti-smoking measures now cover vast areas of public life; smoking in all enclosed public places has recently been banned in France; smoking is restricted in public places in Canada and Australia; the British government is considering legislation to outlaw smoking in all public places and in the work-place; and Singapore is aiming to become the first smoke-free city.

The 1980s and early 1990s have seen a decrease in the potency of legal substances. Motivated in good part by health concerns, smokers are turning increasingly to lower tar and nicotine tobacco products, alcohol drinkers from spirits to wine and beer, with an increasing number of low-alcohol beers appearing on the market, and even coffee drinkers have turned to decaffeinated coffee in increasing numbers. The dangers to public health from alcohol consumption and cigarette smoking are well documented, and all of the health costs associated with the abuse of illicit drugs pale in comparison with those resulting from tobacco and alcohol abuse. Griffith Edwards, head of addiction research at the Institute of Psychiatry in London, stated that 'Only by the most wilful mytholo-gising can we maintain the myth that the dominant problem we are encountering with drugs results from illicit substances.'[62] The total cost of alcohol abuse to American society is disputable, but it has been estimated to be as high as $100 billion annually[63] and, in some European countries, at between 5 and 6 per cent of gross national product.[64] A recent report published in the United King-dom estimated that alcohol problems cost British industry £2 bil-lion annually.[65] Although alcohol is recognised as 'the most widely abused *substance* [emphasis added] in America' by the Office of National Drug Control in their strategy for a 'Drug-Free America', it is not viewed as a drug by the report, 'because it is not a con-trolled substance under the law'.[66] This dichotomy between alcohol and other drugs is a relatively recent phenomenon and owes little to the lessons of history, such as Prohibition, which treated alco-hol as a dangerous drug. The health costs of tobacco use are different but of similar magnitude. Cigarette smoking is the single greatest cause of preventable deaths in dozens of countries, and it is also indisputably linked to the premature deaths of millions of people each year. In the United States alone, an estimated 320,000 people die prematurely each year as a consequence of their consumption of tobacco. For 1984 it was estimated that cigarette smoking cost the United States approximately $54 billion.[67] By comparison, the figures associated with deaths from the use of all illegal drugs has been estimated at a fraction of this figure.[68] Yet despite this, alcohol and tobacco still remain, for many, the acceptable face of drug consumption.

The term 'drug' is commonly not defined in academic and policy-making literature. Policy-making literature refers to 'drugs', 'narcotics', 'psychoactive substances' and 'dangerous drugs' with little explanation of the reasons for the various terms. As with the understanding of the concept of an 'issue' and the lack of any rigorous academic use, there is a great difference between the medical or pharmacological and public perception of the term 'drug'. For the public the term has negative connotations, encouraged by the description of a 'war' on drugs, yet the use of the term is not based on any objective criteria.

The commonly used term 'narcotic drug' is defined by the 1988 United Nations Convention Against Illicit Traffic in Narcotic Drugs and Psychotropic Substances as 'any substances natural or synthetic in Schedules I and II of the Single Convention on Narcotic Drugs of 1961, and that Convention as amended by the 1972 Protocol Amending the Single Convention on Narcotic Drugs, 1961'.[69] The term 'narcotic' in the field of pharmacology refers to the sedative effects produced by a group of substances, mainly opiates and alcohol. However, the 1961 Convention (the keystone convention on drug control) considers as 'narcotic' such substances as cannabis, cocaine, stimulants and psychedelics, but not alcohol. Terminological confusion is added to by the fact that cannabis and heroin are listed in Schedule IV of the World Health Organization's classification of controlled substances. The position of cannabis in Schedule IV with heroin can be seen to be not because of its dangers, but because of its widespread recreational use and the fact that it has no medical use. The term 'narcotic drug', therefore, is used to define substances according to their legal status as socially disapproved substances rather than by any scientific criteria. All illegal drugs are included, with alcohol and tobacco excluded. Also excluded are the barbiturates and amphetamines and other substances that are frequently obtained both legally and illegally for illegal use.

Other key terms in the prohibition of certain drugs such as 'drug addiction' and 'drug abuse' elude clarification. In 1975 the WHO itself recognised that the term 'abuse' had been used within an arbitrary and non-scientific approach:

> Drug abuse is a term in need of some clarification ... The term is really a convenient, but not very precise way of indicating that (1) an unspecified drug is being used in an unspecified manner and amount ... and (2) such use has been judged by some person or group to be wrong (illegal or immoral) and/or harmful to the user or society, or both. What might be called drug abuse by some would not necessarily be considered so by others ... For these reasons, the term 'drug abuse' is avoided here.[70]

Despite this, WHO publications have continued to use the term. Whenever illegal substances are referred to in either WHO or UN publications, they are always referred to in terms of drugs of 'abuse'. As the United States' National Commission on Marijuana and Drug Abuse stated in their report entitled *Drug Use in America: Problem in Perspective*, this has the effect of 'rallying all parties to a common cause since no one could possibly be *for* abuse of drugs any more than they could be *for* abuse of minorities, power or children'.[71] The term 'abuse', then, has no functional use yet discredits the non-medical use of drugs suggesting medical authority for doing so.

The concept of 'addiction' has been used to justify strict legal and social control on illegal drugs and yet again there is no agreement on the term by those that use it. Sociologists speak of 'assimilation into a special life style of drug taking'. Doctors speak of 'physical dependence', an alteration in the central nervous system that results in painful symptoms when the drug is withdrawn; 'psychological or psychic dependence', an emotional desire, craving or compulsion to obtain and take the drug; and of 'tolerance', a physical adjustment to the drug that results in successive doses producing smaller effects and, therefore, in a tendency to increase doses. Statutes speak of habitual use; of loss of the power of self-control; and of the effects detrimental to the individual or potentially harmful to the public morals, safety, health or welfare. In 1957, the World Health Organization classified two types of drug dependence: 'addiction', that is, qualified by physical dependence and tolerance; and 'habituation', qualified by psychic dependence and no tolerance. These terms were replaced in 1965 by a definition which stated that:

> Drug dependence is a state, psychic and sometimes also physical, resulting from the interaction between a living organism and a drug, characterised by behavioral and other responses that always include a compulsion to take the drug on a continuous or periodic basis in order to experience its psychic effects and sometimes to avoid the discomfort of its absence. Tolerance may or may not be present.[72]

This suggests that almost everything we do, even the regular morning cup of tea, could be described as an addiction. Nine specific dependencies were listed and discussed: alcohol; amphetamines; barbiturates; cannabis; cocaine; hallucinogens; khat; opiates; and solvents. Yet there was no explanation of the reason for the inclusion of alcohol but the exclusion of tobacco. Although alcohol was officially included in the WHO classification of dependence-producing drugs, alcohol (and tobacco) have never been mentioned in any of the United Nations' drug control conventions despite universal global acceptance of their dependence-producing nature, and acceptance of the dangers to health associated with them.

The concept of drug addiction, or drug dependence as it is now referred to, suffers from a high degree of conceptual confusion and is indeed 'a monstrous tangle of social, psychological and pharmacological issues',[73] that is difficult for policy-makers to unravel. All types of illegal drug use are seen as equally dangerous and threatening and all levels of use are seen as equally dangerous and threatening, 'experimental first use, casual use, regular use, and addiction alike.'[74]

There is confusion within the expert community on the three major drugs that authorities seek to control: heroin, cocaine and cannabis. Although the dangers associated with acute and chronic consumption of heroin are on the whole not disputed, a variety of research has shown that although heroin is likely to be addictive it is not automatic. If taken in chemically pure form (unlikely with its present illegal status), consumed occasionally or on a regular basis, there are no adverse side effects other than mild constipation.[75] On this basis in the early twentieth century in the United States, opiates were used to treat alcoholism, since opiate addiction was seen to be a preferable condition to alcoholism by the medical profession when abstinence was not a realistic option.[76]

Similarly, as recently as the later half of the 1970s, cocaine was described as non-addictive and relatively harmless by numerous observers.[77] Although much of the current literature views cocaine consumption with considerable alarm, addiction to cocaine has been described as uncommon (but possible, particularly when used in 'crack' form) and studies have shown that it is rare for moderate use to lead on to heavy use. Among heavy users there is increased likelihood of heart attack, brain haemorrhage, liver damage, psychotic episodes, delusions and violent behaviour, and most recently, strokes, but use when controlled leads to few adverse effects. However, much of the research on cocaine use has concentrated on the crack-cocaine use in urban ghettoes, rather than the cocaine use that has been described as analogous to social drinking. Grinspoon and Bakalar go as far as to state that many Americans accept cocaine use as a 'relatively innocuous stimulant, casually used by those who can afford it to brighten the day or evening'.[78]

Perhaps the strongest example of the lack of scientific consensus, however, can be seen with cannabis use. On the one hand, researchers claim that cannabis causes harmful physiological effects,[79] and on the other hand, researchers claim that cannabis has few harmful effects.[80] The first reference to the question of the international control of cannabis was at the Hague Conference in 1912. However, it was not until the early 1970s that the Commission on Narcotic Drugs voted for a resolution strengthening control measures for cannabis, while again requesting a study of the medico-social aspects of cannabis use to be carried out by the Division of Narcotic Drugs. The study, according to the French delegate, 'would draw attention to the medical and social dangers of cannabis and would explain the reasons for its having been placed under international control by the narcotics treaties'.[81] The decision was made therefore to control cannabis use before scientific studies had been carried out, and based on 'preconceived ideas, beliefs and traditional value judgements imposed on the international bodies'.[82]

Cannabis was included along with heroin in Schedule IV of the 1961 Single Convention due to its 'addictive' nature, defined in terms of the 1957 WHO definition of 'physical dependence'. However, the addiction-producing properties of cannabis were 'not possible to assess' at that time, according to a WHO representative speaking at the XIV Session of the UN Commission on Narcotic Drugs, as has already been suggested. Furthermore, the 1965 WHO definition of 'cannabis-type dependence' (described earlier), stated that there was 'little, if any, physical dependence' associated with cannabis use. As Arnao notes: 'Paradoxically, the inclusion of cannabis in Schedule IV by the Single Convention was based on a WHO classification, which was latterly disproved by the WHO itself.'[83] The inclusion of cannabis in Schedule IV by policy-makers can be seen to be due to its wide recreational use and lack of medical use.

However, the use of cannabis for medical purposes has received widespread documentation. Its history as a western medicine lasted from the 1840s to the 1940s, during which period it was extensively used to treat a wide variety of diseases such as depressive mental conditions, and the muscle spasms of tetanus and rabies.[84] The use of cannabis for medical purposes has recently been the subject of some debate again in the United States and the United Kingdom. Patients suffering from a wide range of serious illnesses such as leukaemia, epilepsy and multiple sclerosis have claimed benefits from taking the drug.[85] It has been claimed that cannabis relieves the nausea associated with radiation and chemotherapy and can alleviate the pain in some victims of multiple sclerosis.[86] A side-effect of marijuana, its ability to boost the appetite, has increased the pressure to legalise the drug for medical use in the United States recently, led by America's AIDS activists. AIDS patients have used marijuana to stimulate their appetites, countering the deadly wasting that can be caused by the disease.[87] The use of the drug for patients suffering from glaucoma has been the subject of research since the 1970s. Glaucoma sufferers claim that it can lower the pressure within the eye, so avoiding the onset of blindness.[88] In 1989, the United States administrative law judge of the Drug Enforcement Administration recommended that marijuana could be legally available for such patients in the United States on compassionate grounds, but the DEA rejected the recommendations of its own judge to reclassify marijuana as a Schedule II drug, which would have made marijuana available on a prescription basis.[89] Judge Francis Young called marijuana 'one of the safest therapeutically active substances known to man' and argued: 'It would be unreasonable, arbitrary and capricious for [the] DEA to continue to stand between those sufferers and the benefits of this substance in light of the evidence in this record.'[90]

In order to utilise the possible medical benefits of cannabis, however, cannabis would have to be legalised, since it is unlikely that cannabis could ever be licensed. This is because the stringency of the drug trials and testing procedures would mean that it would be a risky investment for a drug company, since the chance of the company securing a licence at the end of it would be too small. Cannabis is also not just one drug but a myriad of chemicals which would take years to analyse.[91]

As the 'drugs problem' needs to be understood not as a single issue, but as an amalgamation of various issues, involving various values and stakes, so too is it important to understand and distinguish between the various illicit drugs, because their markets, problems and potential solutions differ. As has been demonstrated, it is not the chemical properties of the substances that policy-makers are interested in. Drug-taking is seen as challenging established values and established social norms. To sum up, drugs that are illicit are the problem; all drugs that are illicit are defined as equally problematic, and it is drug-taking itself which is seen as harmful, rather than its consequences. The seemingly scientific categorisation of drugs, and the rationale behind drug control, are based rather on the proscription of substances whose supposed effects on humans are by social norm and by law considered to be wrong. The evolution of these norms and values therefore needs to be explored.

THE STRUCTURE OF THE BOOK

As has already been emphasised, the 'drug problem' can be seen as not a single issue at all, but an amalgamation of a variety of separate issues involving various actors and various stakes in distinct issue-systems, within a similar context of what can be described as drug-related activity. The spread of Acquired Immune Deficiency Syndrome (AIDS) and measures to combat it; increasing use of illicit drugs among minors; money laundering by criminal organisations; the link of drugs to international terrorism and arms sales; the usurpation of government by cocaine barons in Colombia; the corruption of governments, are all concerns which would now appear to have the status of global issues, due to their importance on the international agenda and the increased international action over how best to combat them. Conceptually, these issues can be seen as separate, but behaviourally these concerns are seen as linked by policy-makers. Exploring the relationship between issue-systems and international regime analysis can help clarify the context under which an issue is regulated. However, the concept of regimes and the concept of issues both suffer from lack of clarification in International Relations literature.

Chapter 2, will therefore explore the scope and nature of the drug phenomenon and in so doing highlight the complexity of the nature of the issues. The International Relations literature on issues will be reviewed with the aim of understanding why international action on drug control has moved higher up the international agenda during the 1980s and early 1990s. Chapter 3 will explore the evolution of the values and stakes involved with international drug control during the nineteenth century in order to understand the nature of values and the evolution of issues on the international political agenda.

Chapter 4, in reviewing international co-operation to date on drug control, will propose that a single international drug-control regime is not possible, due to the multi-issue nature of the drug phenomenon. Furthermore, international consensus over the need to control global drug trafficking has only produced a weak regime. With a greater understanding of the evolution and nature of issues, a more thorough understanding of regime creation can be attempted in Chapter 4. Chapter 5 will show that in order for an issue to become regulated by the creation of an international regime, the process of contention over values must lead those for whom the issue is salient to a high level of consensus over an agreed norm on which the regime can be based. Chapter 5 will proceed to identify the norms in the international politics of drugs. Of the norms involved, it is the norm that 'Banks should not profit from criminal activity', concerned with the tracing, freezing and confiscation of drug-traffickers' assets, that can be seen most clearly to be regulated by a regime. The banking and finance issue-system can be seen to feature a high degree of consensus over this norm in order to protect the soundness and stability of banks, and an international regime has emerged to regulate the issue of money laundering. The evolution of this regime will be the focus for Chapter 6. Finally, the current debate concerning the legalisation of illicit drugs will be explored in Chapter 7 in relation to regime formation. Current pressures towards liberalisation of drugs policy emphasise the importance of understanding the dynamics of changing values, central to the author's approach to regime creation. Present concerns with the increase in drug trafficking, the scale of the profits generated and the internationalisation of organised crime have led many to reconsider current drugs policy. It will be shown that current enforcement practices towards drug trafficking are ineffective and unless the technology for preventing drug trafficking improves, the pressure towards liberalisation of current drugs policy will continue. It will be argued that an understanding of issues, in terms of contention over values, is central to the study of International Relations, contrary to the current Realist understanding of the nature of international politics as the struggle for power in an anarchic world.

CONCLUSION

The drug phenomenon is a complex and multi-faceted phenomenon which challenges the traditional Realist approach to International Relations to explain its complexity. This complexity requires precisely the issue-specific approach of international regimes as understood by the Global Politics paradigm. However, the clarification of key terms used in the literature on international regimes is necessary for an understanding of the emergence of international regimes that is not based on Realist hegemonic-power theory.

Within the field of International Relations there has been very little research done on the emergence of issues and the significance of values and norms in international politics. In attempting to understand the values and stakes involved in the drug phenomenon, a greater understanding of the phenomenon can be reached which does not ignore the lessons of history. As Zimring and Hawkins remark in *The Search for Rational Drug Control*, 'the immunity to historical evidence that characterizes the contemporary discussion of drugs in the United States is peculiarly pervasive'.[92] The same can be said of international drug control. In developing an understanding of value and norm emergence, issue dynamics and regime evolution can be explained.

2 The Scope and Nature of the Drug Phenomenon

INTRODUCTION

The last ten years has seen the wider availability and growing consumption of cheaper and more potent forms of illicit drugs, and increasing concern over how best to combat drug use by the international community. In the 1980s, the cocaine supply increased dramatically. Between 1947 and 1980, 35 metric tons were recorded as having been seized globally. During the three-year period from 1983 to 1985, 94 metric tons were recorded seized in the Andean region alone, the main coca-growing area in the world.[1] Due to over-production, cocaine prices were estimated by one United States report to have dropped by as much as 80 per cent by the end of the decade, and to have reached a level of production to satisfy four times the annual estimated cocaine market.[2] During the 1980s, the media and various international conferences focused on cocaine use, giving the impression that cocaine use was a relatively recent phenomenon. That this is not the case is illustrated by the next chapter, which shows how mass cocaine consumption first appeared in the early nineteenth century. The focus on cocaine has been fuelled by the media publicity given to the drug 'crack' and its association with inner-city use and increasing crime.[3]

This focus has also blurred the fact that there has also been a increase in heroin and cannabis production and consumption. The world's illicit opium production increased four-fold, from 990 tons in 1971 to 4,200 tons in 1989.[4] Illicit opium production in the main producing area of South-East Asia, the Golden Triangle, doubled in 1988/9, from the previous year's production, to some 2,000 tonnes, with a corresponding surge in opiate availability.[5] There has also been a diversification from cocaine production to opium poppy production in many Latin American countries. Opium production in Colombia has been estimated as equalling the size of the area under illicit coca cultivation.[6] The purity of heroin at the retail level in the United States, for example, has also increased significantly, averaging over 36 per cent compared with less than 10 per cent in the 1970s and early 1980s.[7] Cannabis is still the most popular illicit drug in Europe, Asia and Africa. New technologies for production have led to increased production and consumption patterns. Hydroponic equipment facilitates year-round cultivation of cannabis. This technology has also increased the potency level of the drug.[8]

Increases in technology have led to new, so-called 'designer drugs', such as 'Adam', 'Eve', 'China White' and most recently, and with most notoriety, 'Ecstasy'.[9] These synthetic drugs add a worrying new dimension to the drug phenomenon for governments and law enforcers since their production is relatively easy and inexpensive. They are synthesised from readily available chemicals, may be derivatives of pharmaceuticals, are very potent, and in addition are marketed towards youth culture. Little data or research is available on these synthetic drugs, and the international regulatory procedure is not able to respond swiftly enough to the increasing numbers of new substances requiring investigation and possible control. Recent international control efforts have focused on the need to control diversion of precursor chemicals used in the manufacture of these, and other illicit drugs, from European manufacturing and exporting countries to illicit channels in parts of Africa and Asia. Diversions are generally the result of deficiencies in the application of control measures in international trade.

All these developments have led to increasing concern within the international community over how best to combat illicit drug use, and to increased international action. In 1985, the Secretary General of the United Nations, Perez de Cuellar, took the unusual step of calling for a United Nations Conference on Drug Abuse and Illicit Trafficking.[10] This was followed by the creation of the Convention Against Illicit Traffic in Narcotic Drugs and Psychotropic Substances initiated by the government of Venezuela.[11] The Convention, known as the Vienna Convention, was the first United Nations drug control document in eighteen years and came into force on 11 November 1990. This was followed by a United Nations General Assembly Special Session, called for by the President of Colombia, which served to emphasise the importance of drug control on the international agenda, with the announcement of a United Nations decade against drugs.[12] In April of the same year, a World Ministerial Summit to Reduce the Demand for Illicit Drugs and to Combat the Cocaine Threat took place in London.[13] The drug phenomenon was also discussed in a large number of meetings of heads of governments: a summit of the Non-Aligned Movement, the Commonwealth, the Group of Seven industrialised nations, the European Council, and a regional summit where the heads of state of Colombia, Bolivia, Peru and the United States met together at Cartagena de Indias, Colombia, in February 1990, followed by a second meeting in San Antonio in February 1992.[14] This increase in international co-operation on drug control shows how the need to control the illicit use of drugs has increasingly been placed higher on the international political agenda. That this has come about is not merely due to an increase in drug consumption throughout the 1970s and 1980s, and its serious impact on human health, highlighted by the spread of AIDS, but rather as a reflection of an enhanced understanding of its adverse effects on political and economic dimensions of domestic and international security in an increasing number of countries. The international community has become increasingly aware of the inadequacy of previous multi-lateral treaties to deal with the new developments.

In order to understand why drug control has moved up the international agenda, a greater understanding is needed as to what constitutes an 'issue' in international politics. The drug phenomenon is a multi-dimensional and multi-faceted problem and cannot be analysed as a single issue, as it often is. This necessitates a re-examination of the issue-centred approach to politics offered by the Globalist paradigm, and inevitably necessitates a new approach to agenda-formation, one that is not dominated by hegemonic-power theory. Many Realist writers accept that there are issues on the international agenda other than the issue of power and security, but the significance of these new issues is limited, since they still view the struggle for security, optimised by the pursuit of power, as the dominant issue. In this context agenda-formation is based on power-as-capabilities, determining actors' abilities to put an issue on the agenda. Within the alternative Globalist paradigm a regime approach to understanding the evolution of co-operation in international relations is given a sounder theoretical footing by placing it firmly in an issue-centred paradigm. With this approach, the emergence of issues on the agenda is not dependent on Realist hegemonic-power theories. After the problems associated with drug use and drug trafficking have been outlined, this chapter will examine what we mean by an issue and how issues arise on the international agenda.

THE NATURE OF THE DRUG PHENOMENON

The drug phenomenon challenges traditional approaches to international relations since a social problem, drug-related activity, is seen as a threat to national and international security by many governments. The alliance of terrorist and insurgency movements with drug producers in the 1980s has been a significant development for international drug-control efforts. Insurgency groups have used drugs to fund their operations, directly or indirectly. In the coca-growing regions of South America, terrorist and insurgency groups have supported the cocaine trade in order to strengthen their political position and acquire funds, even though they may claim to be ideologically opposed to the drug trade itself. According to the United States State Department, during the 1980s there were clear connections between left-wing Colombian guerilla groups and drug traffickers despite the fact that many of the drug traffickers were ideologically to the right. The seige of the Palace of Justice in 1985 was seen as linking Colombia's drug barons with communist insurgency groups.[15] Press releases on the involvement of terrorist or insurgency groups with drug production have used the key term 'narcoguerilla'. It is said to have been introduced in 1984 by the US Ambassador to Colombia, Lewis Tambs, who had announced a successful raid on a jungle-based drug complex and had claimed that communist rebels had been guarding the facilities.[16] During the 1980s, according to the Peruvian government and United States State Department reports, the Maoist group in Peru, the Sendero Luminoso or Shining Path, established close ties to international narcotic traffickers and received arms and money in return for protection against law-enforcement authorities. One of the motives behind their involvement with drug production could be seen to be the desire to gain peasant support, by campaigning against the United-States-backed coca-eradication programme and United States involvement in the domestic affairs of the country.

In the Golden Triangle of Burma, China, Laos and Thailand, the opium trade has helped finance insurgency groups. In Burma, insurgency groups include those directly involved with the narcotics trade, such as the Shan United Army who are involved for profit motives, and the ideological revolutionaries such as the Burmese Communist Party (BCP), who use drugs to fund their political operations. Separatist terrorists in Sri Lanka are said to have become involved in drug trafficking in order to finance their arms and ammunition purchases. The United States-supported 'Contras' in Central America were repeatedly accused of links with drug traffickers, in order to supplement United States funds, with the full knowledge of the United States.[17] A link is also visible between insurgency groups and the drug traffickers in the Bekka Valley in Lebanon. Furthermore, these links between drug traffickers and terrorist or insurgency groups means that the trade in drugs and arms is becoming increasingly connected.

There are numerous examples of how drug production and the vast profits to be made from drug trafficking have corrupted the governments and the military of many countries throughout the world. In the early 1980s, government and military leaders in Bolivia were pre-eminent in the drug trade and the international narcomafia. Drug traffickers provided financial backing for the 1980 'cocaine coup' led by General Garcia Meza.[18] A 1989 United States State Department report noted that the corruption of the criminal justice system in Colombia was so complete that it was 'virtually impossible' to arrest and convict drug dealers or to do serious damage to their organisations.[19] The phenomenon is not confined to Central and South America. Drug corruption in Mexico has been described as 'endemic' and extending to the highest levels of the Mexican government. In Pakistan, the entire Pakistani Cabinet offered its resignation in December 1986 over riots in Karachi, orchestrated by the drug barons, to disrupt a police operation against powerful drug dealers. Important figures in the government were implicated as being involved in the drug-smuggling operations and the military was also implicated in the increasing heroin trade. The United States considered the Laotian government to be heavily involved in the production and export of heroin, or at the very least of condoning it, during the 1980s. After repeated allegations, beginning as early as 1983, over the involvement of the government of Cuba (with or without Castro's blessing) in the smuggling of illicit drugs into the United States, Castro finally acknowledged the problem within his government and had the principals tried and executed. The corruption of governments and the state by drug traffickers is clearly illustrated by the case of Panama, where the military and the very highest leaders were implemented in promoting off-shore banking and other facilities for Andean drug traffickers. The role of the Panamanian military in the laundering of what has been termed 'narcomoney', has led to the adoption of a new term, the 'narcomilitary state'.[20]

The drug phenomenon can be seen as a direct threat to the governments of drug-producing countries. Colombia in particular has experienced what has been called 'narco-terrorism', with an open war with the Medellin cocaine cartel declared by the drug traffickers. During the latter half of the 1980s, several prominent politicians, and over 3,000 military and police personnel, were killed or wounded.[21] Colombia has been in a state of seige for the greater part of the 1980s. The drug barons threatened the very heart of the Colombian judiciary by systematic threats and corruption which led to the virtual collapse of the judicial system in the latter half of the 1980s. The Medellin cartel declared a 'total war' against the government of Colombia after the major offensive launched against the cartel by the then President, Virgilio Barco Vargas, following the drug-financed assassination of the presidential candidate, Luis Carlos Gatan, in August 1989. The Colombian extradition treaty with the United States government, agreed in 1979, was overturned in 1987, leading to a nation-wide debate about how best to bring the traffickers, 'Los extraditables', to justice. Government negotiations with the leaders of the cartels, such as Pablo Escobar Gaviria, were described by senior officials at the time as being akin to a 'pact with the devil'.[22] However, negotiations led to the surrender of many leading drug barons and Colombia seems to be entering a new stage in its attempts to control drug-related violence.

The influence and organisation of the Colombian cocaine cartels during the 1980s had spread to the point where they were described in the 1989 United States Department of Justice Report as a state-within-a-state in Colombia, operating openly and with impunity. As Rensselaer W. Lee III states, 'Drug barons today are major political forces in countries such as Bolivia, Colombia and Peru, carving out states within states in coca-producing regions.'[23] The estimated world-wide financial transactions in cocaine for 1986 exceeded the reported 1984 gross domestic product of 88 of the world's market economies, including Argentina, Belgium, Indonesia, Nigeria, Pakistan, the Philippines and Turkey, making the drug traffickers very wealthy men.[24] The 1989 Kerry Commission Report estimated that the Colombian drug cartels earn $8 billion annually, and *Forbes* magazine listed Colombian cartel leaders Ochoa and Escobar as among the richest men in the world. The drug barons and traffickers can therefore afford huge private armies that are often better equipped than many countries' official military forces, as in Colombia. The incredible wealth generated by illicit drug trafficking has meant that cocaine barons have even spoken of using their financial power to take over countries, and have challenged governments to participate in a contest for state power.[25] In Bolivia in the early 1980s, the drug trafficker Roberto Suarez Gomez offered to pay off two-thirds of Bolivia's foreign debt (then at $3 billion) in cash, in exchange for immunity to run his cocaine business.[26] Their wealth has also been used to provide some of the traditional facilities that a government usually provides: hospitals, educational facilities, clinics and sports plazas; and Escobar had reportedly constructed more public housing in Medellin than the government itself. In Burma, Khun Sa, one of the opium warlords of the Golden Triangle, has held press conferences to boast of his huge wealth. It is alleged that the Thai government negotiated with Khun Sa to enable the government to import wood from the territory under Khun Sa's control, because Thailand has depleted its own forests. In exchange the government have reportedly offered immunity from arrest for Khun Sa while on Thai soil.[27] This incredible wealth, and the influence it provides, makes the drug barons major political actors in the area of drug control and challenges the Realist concept of 'state sovereignty'.

A great deal of research has been done on the importance of the drug trade to the economies of many developing countries, and for Latin American countries in particular. Cocaine is deeply integrated into the economies of Peru, Bolivia and Colombia. Its production employs thousands and supplies much needed export earnings for the governments. In Peru an estimated 110,000–186,000 of the adult work force are employed directly by the production of the drug. In Bolivia the figure is estimated at 350,000–400,000 (or approximately 7 per cent of the population), and in Colombia approximately 300,000 were estimated as employed in drug production in 1988. The revenue generated by coca production has been estimated at $1 billion a year in Peru, and approximately $1.5 billion in Bolivia and Colombia.[28] Once in the financial system, the huge amounts of money generated from cocaine production can be used to meet many foreign exchange needs, including servicing the countries' foreign debt. Cocaine has been estimated at providing from 20 to 30 per cent of Peru's foreign exchange and well over 50 per cent for Bolivia in 1989.[29]

This challenge to the stability of governments by illicit drugs is not confined to producer countries, but also affects the traditional consumer countries of the developed world. The demand for drugs has been linked by governments to increasing crime rates, seen as increasingly threatening to the domestic security of developed countries. However, since the source of illicit drugs is primarily international, their control becomes a part of a government's foreign policy. The threat to security posed by illicit drugs was recognised as long ago as the early 1970s. In 1971 Nixon was the first United States President to declare a 'War on Drugs'. Drug abuse was described as a 'national emergency', and drugs as 'public enemy number one' needing a 'total offensive'.[30] The effect of the war, the successful eradication programmes, for example in Turkey, and the destruction of long-established trafficking networks, was to disperse production and consumption around the world, making control more difficult. The war can be seen to have had the effect of breaking up the established drug trafficking network between Turkey–Marseilles–New York into smaller and less detectable routes, and moving production from established areas to new areas, particularly into the Third World. For the first time, First World drug users were connected to Third World producers. Another effect of the war was to encourage the diversification of traffickers into other substances. The cost of drugs such as cocaine and heroin also increased in price in the United States due to the success of Nixon's programmes, making the profit margins that much more attractive for traffickers and encouraging further trafficking operations. As McCoy and Block note, 'America's first attempt at an international solution had, over the long term, compounded the problem'.[31]

In October 1982 President Reagan announced the start of the current 'War on Drugs', which was taken up by his successor, George Bush. In 1989 William J. Bennett, then head of the Office of National Drug Control Policy, declared:

> The source of the most dangerous drugs threatening our nation is principally international. Few foreign threats are more costly to the U.S. economy. None does more damage to our national values and institutions and destroys more American lives. While most international threats are potential, the damage and violence caused by the drug trade are actual and pervasive. Drugs are a major threat to our national security.[32]

Attempts by governments to control the distribution and use of illicit drugs can therefore be seen to destroy another tenet of the Realist approach to international politics, that there is a clear divide between domestic issues and domestic politics, and international issues and international politics. Charles Rangel, Chairman of the House Select Committee on Narcotics Abuse and Control, stated that,

> If Colombia falls [to the drug cartels], the other, smaller, less stable nations in the region would become targets. It is conceivable that we would one day find ourselves an island of democracy in a sea of narcopolitical rule, a prospect as bad as being surrounded by communist regimes.[33]

The control of illicit drugs, once seen as an issue far removed from the 'high politics' of government, has become the United States' highest diplomatic priority in relations with Colombia and a vital component of United States relations with Latin America in general.

The 1980s attempts to control drugs differed from previous ones by the scale of the resources allocated, and by the use of the military. George Bush consistently reaffirmed his commitment to further escalation of the war on drugs throughout the late 1980s. Specific mention of drugs in his inaugural address, direct United States military involvement in the invasion of Panama in December 1989, the consideration of plans for a battle fleet off the coast of Colombia, the sending of millions of dollars' worth of military equipment, and the dispatching of the Green Berets to Peru, have all confirmed this. Deploying the armed forces of the United States to assist drug enforcement operations necessitated, in 1981, the repeal of the 1878 Posse Comitatus Act, which restricted military involvement in federal law enforcement. The militarisation of the war on drugs deployed not only the armed forces in interdiction exercises, but also the Central Intelligence Agency (CIA) in the supplying of intelligence about foreign drug sources, and the National Aeronautics and Space Administration (NASA), in carrying out satellite-based surveillance of illicit drugs under cultivation. During the period 1989–1990 there was a steady expansion of the role of the United States military along its borders and overseas, and intensified pressure was put on other governments in the hemisphere to assign a greater role to their own armed forces in combating drug trafficking.[34] In mid-September 1989 Secretary of Defence Richard Cheney declared that 'detecting and countering the production and trafficking of illegal drugs is a high-priority, national security mission' for his department.[35]

The recent political and economic changes in Central and East European countries have resulted in a substantial increase in the

movement of peoples, goods, services and capital within and outside Europe. This has resulted in a corresponding increase in drug
trafficking and drug use in Europe. With the emergence of free-
market economies in the former Eastern bloc, the manufacture,
export, import, domestic trade and distribution of pharmaceuticals
in Eastern Europe, previously monopolised by the state, were now
in the hands of hundreds of new manufacturing and trading companies. The nascent democracies are also experiencing an upsurge
of crime and corruption, providing opportunities for well-organised
criminal networks, which profit from illicit drug trafficking. European concerns in the late 1980s and early 1990s have therefore
focused on fully integrating the former USSR and Eastern bloc
countries into the European and international drug control system.

Within Western Europe, the implementation of the Single European Act allows in principle for persons, goods, services and capital to move more freely within the Community. The signing of the
Schengen Convention in 1990 by eight of the Member States of
Europe, with Greece signing in 1993, is a move towards the abolition of frontier controls. However, the United Kingdom, the Irish
Republic and Denmark remain outside the Schengen Group. The
outside borders of the Community are feared by some as becoming the only barriers for drug traffickers to penetrate. Significantly,
drug seizures have also increased, suggesting that the amount of
trafficking has also increased. In 1992, 4.5 tonnes of heroin were
recovered in Europe, as against three tonnes in 1991, cocaine seizures increased by 42 per cent in the first half of 1993, and cannabis seizures increased from 80 to 91 tonnes.[36]

The European Community has recently focused its drug-control
efforts on combatting drug-money laundering. Close co-operation
has been achieved throughout the Community with various financial institutions in efforts to tighten the regulation of financial institutions and to prevent the utilisation of the banking system and
financial institutions for the purpose of laundering drug money.
The Financial Action Task Force (FATF) was set up in July 1989
in Paris by the heads of state or governments of the Group of
Seven industrialised countries, and the President of the Commission of the European Communities, with the aim of fighting money
laundering.[37] A European Economic Community Directive, adopted
in June 1991, obliges all Member States to introduce measures against
the use of the financial system for money laundering.[38] France has
made it mandatory for financial institutions to make a declaration

whenever they have reason to believe that funds stem from drug trafficking. In Germany, new legislation has been enacted to close the loopholes that have been used by traffickers to re-route into legal channels proceeds from illicit activity. Switzerland has seen the abolition of the traditional anonymous money deposits in Swiss banks. In 1991, the Swiss Criminal Code contained the specific offence of money laundering and a general obligation to identify the customer as well as any possible beneficial owner of the funds. Luxembourg has also amended its laws on money laundering, but only for funds that have been tainted with drug-related activity. Austria, Italy, Spain and the United Kingdom have also enacted similar legislation.

The scale of crime and public disorder associated with drug use and trafficking has led many European countries to dramatically rethink their attitude to drug control. High-level public officials in several European countries have called for the debate to be opened on the decriminalisation and legalisation of not only marijuana, but also cocaine, heroin and other illicit drugs. In the United Kingdom, senior police officers have spoken out in favour of some form of legalisation, as have a national newspaper, a prestigious magazine, members of the judiciary, and a senior economist. In Spain, eminent judges and lawyers, including law professors from half of Spain's universities, have been campaigning to legalise the sale of drugs, as part of an alternative approach to Spain's serious problems with drug use and trafficking; Spain is now the major point of entry for cocaine from South America and cannabis products from northern Africa destined for Europe. In Italy in 1993, in an attempt to control the increasing mafia-related crime, one of the eight separate referendums was concerned with de-penalising personal drug use. Chapter 7 of this work will explore further the current debate on the legalisation of drugs.

The threat posed to European countries is a perceived threat to national stability and security, due to the link of illicit-drug distribution to international criminal networks, such as the Hong Kong Triads and the Japanese Yakuzas (see later). The defining of the non-medical use of certain drugs as a criminal act has allowed the growth of the largest criminal enterprise ever seen. Estimates of the annual turnover from the drugs trade vary enormously due to problems of collecting data. Because drugs are illegal, criminals, terrorists or insurgency movements can gain large profits from the various stages of production and marketing. Drugs profits have become by far the largest single source of revenue for organised crime in developed countries (see Chapter 6). This increase in crime and instability has led many European countries to begin to re-evaluate their drug-control programmes. Switzerland and the Nether-lands are frequently cited as archetypal of this alternative approach, providing drug users with their chosen narcotics in an attempt to drive the criminal traffickers out of business.[39]

All the above examples serve to illustrate the fact that the drug phenomenon affects different countries in different ways, highlighting the complexity of the phenomenon. Different governments have different stakes to preserve. In Colombia, the concern for the govern-ment is centred on ending the mafia violence or narco-terrorism, 'the principal threat against [our] democracy', rather than on end-ing the cocaine trade itself.[40] In Peru and Bolivia the dominant issue facing the governments is the threat from the insurgents, often allied with the coca-growers. In Peru the alliance of the Sendero Luminoso with the coca-growers presents a difficult dilemma for the government. Destroying coca production allies more and more peasants with the guerillas. In 1990, President Fujimori suspended the United-States-supported anti-cocaine enforcement programme for fear that it would further strengthen the guerilla insurgency led by Sendero Luminoso. Similarly, the government of Thailand has also been wary of moving against some of its poppy-growing peasants, remembering that it was an earlier destruction of opium fields that allowed communist guerillas to infiltrate and win over many hill tribesmen to an anti-government position.[41] Competing stakes for the Peruvian government meant that in March 1990 two separate missions of United States helicopters carrying Peruvian anti-drug police were fired upon by army soldiers. Similarly, in June 1989, a Bolivian navy detachment shot at helicopters carrying Bo-livian anti-drug police and United States Drug Enforcement Agency advisers.

The traditional consumer countries of the developed world see drug trafficking as a threat to their security in relation to the rising cost of crime and social unrest associated with illicit drug use. Furthermore, the increase in the laundering of profits made from the increasing sales of illicit drugs, and recent financial scandals involving drug money, such as the Bank of Credit and Commerce International (BCCI) affair, threaten the economic stability of de-veloped countries, as will be discussed in Chapter 6. For the tra-ditional producer countries, drug trafficking threatens to undermine political and judicial systems in several countries, and forms an integral destabilising component of the economies of several countries. There is also concern that the drug trafficking–insurgency connection will increasingly enable terrorist groups to force their agendas onto governments. The domestic political reaction therefore can be seen to be due to the problems of stability and security, resulting from increased trafficking and from the link between drugs and crime. The international agenda has subsequently been affected accordingly.

THE INCREASE IN DRUG TRAFFICKING

From the 1950s onwards there has been a steady increase in drug trafficking due to a number of factors, as will be outlined briefly below.

Increasing communications between regions and increased transport links with regular flights, for example between South America and Spanish cities, and between the United States and Sicily, have facilitated consumer–producer links. The report of the United Nations International Narcotics Control Board for 1990 cites how new air services linking Angola, Nigeria, and Mozambique with South America have led to an increase in illicit drug trafficking in these countries. Furthermore, the increase in tourism world-wide has spread the problems related to the use of drugs. In Sri Lanka the increase in tourism has led to an increase in the use of heroin among young people.[42] Increasing communications have contributed to increased migration flows, with large diasporas of some ethnic groups now residing in strategic parts of the world, whose blood ties have been utilised by traffickers in the formation of illicit networks.

In Viet Nam, changes in its economic system have resulted in an increase in the movement of both peoples and goods, both within the country and in neighbouring countries. This has led to drug traffickers targeting it as a source of illicit drugs, as a transit route (due to its proximity to the Golden Triangle) and also as a potential market. More recently, the abolition of many of Europe's customs posts (particularly among the signatories of the Schengen Convention) and the promotion of free trade has led to increased movement of peoples and an increase in illicit drugs available. Similarly, reports have been made of Colombian drug cartels setting up factories, warehouses and transport companies in Mexico to exploit the flood of cross-border commerce expected under the North American Free Trade Agreement, which is awaiting endorsement.[43]

The increasing migration flows between countries, and the collapse of economic barriers are often due to increasing economic growth. Economic growth has led to expanding markets in countries such as Japan, Germany and the former Eastern bloc countries, such as Poland. The increase in commerce between China and Hong Kong and Macao has led to increasing movements of heroin across China's southern borders.[44] The opening up of the former Eastern bloc countries has led to new markets, where non-convertible currencies had previously meant that there was little profit to be made by drug traffickers. Greater freedom of movement and economic growth has allowed Italian mafia groups to buy up sectors of the new economies, in order to launder drug money.[45] In 1985, the Balkan heroin route from Czechoslovakia, Yugoslavia, Romania and Bulgaria via Turkey accounted for an estimated quarter of all the heroin reaching Western Europe. It has been estimated to have increased by 70–80 per cent in 1990.[46]

One of the most significant factors in the increase in drug trafficking has been the involvement of organised criminal groups, beginning with the mafia in the 1950s in the United States. Since drugs are an illegal activity, vast profits can be made from their distribution. Some large multi-national illicit drug distribution organisations existed as early as the 1930s. The 'French Connection' between refiners, traffickers and producers in Marseilles and Turkey supplied heroin to the United States from the 1930s until 1973.[47] Today the main competitors are the Japanese Yakuza,[48] the Chinese Triads,[49] the Colombian cartels,[50] the Mexican mafia[51] and the Sicilian mafia.[52] With the fall of the Berlin Wall and the collapse of communism, the former Eastern bloc has become accessible to Italian and Colombian mafia groups. Mafia groups have also been reported to have been working together in unprecedented co-operation in order to expand their businesses. There have been reports of the Italian mafia signing deals with underworld gangs in the former Soviet Union to set up a global ring in narcotics and nuclear-weapon materials.[53] South American and western European organisations have used each other's routes in a joint venture to smuggle cocaine to Europe and heroin to North America. Seizure data also shows linkages being established between South-East-Asian traffickers and criminal organisations elsewhere.[54] The increase in the use of the western and northern sub-regions of Africa as transit countries for cocaine from South America has seen a corresponding increase in the activities of European and South American criminal organisations in the region.[55]

The present international economic order, debt, falling commodity prices and poverty can be seen to have helped pave the way for increased drug production in the traditional producer countries of the developing world. According to United Nations analysts, the decline of prices for commodities between 1980 and 1988 (sugar by 64 per cent, coffee 30 per cent, cotton 32 per cent and wheat 17 per cent) meant that farmers turned to cash crops like the coca bush and the opium poppy for economic survival. Furthermore, the export of illicit drugs often took up the slack of foreign exchange reduced by falling prices for agricultural goods as well as for minerals, including tin (down by 57 per cent in the 1980–1988 period), lead (28 per cent), crude oil (53 per cent) and iron ore (17 per cent).[56] In July 1989, the 74-nation International Coffee Organisation's price maintenance system collapsed and coffee prices halved. Coffee is Colombia's largest legal export, and accounted for about one-third of Colombia's total exports. Before the collapse of the coffee agreement, Colombia had been producing 10–12 million 60-kilogram sacks per annum. Until the price collapsed, a Colombian farmer could earn almost as much from growing coffee as from growing coca bushes.[57] A 1990 United Nations Drug Programme study quotes potential incomes per hectare per year in Peru from possible coca substitutes such as cocoa ($1,615), coffee ($1,114), palm oil ($833), and rice ($885) using the best available technologies, compared to $4,500 per hectare (in 1985) for cultivating coca.[58] A similar discrepancy between prices for legal produce and for illegal coca exists all over the Andean region of Latin America.

Throughout the 1980s, the economy in Peru was in a serious state of decline, with an external debt of approximately $18 billion by the end of 1988.[59] President Alan Garcia angered international bankers by limiting debt repayments to 10 per cent of export earnings (no exports, no payments). The country quickly became capital starved and, since relations with international creditors were poor, money from cocaine production, or 'narcodollars', provided some respite. Garcia stated that those demanding drug control should be aware that 'the only raw material that has increased in value is cocaine' and that 'the most successful effort to achieve Andean integration has been made by the drug traffickers'.[60] He challenged the current economic order, and the emphasis of the international community on controlling drug production, by stating 'it is an equally grave crime against humanity to raise interest rates, lower the prices of raw materials and squander economic resources on technologies of death while hundreds of millions of human beings live in misery or are driven to violence'.[61]

In Bolivia, from 1981 to 1982, the GDP contracted by more than 9 per cent; inflation soared from 123.5 per cent in 1982 to 11,750 per cent in 1985; and unemployment tripled to 20 per cent by 1985.[62] Tin, natural gas and to a lesser extent oil, were Bolivia's natural exports. The collapse of the buffer-stock operations of the International Tin Council in October 1985 and the 1986 downturn in oil prices had a dramatic effect on the economy of the country, which was already struggling. By the mid-1980s, a complex web of drugs, economic development problems, external debt, and political instability had brought Bolivia to the edge of a crisis. A former finance minister explained, 'Bolivia has gone from the economy of tin to the economy of coca. If narcotics were to disappear overnight, we would have rampant unemployment. There would be open protest and violence.'[63] Similarly, the expansion of the coca trade into Venezuela, Ecuador and Chile in the late 1980s can be seen to be due to declining economic conditions.[64]

The relationship between decreasing economic conditions and the increase in drug production is not only illustrated by Latin American countries. The cuts in the United States sugar quota system in the 1980s, for example, have been advanced as a key force in pushing farmers in Belize and Jamaica out of sugar and into marijuana cultivation.[65] There has been also been an increase in drug trafficking in many parts of Africa in recent years, with the global economic recession combined with severe drought, famine and civil war as major contributing factors, according to an International Narcotics Control Board report.[66] Large quantities of heroin from South-East and South-West Asia are being routed through African cities for distribution on illicit markets in other parts of the world. Countries in the western and northern sub-regions are increasingly being used as transit countries for cocaine from South America.[67]

For many producer countries in the developing world, the problems associated with attempts to control drug production are inextricably linked to the problem of economic development and to the question of trade rights. A 1991 report by the International Narcotic Control Board stated that 'It is axiomatic that if programmes designed to provide alternative income possibilities for growers of narcotic crops are to succeed, marketing opportunities and fair export prices for such alternatives must be established.'[68] The report suggests that other governments should take note of the actions by the European Economic Community to include Bolivia, Colombia, Ecuador and Peru into its preferential customs system for a number of agricultural and industrial products.

The increase in illicit drug trafficking since the 1950s has come about due to the increasing interdependence of peoples and economies and an increase in economic growth and markets. The development of the current economic order, and the involvement of national and international criminal organisations, has led to the fact that trafficking groups have succeeded in making available increasing amounts of illicit drugs, in particular cannabis, cocaine, and heroin, virtually anywhere in the world.

PROBLEMS TO CONTROL

Throughout the latter half of this century drug trafficking has increased, despite increasing international action through the main international control body, the United Nations, and other international institutions to prevent it. The success of United Nations efforts since the 1940s, (12 multi-lateral treaties in all) has been limited in controlling the problem. There are many difficulties involved in attempts by a legal structure to control an illegal activity.

Initial United Nations attempts focused on supply reduction, as emphasised by the keystones in United Nations drug control, the 1961 Single Convention on Narcotic Drugs, as amended by the 1972 Protocol, and the 1971 Convention on Psychotropic Substances.[69] The combination of crop-eradication and crop-substitution programmes, financial inducements and punitive measures against growers have met with mixed success. There are many obstacles in attempting to control supply. Coca leaves, which provide the alkaloids from which cocaine is derived, grow on bushes on a wide range of soils. The coca plant can be grown in virtually any subtropical region of the world that receives between 40 and 240 inches of rain per year, where it never freezes and where land is not swampy or waterlogged. In South America, this comes to approximately 2,500,000 square miles, of which less than 700 square miles are currently estimated as being used to grow coca.[70] In the proper climate, therefore, coca bushes will grow on soils so infertile as to be unsuitable for any other cash crop. Coca bushes also mature sufficiently in three years for the leaves to be picked from three to six times annually, which is an excellent cash-cropping pattern. Also, after the bushes have matured, little cultivation is required. Cannabis can be grown year-round if water resources are sufficient, and hydroponic equipment also facilitates year-round cultivation and increased potency. Opium can be grown in a wide variety of locations. The opium poppy stores well, does not spoil, can be grown in high terrain, can be grown without fertiliser or much irrigation, and can be harvested without machinery. Now some developing countries also have the technology to do their own refining.[71]

Problems of trying to control supply also involve problems with the identification of illicit cultivation. It is often difficult to locate illicit drugs, especially with regard to coca production in and near the Andean region, in the remote areas and in mountainous terrain. In places the drugs are also grown interspersed with other plants, which makes locating and eradicating them more difficult. In 1989, for example, less than 1 per cent of Peruvian and Bolivian coca products were interdicted.[72] The areas are also difficult to control for law-enforcement agencies. The eradication of illicit drugs, in a small number of cases, poses problems that are not only practical in nature. In some areas, eradicating production would be environmentally damaging. In the Chu valley in Kazakhstan, cannabis is the only plant which grows in the sand. Its immediate eradication would result in an ecological disaster, transforming the valley into a desert.[73]

The drugs phenomenon is mutable in form, changing over time. Suppression of one form of production, one form of traffic and one pattern of drug abuse leads to the emergence of others. In the late 1970s, under pressure from the United States government, the relatively successful attempts by the government of Colombia to eradicate marijuana production led to the expansion of the production in Mexico. When the United States put pressure on Mexico to eradicate production, crop cultivation rapidly increased in the United States, where domestic production now fulfils over one-third of demand.[74] When the Turkish authorities clamped down on the illicit cultivation of opium poppies in the 1960s, drug-producing organisations shifted production to the Golden Triangle region of South-East Asia and to the mountainous regions on both sides of the Afghanistan–Pakistan border. More recently, new growing areas of Ecuador and Brazil have seen a shift from cocaine to opium and marijuana production, due to successful government programmes aimed at the eradication of cocaine. Illicit opium-poppy cultivation is also increasing in Guatemala.[75] In Colombia, the area under illicit poppy cultivation has expanded to an estimated 18,000 hectares, thereby equalling the size of the area under illicit coca-bush cultivation.[76] Ironically, the dismantling of the Medellin cartel handed much of the business over to the competitive Cali cartel, described as 'the most powerful criminal organisation in the world', and seen as a greater threat to security by law-enforcement authorities.[77] Furthermore, drug trafficking activities have dispersed to neighbouring countries, such as Bolivia, and throughout the continent, thereby exacerbating drug control efforts.

Methods of transporting the drugs from producer to consumer countries are also flexible and difficult for law-enforcement agencies to control. The effective implementation of the United States National Air Interdiction Strategy forced drug traffickers to abandon private aircraft as the favoured mode of transporting cocaine into the United States and to resort to other, more complex, modes of smuggling, such as commercial maritime cargo concealment.[78] Many recent cases of drug smuggling have involved individual 'swallowers', who carry the drugs inside their bodies, often in condoms, while travelling on commercial airlines. In this form a 'Nigerian Connection' for heroin traffic appeared in the early 1990s and has reportedly taken control of as much as 40 per cent of the heroin market in the United States.[79]

Most drug-enforcement authorities have focused their efforts on combatting trafficking in heroin and cocaine. Less attention has been given to the world-wide trafficking in psychotropic substances that have similar abuse potential. Increased action is required in this area in the light of evolving seizure data regarding amphetamines, MDMA and LSD. Trafficking in, and abuse of, stimulants and sedative hypnotics are widely occurring in Africa, Asia, Latin America and also Europe and North America. The diversion of precursor chemicals for illicit drug production, is also increasing. In one recent case, large quantities of a precursor were exported from a European country to a Latin American country where it was used to manufacture MDMA, a Schedule 1 psychotropic substance. The product, in tablet form, was registered with the Ministry of Health as a slimming pill and exported to North America, where it appeared on the illicit market as 'Ecstasy'. Effective implementation of the provisions of the Vienna Convention to prevent diversion of precursors requires adoption by governments of practical control methods. The establishment of the Chemical Action Task Force (CATF) by the Group of Seven major industrialised countries went some way towards trying to combat the situation.[80]

The ever-increasing new 'designer drugs', referred to at the start of this chapter, are a growing problem for drug-control agencies to regulate. Designer drugs are substances intended for recreational use, and have been modified from legitimate pharmaceutical agents in order to circumvent legal restrictions. The legal definitions of drugs on the controlled substances list are often very narrow, both in order to enhance the strength of cases brought in the legal system, and in order not to unduly inhibit or discourage legitimate chemical and pharmacological research. The challenge for regulatory and law-enforcement authorities is to keep pace technologically with new screening techniques capable of detecting a wider variety of chemical substances, as well as more sensitive methods that can detect these drugs and their metabolites at the nanogram and picogram level.[81] The production and sale of designer drugs has been estimated to be a million-dollar industry.

These new developments emphasise how illicit-drug production and consumption patterns cannot be separated. The traditional divide between producer and consumer countries is no longer valid. Consumer countries now produce illicit substances such as designer drugs, and there has been a steady increase in consumption patterns among the traditional producer countries. The availability and abuse of cocaine is expanding in many traditional producer countries, such as in South and Central America. The smoking of coca paste mixed with tobacco or cannabis (basuco and pitillo) is the most frequent form of drug use in countries such as Bolivia, Colombia and Peru. Drug use amongst children has reached alarming proportions in many urban areas, particularly in Brazil.[82] This again emphasises that different countries face different and often changing problems with regard to controlling drug supply. Despite this, the United States administration has continued to emphasise supply-reduction policies. Seventy per cent of the 1991 anti-narcotic budgets went on supply-reduction programmes.[83]

During the 1980s, however, a new focus emerged, emphasising control of the demand for illicit drugs and a high level of international consensus against drug trafficking. The 1988 United Nations Convention Against Illicit Traffic in Narcotic Drugs and Psychotropic

Substances and the World Ministerial Summit to Reduce the Demand for Illicit Drugs and to Combat the Cocaine Threat both
emphasised the necessity to attack drug-trafficking and the vast
profits to be made. The United Nations, which has been through
the decades at the forefront of drug control, has not the necessary
authority to deal with this emphasis on drug-trafficking control and
the focus on traffickers' profits. In its present form it has no authority
to implement global enforcement and policing powers, nor has it
the authority to deal with banking regulation and traffickers' assets.
The United Nations drug-control bodies are also under-staffed and
under-funded to deal with the situation, as we will see in Chapter 4.
Drug control in a state setting implies the participation of many
branches of governmental machinery: those organs concerned with
public health, education and social welfare, the judiciary, law
enforcement, economic affairs, and also research and academic
bodies and non-governmental organisations. In the United States,
only two of the twelve federal government departments do not have
a role in the drug war, with at least twenty-five agencies having a
mandate and committing resources. Co-ordinating the activities
of these agencies is therefore a difficult task. At the international
level, similar complexities are faced in efforts at international co-
operation, particularly within the United Nations system. International
co-operation is dispersed, which creates difficulties for policy co-
ordination. Furthermore, the total annual expenditure of the
United Nations, in the drug-control area, was approximately $37m
in 1988–1989 (0.5 per cent of the regular budget), which equals
just over 0.007 per cent of the estimated level of the world's illicit
trade in 1989 ($500 billion), or only 39 minutes' turnover in the
trade.[84]

Lack of success by the United Nations, in combatting the spread
of illicit drugs, can be seen to be due to a number of factors. Drugs
are the archetypal free-market commodity: as has been discussed,
they are easy to produce, easy to transport, easy to conceal and,
due to their illegality, have a high added value at each stage of the
trading chain. *The Economist* notes, 'The drugs trade is a fine speci-
men of unrestricted competition, which efficiently brings down prices
and pushes up consumption.'[85] In 1987, for instance, the price of
coca leaves sufficient to produce one kilogram of cocaine was between $500 and $750. As coca paste, it was worth from $500 to
$1,000; as cocaine base, from $1,000 to $2,000. After processing in
laboratories, the kilo of cocaine would be worth between $3,000

and $6,000. Once exported to the United States, it would be worth
$14,000–21,000 at the wholesale level, and more than ten times
that price, between $160,000 and $240,000, at the retail level (where
it would be diluted with other substances).[86] The focus on supply
reduction has yielded unimpressive results. In some cases, such as
in Latin American countries, efforts have had far-reaching consequences in terms of threatening social order and stability. Efforts
to control trafficking routes have led simply to diversification by
traffickers, from one method of transportation to another, and from
one region to another. Attempts to eliminate patterns of drug use
have led to the emergence of new, often more potent and more
dangerous varieties of drugs. The international community has been
slow to respond to the advent of these new designer drugs, which
helps to illustrate how complex differing interests and perspectives
are on the phenomenon of drug control. In the past, three clearly
identifiable groups have emerged with regard to international co-
operation on drug control: consumer countries, producer countries,
and transit countries. Today, countries do not fit neatly into any of
these categories. Most producer countries are also consumer countries, most consumer countries are also transit countries and most
transit countries are also consumer countries. Also, traditional producer countries relate the drug problem to the wider problem of
economic development (especially in Latin America), whereas traditional consumer countries are more concerned with the role that
illicit drugs play in the increase in domestic and international crime,
and the increase in money laundering. Lack of success in combatting the spread of illicit drugs can be seen in part to be due to the
conceptualisation of the drug problem as a single issue, as the problem is too disparate to be viewed in this way.

DRUG CONTROL AND ISSUE-POLITICS

Attempts to control illicit drugs by the international community
date back to 1909,[87] but as has been demonstrated, the drug phenomenon has recently acquired new characteristics. The increase in
trafficking and the associated large amounts of money to be made
from the activity have become a threat to the political and economic dimensions of domestic and international security of nearly
all the countries of the world. The size and complexity of the international drug phenomenon, involving environmental, health,

education, crime and development concerns, as discussed in Chapter 1, means that it must be viewed not as a single issue. Rather, it is an amalgamation of a variety of interconnected, but separate issues. For the purpose of this book a disaggregation of what is often conceptualised as an 'issue' is needed. The current 'drugs problem' can be seen not as a single issue at all, but as an amalgamation of a variety of separate issues, involving various actors and various stakes, in distinct issue-systems, within a similar context of what can be described as drug-related activity.

The undeniable growth in transaction flows, the recognition of international actors other than states, the disaggregation of the state, the blurring of borderlines between national and international politics, and the increasingly minor role of military force in the international system since the 1970s, have all been subsumed under the Keohane and Nye concept of *interdependence*.[88] Two key concepts have emerged from this literature:

1. The concept of *international regimes*, predominantly explored by Realist writers in the face of the challenge from interdependence.
2. The concept of *issues* forming distinct *issue-systems* governing behaviour within a state of interdependence.

Previously the two concepts have been developed principally in isolation, and have both suffered from lack of clarification. To develop a theoretical framework for an analysis of drug-related activity this section will attempt to clarify and develop the concept of an 'issue', in order to prepare the way for a more thorough understanding of the emergence of international regimes.

THE INTERNATIONAL RELATIONS LITERATURE ON ISSUES

For Realists, all issues in international politics are dominated by the struggle for security, which is optimised by the pursuit of power. For Realists, an issue reaches the international agenda through the power of a state putting the issue on the agenda, or through changes in the balance of power transforming the agenda. Despite this emphasis on states and power, Realists have acknowledged the existence of transnational relations in an ever-increasing interdependent world, and accommodate it within their theory of international relations. Issues are classified into either 'high politics' issues or 'low politics' issues. Issues of high politics affect security and diplomatic prestige, involve the highest decision-makers in government, may lead to crisis, and are dominated by states. Low politics consists of economic, social, technical or environmental issues, involves government bureaucrats (if it involves governments at all), is handled routinely, and may be dominated by transnational actors.

An alternative view, advocated by the Globalists, is that *all* issues may affect security, involve the highest decision-makers, produce crises and be dominated by governments.[89] As we have seen, the drugs phenomenon does affect the security, or perceived security, of several countries, involves the highest decision-makers in government and has led to crisis, particularly in the case of several Latin American countries. On 15 February 1990, the Presidents of Colombia, Bolivia and Peru met with the President of the United States in Cartagena de Indias, Colombia, to review co-operation with respect to drug control. The issue for the United States administration was viewed as important enough for the President himself to attend the meeting.[90] In order to understand the nature of issues and their emergence onto the international agenda without the Realist high/low power politics structure, the concept of issue *salience*, developed by the Global Politics paradigm, will be used.

For the Globalists, debate on interdependence has led to the acceptance that there is not a single international system, as understood by the Realists, but rather, multiple issue-based systems, with each system featuring a unique cast of governmental, inter-governmental and non-governmental actors. The actors in a Globalist system are those for whom the issue is relevant and important. Stated more formally, 'One issue is more salient than another issue, for a specific political actor, if it is perceived by that actor to be of greater priority for the optimisation of the actor's own set of value preferences.'[91] Therefore, the salience of an issue will vary from one actor to another and may vary over time. The advantage of the concept is that it does allow for actors other than governments to be included in an analysis of change in the global system. However, the concept of issues and their formation into issue-systems first needs to be clarified. This involves a clearer understanding of the concept of an issue than is currently the case.

TERMINOLOGICAL CONFUSION

The concept of an 'issue' is central to the paradigm approach variously known as pluralism, interdependence and transnationalism, the multi-centric approach or, the term favoured here, globalism. Writers such as Rosenau, Mansbach and Vasquez, Willetts, Keohane and Nye, have all written with the implicit theoretical assumption that we can recognise distinct 'issues' on the global agenda. Despite this, an authoritative theoretical literature defining the concept of an issue remains elusive. Indeed, Rosenau's initial work in the area, his article on 'pre-theories' (1964) and later, *The Scientific Study of Foreign Policy* (1971) do not even include a definition of what is understood by an 'issue'.[92] Rosenau's work sought to bridge the artificial divide between domestic and international politics, seeing different levels of analysis, (local, national and international politics) as forming horizontal systems, cross-cut vertically by what he termed 'issue-areas'.

Rosenau, in *The Scientific Study of Foreign Policy*, defines an issue-area as consisting of:

> (1) a cluster of values, the allocation or potential allocation of which (2) leads the affected or potentially affected actors to differ so greatly over (a) the way in which the values should be allocated or (b) the horizontal levels at which the allocations should be authorized that (3) they engage in distinctive behaviour designed to mobilise support for the attainment of their particular values.[93]

Rosenau stated that there were only four types of issue-area to be considered: 'status area', 'human resources area', 'territorial area' and 'non-human resources area'. From this typology, Rosenau hypothesises that conflict over Berlin and conflict in Princeton, New Jersey, since they were both located in the territorial area of his typology, would generate different types of behaviour from the three other types.

The later work on issues by Mansbach and Vasquez, *In Search of Theory*, at first seems entirely compatible with the Rosenau work. Mansbach and Vasquez describe an issue as follows:

> It is the perceptions of contenders concerning the way in which these various proposals about stakes are related that shape issues. Proposals that are seen as related (either because actors con-

sciously claim they are or behave as though they were) are perceived to constitute an issue ... stated more formally: *An issue consists of contention among actors over proposals for the disposition of stakes among them.*[94]

However, the two definitions are not compatible. Rosenau clearly states that an issue-area consists of *many* issues. Issue-areas are described as persistent and general, whereas issues may be temporary and situational. Mansbach and Vasquez, however, take Rosenau's definition of an issue-area to be a definition of an issue. In fact, Rosenau's description of the differences between actors over the allocation of values leading to mobilisation of support refers to the concept of an issue, and the cluster of values generating distinctive behaviour was the basis for defining how different issues may be categorised into a common issue-area. The concept of an issue-area, as used by Rosenau, is not useful because it encompasses two concepts, the idea of concrete political processes that produce the relationships, as well as the idea of abstract values. However, for a clarification of the term 'issue', the idea that there is both an ideological (perception) and behavioural aspect to the term needs to be clarified.

The work of Keohane and Nye, writing a decade later, shows how much confusion was generated from the above work. Whereas Rosenau talked about issue-areas as an area to be conceptualised at a high enough level of abstraction to encompass a variety of vertical systems, Keohane and Nye equate issue-areas, from this description, as consisting of aggregations of Rosenau's vertical systems, or the term favoured by this writer – issue-systems. As Keohane and Nye explain in *Power and Interdependence*, 'When the governments active on a set of issues see them as closely interdependent and deal with them collectively, we call that set of issues an issue-area'.[95]

The use of systems analysis in political science was pioneered by David Easton. For Easton a political system is 'any set of variables selected for description and explanation'.[96] Furthermore, if a system can be conceptualised wherever one can identify interdependence or behaviour modification in a given area of consideration, then this is in line with the Mansbach and Vasquez concept of an issue as 'contention among actors over proposals for the disposition of stakes among them'. The concept of issue-systems is more analytically useful than the term issue-area, because it need not

evoke the behavioural processes that Rosenau associated with the
term issue-area. We can instead concentrate attention on the contention over values of the actors concerned. The Keohane and Nye
definition of the term 'issue-area' represents common academic usage
of the term 'issue' in International Relations theory, but it takes
little theoretical footing from the original Rosenau work.

The much overlooked work of Mansbach and Vasquez, in concluding that Rosenau's typology of issue-areas was not useful, but
agreeing with Rosenau's emphasis on the tangibility of issues, can
help explain the nature of issues and the formation of issue-systems.
In concentrating on the means available for winning support, rather
than the tangibility of the ends, Mansbach and Vasquez posed that
a substantive typology could be arrived at deductively from the values
that are invoked by an issue. This is possible, they say, because
there are a limited number of values that people pursue. This will
be explored further in the next chapter. Mansbach and Vasquez
return to what they see as the original definition of an issue offered by Rosenau, namely, that 'an issue consists of a cluster of
values that are to be allocated', with an issue consisting of 'contention among actors over proposals for the disposition of stakes among
them'. Mansbach and Vasquez state that since values are abstract
and intangible they cannot be obtained directly, therefore they are
represented by objects or *stakes* for which actors contend.[97]

What needs to be explored, therefore, is how an issue becomes
a matter of contention. As Mansbach and Vasquez state, issues
come on to the agenda when an actor wishes to bring about some
change in the current authoritative allocation of values by creating
new stakes, reviving old ones, or altering the values ascribed to an
existing stake. The next chapter will explore further the relationship between values and stakes. Furthermore, since values are not
stakes, but the criteria by which we choose stakes, the evolution of
conceptions of what is to be preferred needs to be explored, with
reference to the work on epistemic communities, discussed in the
next chapter.

ISSUES AND AGENDA-FORMATION

For the Realist, issues come on to the international agenda through
changes in global power. As Kindleberger states,

Power politics constitutes the principal determinant of collective outcomes in international society in that outcomes flow directly from interactions among autonomous states, each of which is attempting to maximise its own power.[98]

For Kindleberger (1973), as for Keohane (1984) and Krasner (1976, 1983) agenda-building in international politics is dominated by the theory of hegemonic stability. Hegemonic-stability theory was originally presented as an explanation of patterns of international economic co-operation. A state, acting as a rational actor, possessing sufficient power in terms of capabilities to become the leader on an issue, would control its movement on the international agenda on the basis of a cost-and-benefit judgement. According to this perspective, state power and 'state interests' explain which issues come on to the international agenda and which issues remain on the periphery. However, as we will see in the next chapter, the inclusion of opium regulation on the international agenda in the early part of this century was not through the power of a single dominant power, or hegemon, controlling the issue. The concept of hegemony has been used to explain the evolution of international regimes and will be discussed further in Chapter 5.

An alternative approach to agenda-building is proposed by the work of Mansbach and Vasquez, but is not fully developed. As they state, work on agenda-formation is practically non-existent in International Relations literature.[99] This is partly as a result of the Realist emphasis on the anarchy of the global system, rather than viewing world politics as the co-operation and conflict of actors over efforts to allocate values authoritatively in multiple systems. Mansbach and Vasquez suggest that issues influence actors to differing extents at different times, and have different impacts on agenda formation, by using the idea of an issue cycle: 'During its life, an issue may be characterised by changes in stakes and variation in the cast of actors that are contending for them'.[100] The key stages they identify, through which an issue passes before it may be resolved, are crisis, ritualization, dormancy, decision-making and administration. An issue is described as in the 'crisis stage' when it creates a sufficient sense of urgency for action, or creates shifts in political order, or threatens accepted norms of behaviour. The next stage of ritualization evolves when the actors affected by this crisis develop 'patterned sets of expectations', with tacit sets of rules and procedures between actors as to how to deal with this crisis. Once

this has occurred, according to Mansbach and Vasquez, the next
stage is for the issue to be removed from the agenda through either
direct resolution, where a decision will be made, or dormancy. During
the dormancy stage, the issue may for a time be relegated to the
periphery of public attention, which then may lead directly to the
decision-making stage; or the issue may remain unresolved in a
state of atrophy. But their analysis is applied only to 'issues that
dominate the attention and energy of the major actors – critical
issues',[101] and therefore does not claim to have general application. There is no accounting for 'non-critical' issues in this evolu-
tionary cycle. The analytical use of the concept of salience, as
previously described, is a more fundamentally useful theoretical concept for understanding issue formation and evolution, because it
shifts the 'critical' property from the issue to the actor. Applying
this concept allows us to challenge the Realist high/low politics
distinction that Mansbach and Vasquez are in effect falling into
with their explanation of 'critical and non-critical' issues. The threat
of an invasion of a country by a foreign army is a threat to the
security of a country. However, applying the concept of salience
also allows us to consider that the greatest probable security threat
to the government of Bangladesh is a major monsoon; in Niger it
is drought; for small island states it is the threat caused by global
warming; and in Colombia, as has been demonstrated, it is conflict
with the drug barons.

As has already been stated, issue-systems arise because actors
seek to generate support for a particular value. Values are abstract
and intangible and actors are in contention over proposals for the
disposition of stakes that each actor perceives as being salient to
the value under contention. An issue therefore can be seen as contention by a group of actors over a set of related stakes. Therefore
we can define an issue-system as a point of contention about concrete
stakes involving abstract values. The values evoked explain the
behaviour of the actors and the formation of an issue-system. This
alternative view of agenda-formation through the salience of values
and the attempts to authoritatively allocate them poses a direct
challenge to the heart of the Realist paradigm. The Realist's assertion
that values are authoritatively allocated only when it is in the interest
of states that they be so, seems to imply that values are somehow
unrelated to interest in the Realist approach to international politics.
Interests cannot be separated from values as the Realist theory
seems to imply, as will be shown in the next chapter.

Regime analysis can help clarify the context under which an issue is regulated. It is possible to conceptualise a link between issues and regimes, since a regime must have an issue that it seeks to regulate. The concept of an issue-area has been widely and broadly used in International Relations literature and the literature on international regimes to refer to the vertical boundary which encompasses the link of actors, processes and outcomes into one functionally significant whole (Rosenau) or the description of a set of issues that governments see as closely related and deal with collectively (Keohane). However, as has been stated, the term issue-area is not analytically useful because of this confusion. By using the term issue-system we can separate the actors' beliefs and values from their behaviour. The actors in each issue-system are in contention over proposals for the disposition of stakes that each actor perceives as being salient for the same value. The extent to which the actors in the issue-system regulate the issue (by authoritatively allocating the values at stake) is variable. An issue-system may or may not form a regime, depending on the success of translating values into the form of an agreed norm, as will be discussed later in this work. Where regulation occurs, based on an agreed norm, the phenomenon of an international regime emerges. Therefore agenda-setting, formation of issue-systems, agreement on norms and the creation of international regimes can be seen as different stages in the same process of global change.

CONCLUSION

The increase in drug trafficking, the threat to the political and economic stability in an increasing number of countries, and the corruption of the international banking and financial networks as demonstrated by the BCCI scandal, has led to the problem of drug-related activity being placed higher up the international political agenda during the last decade. The size and complexity of the phenomenon means that North and South, East and West are all affected by it. International initiatives throughout the century have proved ineffective, and have in some instances aggravated this phenomenon. Efforts to combat drug-related activity clearly demonstrate the increasingly fragmented issue-specific character of contemporary international relations, with different actors facing different problems related to drug activity. Governments are faced with a phenomenon that requires more and more international co-operation, which is taking on a greater variety of forms, as traditional bilateral diplomacy proves unable to address the concern. This fragmentation requires precisely the issue-specific approach of regime analysis.

The concept of issue-areas has been widely used in International Relations literature. From the literature on issue-areas our understanding of the concept of an issue has evolved, yet an authoritative theoretical literature defining the concept of an issue remains elusive. Rosenau's initial work in the area subsumes both decisions that initiate behaviour and those decisions that implement it. There would, however, seem to be a very real distinction between issues as understood as the *perceptions* of actors that certain stakes are related, and the concrete political *behaviour* involved in an issue entering the policy process. The concept of an issue-system avoids this confusion by concentrating attention on the contention over values of the actors concerned.

The drugs phenomenon must be viewed not as a single issue, but rather an amalgamation of many issues, such as the corruption of governments, the influence of cocaine barons in Colombia, the link of drugs to international crime and terrorism, the increasing use of drugs among minors, the increase in money laundering and efforts to combat it, the spread of AIDS and measures to combat it, and so forth. Each issue forms a distinct issue-system, with actors participating in the system, if the issue is sufficiently salient for them. The concept of salience has been utilised in contrast to the Realist hegemonic power-theory of agenda-building. The nature of values, and of the stakes that represent them, will be explored in the next chapter, which will attempt to explain the process through which drug use, a legitimate practice in the nineteenth century, was brought onto the international political agenda and delegitimised.

3 A History of Drug Use: The Dynamics of Change

INTRODUCTION

This chapter is concerned with the changing attitudes towards drug use in the nineteenth century. Prior to the twentieth century opium, and to a lesser extent cocaine and cannabis, were widely available and on open sale in Britain and the United States and no global patterns were discernible in the values and legal sanctions governing their use. Yet the latter half of the nineteenth century saw the establishment of changing values concerning drug use, with the subsequent definition of drug taking as a 'problem' requiring international legislation. The 1909 Shanghai Conference and the Opium Convention of 1912 launched an anti-drugs diplomacy, followed by a specific mention in the Covenant of the League of Nations and eight decades of further restrictive legislation by the international community.[1]

Although the drug phenomenon today bears little resemblance in complexity and scale to its nineteenth-century predecessor, sociologists, historians and policy-makers have frequently drawn parallels. It can be said that the growth of toxicology as a science in the nineteenth century, with new drugs creating new problems, parallels today's concerns with 'designer drugs'; that 'infant-doping' of the previous century has some parallels to the vast prescribing in the United States of drugs to the 'overactive child'; and that nineteenth-century fears of opium as a 'stimulant', with the working classes as the focus of society's concerns, parallels twentieth-century fear of the pleasure-seeking youth culture. The purpose of this chapter, however, is not to draw historical analogies, which can be misleading. An historical perspective will instead focus on the factors responsible for the emergence of restrictions on the sale and use of opiates and, to a lesser extent, of other substances, in order to explain why values towards opium use changed; how practices were delegitimised; and also for considering why states develop mechanisms for co-ordinating policies on restricting particular activities and not on others.

It is impossible within the scope of a single chapter to detail the historical factors involved in the changing attitudes towards drug use. Furthermore, it is also beyond the current discipline of International Relations to analyse in depth the social dimensions, the predominant concern of sociology, which led to such a fundamental change in the attitudes of people towards drug use and more widely to a world-wide change in attitudes and international cooperation and control legislation, before national legislation in the majority of countries was achieved. Traditionally predominant approaches to change in international relations have failed to take into account the advances, concepts and methods from alternative disciplines such as sociology, philosophy or history, to our understanding of change. The connections between the various disciplines lack coherence, and a coherent theoretical relationship needs to be developed. With the example of drug control, these disciplines have obviously a great deal to offer. There is a need to move away from an analysis of change which is focused on states and their power capabilities. Likewise we need to avoid the criticism by Susan Strange of current regime analysis as 'overemphasizing the static and under-emphasizing the dynamic element of change in world politics',[2] by moving towards more of an understanding of social change, making obsolete the traditional approaches which focus on power capabilities and differentiate between national and international politics. An emphasis on values as the means for understanding regime creation also avoids the criticism of the regime approach by writers such as Stein, that it has nothing new to add that current theory cannot deal with.[3] For as Krasner states, 'It is the infusion of behavior with principles and norms that distinguishes regime-governed activity in the international system from more conventional activity.'[4] This chapter will present an overview of the history of drug use through to the nineteenth century, when the significant developments led to changing attitudes towards drug use and the theoretical implications behind this change.

THE CULTURAL TRADITION

The use of drugs for medical and non-medical purposes (with no clear distinction) can be traced back to man's early history.[5] As Aldous Huxley said, 'Pharmacology is older than agriculture'.[6] Coca is the oldest stimulant known to man, and chewing the dried leaf to extract the alkaloids it contains has been utilised by the people in the Andes since prehistoric times to increase physical endurance and to make breathing easier in the thin oxygen at extreme altitudes. The recent discovery of the drug in a mummified South American Indian is the earliest scientific confirmation of coca use, dating use back 2,000 years.[7] In Colombia, some of the idols standing in San Agustín's mysterious Valley of the Statues, dating back to 600 BC, display the characteristic distended cheek of the coca chewer. Coca consumption was, and still is, bound up with religious ceremonies and was regarded as the sacred, living manifestation of divinity, brought from heaven by the first Inca emperor, Manco Capac, and buried with the dead to help them on their journey to another world. The right to chew it was a sovereign gift, bestowed upon priests, doctors, young warriors, the scholars who kept the emperor's accounts and the relay runners who travelled miles a day to deliver messages. Today the people in the Altiplano region still measure time and distance in 'cocado': how far a man can travel while chewing one wad of coca leaf.[8] Throughout South America, an estimated eight million people chew coca leaves, and millions more drink 'maté de coca' (coca tea), which is sold in almost every supermarket.[9]

Cannabis sativa, known as hemp, marijuana, hashish, bhang or ganja, was brought to Europe with opium by the Moorish invaders of Spain and employed from early times as a pain-killer and tranquilliser. Cannabis has many derivatives and various names, as demonstrated. The variety of alternative terms is testimony to the drug's established place in the culture of many countries. In India, Persia, Turkey and Egypt it was in common use for centuries. It had been known to the Chinese several thousand years before Christ, and the ancient Greeks and Romans used it for both medical and social purposes. Cannabis was known in Europe well before the nineteenth century. Its use as an intoxicant, medicine, and even its fibre for clothing, is widely documented. But it was in 1839, on the publication of a monograph by W. B. O'Shaughnessy 'On the Preparation of the Indian Hemp, or Gunjah', that hemp was introduced into conventional nineteenth-century western medicine and described in 1890 as 'one of the most valuable medicines we possess' by the President of the Royal College of Physicians.[10]

Greek archaeological discoveries of seeds and capsules found in ancient pots, and clay tablets describing the cultivation and preparation of the white poppy, *Papaver somniferum*, date back to 5000

BC. Classical references dating back to Homer's *Odyssey* describe opium as a drug that will 'lull all pain and anger, and bring forgetfulness of every sorrow'.[11] Its healing properties were first detailed in the work of the Greek physician Hippocrates (466–377 BC) and later explored by the Roman physician Galen (AD 130–200). Aristotle, Virgil, as well as ancient writings from Egypt, India, Persia and China, all give opium an honoured place in ancient medicine. For many centuries opium use was mainly restricted to the Middle and Far East. It was brought to India by Arab merchants and from there to Europe. Ironically, in Europe people used opiates because they regarded them as a sedative, whereas in the East they were valued as a stimulant, often used by soldiers before battle. This emphasises the confusion surrounding the properties of the various drugs described in Chapter 1.

Trading in opium by Europeans began with the Portuguese traders in the sixteenth century, but the modern era for the opium trade began in 1773 when the British East India Company took control of the export of Indian opium to China. Warren Hastings, the new Governor General of Bengal, established a colonial monopoly on the production and sale of opium. As the company expanded production, opium became India's main export through the company's Calcutta offices to China. Exports of Bengal opium to China increased dramatically over the next 75 years, from 13 tons in 1729, to 148 tons in 1789, and 2,558 tons in 1839, with opium becoming 'the world's most valuable single commodity trade of the nineteenth century'.[12] Opium became a major global commodity of the same proportions as coffee, tea and cacao, which distinguished it from its earlier forms as a folk pharmacopoeia or luxury item.

In both Europe and the United States, by the first half of the nineteenth century opium was distributed in a wide variety of forms: as lozenges, pills, plasters, enemas, and in drinks such as beer and tea, for a large and diverse range of medical uses ranging from treating masturbation, photophobia, nymphomania and violent hiccoughs, to dulling pain, inducing sleep, controlling insanity, alleviating coughs, controlling diarrhoea, and for 'treating' a wide range of incurable diseases including malaria, smallpox, syphilis and tuberculosis.[13] In both Britain and the United States consumption of opium, and numerous preparations containing it, was for non-medical as well as medical use. Opium, and preparations containing it, were on legal sale throughout the century, conveniently and at low prices, with the price of the drug comparable to the price of aspirin today. Pharmacists sold opiates over the counter to customers without a prescription. Corner shops and general stores stocked and sold opiates. Opiates could be ordered by mail from newspaper advertisements and catalogue sales, and in the United States from the medicine show-wagons as they travelled throughout America.

Opium used in Britain at this time was legally imported as just another commodity. There were also small-scale attempts at domestic cultivation of the drug. Berridge and Edwards note that opium played a small part in the moves towards the agricultural improvements of output and productivity in Britain and the establishment of a capitalist agricultural structure paralleling that of industry at the turn of the nineteenth century:

> Opium's inclusion with turnips and rhubarb in the agricultural discussions of the period was one sidelight on the content of agricultural innovation. It was an indication, too, of the drug's acceptability; the 'home-grown' product bore witness to the place of opium in society at the time.[14]

Most of the opium consumed in the United States during the same period was also legally imported and opium poppies were also legally grown within the United States. In 1871 an official reported that opium production in California and Arizona was becoming an 'important branch of industry'.[15] Opium use was therefore not regarded as a social menace or problem for a large part of the nineteenth century. Among those who are known to have consumed opiates are: Elizabeth Barrett Browning, King George IV, Florence Nightingale, Byron, Shelley, Keats, Scott, Darwin, Ruskin, Rossetti, Coleridge, Dickens, William Wilberforce, and Disraeli, who made his famous record-breaking budget speech on a mixture of brandy and opium. Opium consumption was revered for expanding the consciousness and giving access to greater creativity by artists and writers of the period in particular. Unlike the communal activity of ancient times, drug consumption was seen as a private affair.

In the United States drug consumption was clearly associated with alcohol consumption. With the prohibition movement came an increase in demand for drug-based elixirs such as Coca-kola (later Coca-Cola), which came out in 1886 when Atlanta went dry. Coca-kola was originally sold as a quasi-medicinal stimulant and contained cocaine. In addition to Coca-kola there were hundreds of other similar substances on the market. Vin Mariani's Coca wine contained fresh coca leaves and was consumed by such luminaries as the then President William McKinley, inventor Thomas Edison, and Pope Leo XIII.[16] This link between alcohol and drug consumption emphasised the ambiguity between health and pleasure, the blurring of the medical with the non-medical use of drugs, which was the basis for the emerging challenge to nineteenth-century drug consumption.

THE DYNAMICS OF CHANGE

For the purposes of this chapter, the focus is on the consumption and use of opium. Cocaine and cannabis use was not as prevalent as that of opium in the nineteenth century, and they played quite a minor medical role in comparison. Unlike opium, coca never became popular in Europe, and it was not until the mid-nineteenth century, when cocaine, the principal alkaloid in the coca leaf, was successfully isolated, that it began to compete with opium in terms of popularity, particularly in the United States. However, both cannabis and cocaine played a part in altering the perceptions of drug use in a negative sense and were associated with opium in discussions on the medicalisation of addiction. Cannabis was seen to have little medical use and was associated only with pleasure during a time when the medical and non-medical use of drugs was being separated, and the discovery of cocaine illustrated the increasing dangers of new, more potent drugs. At the beginning of the nineteenth century there was no formal regulation of opium use. As Berridge and Edwards forcibly state, 'drug use was embedded in culture and was no more legislated or formally controlled than is at present the eating of peas'.[17] However, changes during the century radically altered the position of opium, and other drugs, in society.

During the nineteenth century moves towards industrialisation led to shifts in populations from country to towns looking for work. This necessitated a change in diet accommodating what was available, coupled with the need to increase the nutritional quality to keep pace with the demands of the new industries. An increase in global trade had made foods high in protein such as eggs and beef, stimulants such as tea and coffee, and sugar, available for this new diet. The modern factory worker would use the proteins, stimulants and glucose to accelerate the body's rhythms to those of the machinery, often for very long hours. The role of narcotics would be to soothe and relax the body and mind artificially during the short hours of rest. In the mid-to-late 1800s patent medicine manufacturers produced increasing numbers of drugs to induce any desired state. As McCoy states, 'the growth of mass narcotics abuse seems part of the transformation of daily living in the 1800s'.[18]

Increase in perceived use among the new working classes led to changing attitudes and the first attempts to control. Throughout the century there was a shift from middle-class use to working-class use. The situation in the United States was slightly different, but also shows a change in users. Early nineteenth-century opiate users were from the middle classes (often women) and also aged between 25 and 45, so that opium use was described as the 'vice of middle-life' and a substitute for alcohol, since it was thought of as unseemly for women to drink during this period.[19] However, in the latter half of the century attention was focused on opium use by immigrant Chinese labourers and their opium smoking in the dock areas of San Francisco.[20] In Britain the emphasis was on working-class use. The belief in working-class 'stimulant' use of opium in Britain helped justify the first restriction on the drug in the 1868 Pharmacy Act (see later). The emphasis here of the growing contemporary concern is not on the drug itself, but on the user and the uses, that is, a separation of the medical and non-medical uses. The question of drug use was becoming linked to social control. This led to a shift from informal to formal controls.

Another significant shift to observe in the changing attitudes towards drug use was changes in medicine itself and the medical profession. The beginning of the nineteenth century saw medical practice as still rudimentary. Western medicine was still dependent on bleeding and blistering. Doctors were impatient to transfer into the fields of biology and medicine the scientific revolution that had fired physics and astronomy, and were disappointed when their efforts were seemingly leading to greater confusions. They built vast theoretical medical systems based more on logic than on scientific method. Many of the new systems were a continuation of ancient lores dating as far back as the second century AD to the Greek physician Galen. Galen's ideas on the nature of disease resulting in an imbalance of the four liquids in the body – blood, phlegm, choler (yellow bile) and melancholy (black bile) – were the dominant force in medical thinking in the nineteenth century. Treatments held the dictum that the worse a medicine tasted the greater its curative power: urine, dung and soil fertiliser were common. In this period of great change medical doctors were the most enthusiastic advocates of opium treatment. As historian Terry Parssinen explains, opium was the Victorian's aspirin, lomotil, valium and nyquil. At a time when Marx claimed that religion was the opium of the people, opium was easily and cheaply available.[21]

However, little specialist training or diagnostic ability was needed to give patients opium or cocaine for their complaints and still have satisfied customers. Furthermore, the widespread habit of self-medication, particularly amongst the poor, also detracted from the desire of the medical profession to exercise its authority. In order to exert influence the medical profession needed to become more professional; to differentiate themselves from the various chemists, druggists, apothecaries and herbalists and others then practising. In addition, there needed to be more professional controls over the availability of drugs. The nineteenth century saw the emergence of numerous separate 'professions' and corresponding organisations in many areas such as accountancy and surveying. There were also moves to establish the medical and pharmaceutical professions as separate, self-regulating bodies.

In 1841 the Pharmaceutical Society was established in Britain with the initial objective to limit the title of chemist to those who had passed its own examinations, as well as gradually to raise the status and quality of chemists already in practice and eventually to achieve a monopoly of practice for its own members. This, however, was incompatible at the time with the dominant free-market values (contradicting the international values later displayed in relation to monopolies and trade with China, as we will see later) and no restrictions on sales were imposed. The society had yet to establish itself as the controlling body of the profession. The establishment of the General Medical Council followed, under the 1858 Medical Act, to represent the newly emerging profession of general practitioner. The Council even attempted to include pharmacy under the ambit of the medical profession. In 1860 the United Society of Chemists and Druggists was formed, to represent the non-members of the Pharmaceutical Society unhappy about the body's perceived failure to secure their interests. The societies all had conflicting interests and positions.

The conflict between medical and pharmaceutical interests was shown by the struggle in the British parliament over the 1868 Pharmacy Act to control dangerous substances. Doctors, and those concerned with public health, wanted opium included in the Act and for its availability to be severely restricted. The pharmacists wanted limited control of the drug to protect their commercial interests. Their concern could be seen to be primarily with the availability of opium rather than its use. The passage of the Bill illustrates the competing influences of the groups on parliament. On first reading all mention of opium in the Bill had been dropped, due to strong protests from pharmacists throughout the country, who compelled the Pharmacy Bill Committee 'against interfering with their [the pharmacists'] business'. Opium, they stated, was one of their 'chief articles of trade'.[22] However, despite this argument, the medical lobby triumphed and 'opium and all preparations of opium or of poppies' was added to the schedule as commodities that could not be sold without being labelled 'poison'.[23] However, the power and influence of the Pharmaceutical Society remained, since the Act failed to restrict patent medicines containing opium such as Dover's Powder, Daffy's Elixir, Godfrey's Cordial (for children) and many others, by 'preparations of opium' being distinguished from 'preparations containing opium'.

Opium control in the nineteenth century was still seen by many as a matter of voluntary self-regulation rather than a matter for state legislation. In the United States, the largely unorganised medical and pharmaceutical industries were not viewed as an appropriate area for central government legislation. The United States free-enterprise system positively discouraged controls on sales of opiates and later cocaine. Federalism, which gave the power of regulation to individual states, allowed for the repeal of medical licensing laws, adopted in earlier days, by state after state in the first half of the nineteenth century. Any form of licensing that might lead to a monopoly by the educated élites was seen as a violation of democratic principles.

The 1868 Pharmacy Act had little effect in reducing the availability of opium or of medicines containing opium in Britain. However, in the area of patent medicines it was becoming increasingly clear to both doctors and pharmacists that they had little influence and that their authority was being challenged. The number of vendors applying for licences to sell patent medicines increased from over 12,000 in 1874 to 20,000 in 1895.[24] The increase in vendors was to some extent due to the provisions of the 1868 Act, which had made ordinary opium preparations more difficult to obtain. Furthermore, in 1875 an Act had reduced the medicine licence duty, leading to an increase in vendors. Therefore there began in the

1880s a new professional campaign against open sale, concentrating on the issue of patent medicines. Patent medicine dealers were the largest newspaper advertisers in the United Kingdom and Australia, and the press consequently had an interest in not publicising information detrimental to sales. This was significant in limiting the spread of information concerning the harmful effects of drug use. In the United States, legislation was slower to materialise, but again came about due to an uneasy alliance between the medical profession and pharmacists. From 1895 to 1915 most states and many municipalities passed laws limiting the sale of opiates.

An initial shift in values therefore came about, due to the growing awareness among an emerging medical profession of the need to increase its influence in the field of opiate use, in competition with the increasing number of non-professional outlets supplying opiates and a newly emerging and competitive pharmaceutical profession, which had hardly existed at all before the 1840s.

A major trend throughout the history of drug use is the increased hazards associated with the use of more potent drugs, either purified plant materials or the new synthetic drugs, such as lysergic acid diethylamide (LSD) and 'China White', as has occurred in the last three decades. Until the nineteenth century drugs came from two sources – unrefined plants and animal products – and were usually taken orally. Eating crude plant material offered a certain safety margin, since biologically active components are usually present in small amounts and overdosing was physically difficult. In the mid-1800s morphine was isolated from opium; in the early 1900s cocaine was isolated from coca leaf and heroin was synthesised from morphine. The emergence of these new, more potent drugs, which were the product of the pharmaceutical industry, in combination with the hypodermic syringe in the 1860s, spurred both consumption of drugs and a gradually increasing concern about their dangers which led to changing attitudes concerning domestic consumption

The invention of the hypodermic syringe was a significant breakthrough for medical science. A more accurate and exclusive means of treating disease was being sought by the medical profession, to separate themselves from the mass of apothecaries, chemists, herbalists, patent medicine vendors and manufacturers, and others then practising. The hypodermic method, and its use with morphine in particular, was hailed as a major breakthrough in treatment, with a more immediate effect obtained, smaller doses needed, and safety assured with none of the unpleasant gastric side effects of opiates administered orally. Enthusiasm for hypodermic morphine was generally accompanied by a denigration of popular opium and self-medication. Promoters of the syringe played upon professional insecurities and implied that those who did not use it would fall behind in their profession. The percentage of American physicians using hypodermic medication grew dramatically, to the extent that by 1881 virtually every American physician had one. The use of the hypodermic syringe meant that the use of morphine was in the control of the medical profession, increasing their influence. Furthermore, organic drugs, such as cannabis, were non-soluble and therefore could not be administered in the more 'scientific' way of intravenous injection, and their medical use therefore declined. However, the enthusiastic advocacy of the new treatment among the profession failed to establish true scientific facts, and unquestioning support for hypodermic morphine medication soon led to increased levels of addiction. The attention of the profession then focused on the problem of addiction it had in effect created, rather than the majority of consumers taking oral opium, where usage and addiction were in general declining.[25]

Towards the end of the nineteenth century specific disease agents for illnesses such as typhoid and cholera were isolated. The desire for scientific discoveries encouraged progress in trying to understand less definable conditions, such as that of opium addiction (a term not in widespread usage until the first decade of the twentieth century). Much of the work in this area sprang from research into alcoholism. This led to the re-classification of illnesses with a large social or economic element in them on strictly biological lines:

> From one point of view, disease theories were part of late Victorian 'progress', a step forward from the moral condemnation of opium eating to the scientific elaboration of disease views. But such views were never, however, scientifically autonomous. Their putative objectivity disguised class and moral concerns which precluded a wider understanding of the social and cultural roots of opium use.[26]

For example, in the United States calls for restricting cocaine use were propelled by the increasing awareness of the medical dangers of cocaine and its association with respiratory failure, combined with widely publicised accounts of 'coke-crazed negros raping white women', which were endorsed by writings and reports from such respected bodies as the American Pharmaceutical Association.[27]

Earlier in the nineteenth century, at a time of wide opiate use for self-medication at all levels of society, opium use at worst was regarded as a bad habit, or minor form of moral failing. By the end of the century, when overall use was in decline, the regular user became more noticeable. Along with these new developments in toxicology and bacteriology came a growing awareness of the dependency-producing nature of opium and morphine use among the medical profession. As has already been stated, the medical profession itself was more organised and eager to develop theories of 'morphinism' and 'morphiomania' to further its own professional goals. Disease theories of addiction were seen as individually orientated (the addict was responsible, rather than the physical or mental condition), but this was nevertheless seen as a proper area for medical intervention. Opium eating was medicalised, but failure to achieve a cure was a failure of personal responsibility. Morality and medical science became mixed.

By the last half of the nineteenth century, the emergence of toxicology as a science, and also the elaboration of a germ theory of disease, began to lead to less of a dependency on the use of opium as a treatment for all conditions. Advances in bacteriology led to public health measures, which reduced the incidence of gastro-intestinal disorders, such as diarrhoea and dysentery, previously treated with opium and morphine. Vaccination against typhoid fever (1896), and chemotherapy against syphilis (1909), began to provide effective alternatives to opium and morphine for a few diseases. The achievement of greater diagnostic precision, made possible by the discovery and classification of pathogenic micro-organisms and by the development of new techniques, such as X-radiation, discouraged the prescribing of opiates for all illnesses. Furthermore, these developments led to a host of new and less dangerous anodynes becoming available. The introduction of milder analgesics, the salicylates and aniline and pyrazolone derivatives, constituted another major reason for the decline in the use of opium and morphine. The discovery of the analgesic properties of aspirin in 1899 and its subsequent role in the household as a general non-addictive pain-killer marked a decisive break with the drug-taking of the past.

By the end of the century the alliance between the government and the medical profession in Britain over the control of drugs had been established. The *laissez-faire* model of drug use had gradually evolved into a model of governmental responsibility for health policy incorporating the medical profession. In Britain the Registrar General's Office, established as early as 1837, was one of the first central government agencies. Throughout the second half of the century it provided the statistics on which the medical and public health case against the use of opium were based.[28] Narcotic legislation was seen as a form of social control of lower-class and criminal usage by the governing élite concerned about class tensions, which had emphasised working-class use of opium. For the medical profession, narcotic policy served as a form of professional self-affirmation. The emerging organisations and institutions and the movement for control complemented and paralleled society's concern with public health and led to the creation of new values, with a progressive medical dominance in society's way of thinking about and responding to drug use. Attitudes were changing towards opium users, who were seen as deviating from the norms of society. However, although domestic concerns about the dangers of drug use were changing in both Britain and the United States, the impetus for more fundamental change came from an international source – China. Towards the turn of the century, international developments were seen to impinge on domestic developments and finally establish society's attitude towards drug use.

THE EASTERN DIMENSION AND CHANGING ATTITUDES

The contemporary 'War on Drugs' as described in the last chapter was preceded by a very different kind of drug war. In 1839 and again in 1856 the British government declared war on China in an attempt to open China's markets to its business. It is not within the scope of this chapter to go into great detail on the Opium Wars (1839–1842 and 1856–1858), but rather to illustrate why values were slower to shift, with regard to opium use and the emerging medical dangers associated with drug use in Britain than in the United States. This can be seen to be due to Britain's involvement in the opium trade from the end of the eighteenth century. The 1842 Treaty of Nanking after the First Opium War opened five Chinese ports (including Hong Kong) to British merchants, and established British control over Chinese customs, allowing the import of opium without restraint. The British East India Company had begun to export opium from British India to China in the eighteenth century, as a convenient exchange for tea and silk, commodities at that time much valued in the West. Their monopoly over the China trade lasted until 1834, when the new reformed parliament cancelled it. Opium exported from India had to be smuggled into China, since the Imperial authorities had repeatedly issued edicts prohibiting its importation and consumption. However, opium was seen as a legitimate international commodity, the Chinese whisky, by the British, European and American traders, and as an integral part of the international financial system.

The aim of the Opium Wars, after the ban on opium by the Imperial government of China, was to force China to accept British rules and values of free trade and diplomacy. The 1858 Treaty of Tientsin after the Second Opium War forced the Chinese to accept the British imposition of the legalisation of opium imports to China. The Opium Wars of the middle of the century had effects in the latter half of the century, with an anti-opium movement emerging in the 1870s opposing England's participation in the opium trade with China, changing perceptions of domestic opium use even though its primary focus was on the Far East.

The early anti-opium movement was a loose alliance between British protestants, Western missionaries and Chinese Imperial officials. As with the anti-slavery movement in the eighteenth century, Quakers emerged as the leaders of the anti-opium campaign and founded in 1874 the Anglo-Oriental Society for the Suppression of the Opium Trade.[29] The British Quakers were strong moral reformers. They were committed to changing what they saw as the social wrongs of the world. There was also support for the anti-opium movement from the alcohol temperance movement. Throughout the Victorian era, the alcohol temperance movement was very active. Many leading churchmen and much of the middle class were members of temperance organisations. The anti-opiumists believed that opium physically and morally destroyed the user and was in itself evil. Furthermore, the anti-opiumists believed that opium was to blame for retarding the progress of Christianity, since the Chinese could not be expected to distinguish between the white missionary and the white opium-peddler.

The early aims of the Society were the abolition of the government monopoly of opium in India and a withdrawal of unfair pressure on the Chinese government to admit Indian opium by the creation of an educated public opinion and parliamentary pressure. For 30 years England's missionaries and moralists campaigned through meetings and petitions to change public opinion towards Britain's opium trade, stressing commercial as well as moral arguments. Although it denounced British involvement in the opium trade, the Society supported British involvement in China through legitimate trade.

Domestic pressure by the anti-opium movement in the United Kingdom was helped by the election of a reform-minded Liberal government in 1906, which led eventually to moves to end the trade. In 1907 Britain and China signed an agreement to reduce the shipment of opium from India by 10 per cent. However, since the 1890s British civil servants and politicians had been increasingly aware that the opium trade was forming a declining proportion of the Indian revenue. During the period of the 1860s and 1880s, British trade with China had hardly increased. China's own cheaper production of the drug was increasing and by 1885 China was probably producing as much opium as it was importing. The opium trade was also strangling other forms of commerce, as the Chinese were too poor to buy British goods due to their dependency on opium smoking. An estimated 27 per cent of the population were opium smokers at the height of the problem, with a level of addiction never equalled by any country before or since.[30] Britain needed to improve its relations with China, by abandoning the opium trade, in order to enhance prospects for other forms of trade. As Berridge states, 'Humanitarianism and economic self-interest coincided'.[31] The promotion of opium control in China resulted from considerations essentially separate from the issue of drug use.

The British anti-slavery and anti-opium agitations had much in common. But unlike its role in the anti-slavery campaign, the principal impetus for a multi-national approach to opium control came not from the British, but from the Americans, initially from missionaries returning from the Far East. As Arnold Taylor states, the role of the missionaries in the anti-opium campaign 'might quite appropriately be referred to as a missionary movement, or better still, as missionary diplomacy'.[32] Towards the end of the century, growing awareness of the public health aspect of narcotics addiction and a growing temperance movement made the issue of opium control increasingly popular among reformers. Furthermore, the United States had taken control of the Philippines following the Spanish-American war of 1898, which produced strategic and economic interests in the Pacific region. The Spanish had previously held the opium monopoly to supply the Chinese in the Philippines, and missionaries in Manila and the United States lobbied hard for the repeal of the trade. The Philippines came under the direct control of the United States federal government, bringing the issue of opium consumption for non-medical purposes to the direct attention of Congress. The Civil Governor, William Howard Taft, set up an Opium Investigating Committee to consider the Philippine opium question. The Committee's investigation lasted five months and was the first multi-nation survey on opium use. It concluded that the opium situation was one of the gravest, if not the gravest, of problems in the Far East, and acknowledged the position of opium as a major source of revenue for significant governments. The Committee also stressed the international dimensions to the problem, stating that opium could not be controlled by the Philippines alone, without international co-operation, since the use of opium in surrounding territories would make opium control in the Philippines unworkable.

The lead taken by the United States government, however, was due to a number of factors other than moral indignation. American companies had themselves been involved in opium traffic to China since the beginning of the nineteenth century, as conveyors of Turkish opium to the Far East. After 1805 they had held a virtual monopoly, due to the policy of the East India Company. The Company barred its own ships from carrying opium and at the same time prevented private English shipping from trading between Europe and China (until the ending of its monopoly in 1834). The American trade with China in Turkish opium was sufficient to cause the Chinese commissioner at Canton in 1839 to think that Turkey was an American possession.[33] After the 1839 Opium War the American companies temporarily withdrew from the trade, but participated again in aiding the smuggling of opium into China, by supplying receiving ships or storeships anchored in waters around the islands near to the Chinese mainland, for carriers from India, Persia and Turkey.[34] The United States was experiencing a period of rapid industrialisation and urbanisation in the later half of the century, with corresponding social and economic transformation and increasing social unrest. Links were perceived between working-class criminal users and foreign users of opium. Immigrant Chinese opium-smoking labourers in the west coast docks, brought in to help build the railways, were seen as a threat to society. Smoking opium began to be imported in significant quantities in the mid-1850s, when the first wave of Chinese immigrants arrived in California. Prior to July 1862, crude opium and smoking opium were reported together. The

Smoking Opium Exclusion Act focused attention away from white, middle-class female crude opium users and onto a new 'subculture' of users.

The economic interests of the United States government can also be seen to have played a vital role. After 1858 and the legalisation of the opium trade with China, the American ships that had been used to help smuggle opium into China were no longer needed. This, combined with a general decline in United States shipping companies during and after the Civil War, meant that United States companies' participation in the drug traffic with China had dwindled to insignificant levels and led to the changing attitude of the United States government to the issue. The change in attitude can be seen to have come about due to the recognition by the American merchants that the opium trade was damaging legitimate business with the Chinese, in restricting Chinese purchasing power and jeopardising relations with the Chinese government. Unlike for the British, direct financial benefits for the Americans of trading in opium rarely accounted for more than one-tenth of the total American trade to China in any one year.[35] The United States administration wished to pursue an Open Door policy with regard to China, but their treatment of Chinese immigrants in the United States led to a widespread boycott of United States goods in China in 1905. David Musto describes advisers suggesting to President Roosevelt that a change in position would help American long-range goals – 'to mollify Chinese resentment against America, put the British in a less favourable light, and support Chinese antagonism against European entrenchment'.[36] The United States therefore took the lead in organising an international conference to discuss the international control of narcotics.

The Shanghai Opium Commission met in 1909. At this time the United States had no federal laws proscribing the opium traffic, nor any reliable statistics on its own opium 'problem'. There were no restrictions on the import of opium to the United States, other than a small tariff. The United States did not export manufactured opiates, not on moral grounds, but because its products were not competitively priced with Europe's. United States per capita import of opium was declining, having peaked in 1896, and other substances were entering the market in competition to opium. In order to present something at the Conference, but to avoid offending the medical profession and drug manufacturers, they instituted in 1909 a ban on the import of opium for smoking. The 1909 Conference produced a number of resolutions. The Conference called for all governments to ban opium smoking; the ban (United States position) or careful regulation (Britain's position) of opium use; and a call for strict international agreements to control the traffic in and use of morphine (United States position). Britain insisted that the responsibility for control should be assumed by the governments concerned within their own territories and commitments. These positions reflected fundamental disagreements among participants, especially between the United States and Britain. There was simply no consensus 'that the use of opium for other than medical purposes was evil and immoral'.[37]

Developments in the nineteenth century outlined above reflect the dynamics that established international regulation of opium use. For the British and American governments, the dominant value in the nineteenth century was free trade. In the nineteenth century Britain was the supplier and China the consumer, and drug control was treated as an economic question, an important element in overcoming Britain's trade deficit with China. In the 1840s Britain waged war on China in order to re-open Chinese markets to the East India Company's opium exports. In the mid-nineteenth century there was no consensus on knowledge that drug use was damaging to the individual. Domestic consumption was not seen as a problem that could not be controlled, despite the latter half of the century seeing an increase in consumption amongst the working classes and an increase in medical knowledge of the dangers of consumption. Despite this, and despite the British hegemonic position, the United States government was able to put drug control on the international agenda, where it has remained firmly ever since. The nineteenth century clearly reflects the mixture of social and technological change, competing domestic interests, changing religious values and competing trade interests all reflecting changing values and norms about drug use, leading to its control. The nature of these dynamics will be explored further in the next section.

VALUES AND AGENDA-FORMATION: FROM THE VALUE OF POWER TO THE POWER OF VALUES

Hans Morgenthau, one of the fathers of the Realist school of political thought, advanced a theory of international politics founded on the concept of the national interest. In *Politics Among Nations* he states that 'Interest is the perennial standard by which political action must be judged and directed',[38] and therefore the 'objective of foreign policy must be defined in terms of the national interest'.[39] He goes on to expand on what constitutes the national interest by defining interest in terms of *power*: 'The main signpost that helps political realism to find its way through the landscape of international politics is the concept of interest defined as power.'[40]

For the orthodox school of International Relations in its heyday, from the 1940s to the 1960s, *the* issue in international relations was the acquisition, maintenance and exercise of power. However, during the 1970s, several writers challenged by developments around them introduced a 'transnationalist' critique to explain a changing international system.[41] But its challenge to Realist international theory has not been fully developed, with, for example, Keohane and Nye's work in the area being seen as only modifying Realism while remaining loyal to the classic formulation of Morgenthau and Thompson that international relations is concerned with international politics, and that the subject of international politics is 'the struggle for power among sovereign states'.[42] For the Realist, the traditional analysis of change in the international system is of change in global power: the traditional unit of change is the state, the replacement of one hegemonic state by another, with states pursuing self-interest understood in terms of power maximisation.

Realist orthodoxy has also dominated in the disciplines of international history and sociology. A state-centred approach in international history dates back to the early 1930s[43] and many present-day historians continue to describe their field as diplomatic history.[44] As with Realist international theory, international history has also concerned itself with 'crises in the politics of power and the officials who wield such power'.[45] Recent studies of the international arena by various mainstream sociologists have also shown a preoccupation with Realist concepts of state and power, seeing social systems as national societies or states and all other interaction patterns as being sub-systemic in character.[46] Although interactions between the disciplines of International Relations and Sociology have been intermittent since the 1930s, the 1970s saw a more systematic attempt to draw on the discipline. Attempts were made to analyse the growth of an international consciousness, the advent of global norms, the sociology of international law and the sociology of world conflict with the work of Brucan, Pettman and Banks, developing Burton's 'world society' conceptions of the subject matter of International Relations, where relations between individuals were seen as important as relations between states.[47]

The concept of an international regime was introduced by the neo-Realists in the same period, as a means of combating the challenges to the power politics approach of a changing world and in the face of what many considered new global problems, such as environmental degradation, resource depletion, and pollution. Stephen Krasner's definition of an international regime implicitly contains the concept of 'values', with the explanation of 'principles' as 'beliefs of rectitude' and the notion of 'implicit norms'. Krasner suggests that 'values' are basic 'causal variables' along with interests and power, but does not expand on this. He emphasises norms and principles in defining regimes and regime change by stating that 'Changes in principles and norms are changes of the regime itself', and that 'Changes in rules and decision-making procedures are changes within regimes'.[48] But for Krasner regimes were understood to rise and fall in terms of the power of the state actors comprising them. He asserts that 'The prevailing explanation for the existence of international regimes is egoistic self-interest.'[49] Puchala and Hopkins in the same volume state that regimes are 'closely linked to two classical political concepts – power and interest'.[50] Furthermore, the Keohane concept of hegemonic stability, the most widely employed explanation of regime formation in the Krasner work, also emphasises the role of dominant states utilising power capabilities for regime creation.[51] This concentration on states denies regimes independent impact, seeing them as merely reflecting the overall structure of power in the international system as it is perceived by the Realists under the challenge of interdependence, making the concept of an international regime virtually redundant.

A clearer understanding of values and norms, their evolution and role, is needed to give international regimes an impact in international relations and is also central for an alternative understanding of the international system where regimes have an independent role. As Mansbach and Vasquez state: 'The belief that the struggle for power is the dominant issue fails to accommodate the multiplicity of values and stakes for which actors both cooperate and compete.'[52] At the turn of the century, the United States was not yet a military power on a par with the global empires but was able to put the question of drug control onto the international agenda. The United States, unable to compete with the interest of the hegemon, linked the free-trade challenge to a moral value – drugs were immoral. Britain, as the hegemon, was forced to accept international legislation that could be seen as going against the national interest from a Realist perspective, as well as facing a domestic value challenge. In 1906 the newly elected Liberal government, pressurised by the increasing disquiet regarding the opium trade among the public and politicians, reached an agreement with China phasing out the opium trade between India and China. Values within Britain had changed; ten years earlier the report of the Royal Opium Commission had declared the consumption of opium was not harmful and that 'opium was more like the Westerner's liquor than a substance to be feared and abhorred'.[53] How much the British government's change of attitude was due to market decline, as previously mentioned, rather than the influence of the new morality of the nation and the work of the missionaries, is difficult to say. However, by their later delaying tactics and lack of co-operation with the international opium legislation, remaining the world's main manufacturer and exporter of opium until as late as the 1930s, it can be suggested that the missionaries made a successful value challenge forcing a change in official policy, challenging the Realist position on value change in the international system.

To sum up, central to an understanding of the concept of issues, and central to an alternative understanding of the concept of change in the international system to that of the Realists, is a re-evaluation of the concept of power as the sole variable for change. The emergence of control on drugs by the international system shows how the dynamics for change came not simply from a powerful state imposing its will, but from changing values and value-linkages. The simplicity of the Realist position on change can be contrasted with the much more complex reality of nineteenth-century drug use. The complex mix of social and technological change and competing domestic interests, changing religious values and competing trade interests, all were shown to have promoted a value shift in attitudes towards drug use. Power relationships can be seen to have been changed by a shift in values, whereas for the Realists change is perceived as the other way round, with the practice of states determining values. Also contrary to Realist understanding, the dynamics of drug control at the turn of the century are an example of international values impinging on national values, since fundamental international legislation came before national legislation.

A different approach to politics that identifies the source and role of values as central is needed. The approach of an alternative school of thought is centred around the work of Rosenau, Nye and Keohane, Mansbach and Willetts. All five writers make reference in their work to the ideas of the American political scientist David Easton. David Easton, writing about American political science in *The Political System*, defined politics as 'the authoritative allocation of values'.[54] This can be seen as a denial of the Realist's understanding of politics as the struggle for power. Little attention has been paid to the significance of these two quite separate definitions of the fundamentals of politics for understanding the essence of the international system. As Mansbach and Vasquez emphasise,

> The Eastonian definition moves the analysis of global politics away from conceptions of power and security and toward the assumption that demands for value satisfaction through global decision making must be at the heart of any theory, and must be the central process that awaits explanation.[55]

However, writers following Easton's work have not established an authoritative theoretical literature defining the concept of a 'value' or expanding methodically on Easton's work in an international context. James Rosenau in his seminal work on 'pre-theories' defines issue-areas as a 'cluster of values', but does little to expand on the fundamental nature of those values or where they come from. Mansbach and Vasquez attempt to expand on the work of Rosenau (as outlined in the previous chapter) in attempting a more thorough analysis of issues and values and their role in the international system. This sadly neglected work will be the focus for elaborating on a clearer understanding of the role of values in the international system as an explanation of the dynamics of change.

THE NATURE OF VALUES

The problem again, as with 'issue', is that 'value' is common terminology in a number of disciplines, obscuring the absence of a common understanding. For economists, the term refers to 'utility generating property' or 'valuation revealed in a preferential choice'. For sociologists, the term denotes some kind of 'world view' or 'taken for granted belief or normative standard by which human beings are influenced in their choice among the alternative courses of action which they perceive'.[56] Sociologists emphasise the criteria governing evaluation (why we choose what we choose is based on our values), economists are concerned with the valuations themselves.

An authoritative literature on the source and role of values in the discipline of International Relations is lacking. Analysis of values is central to the discipline of Sociology, concerned as it is with social transformations, but has traditionally been approached on a national rather than an international level. However, a concern for the international aspects of social transformations was shown, as early as the first half of the nineteenth century, in the work of Saint-Simon, Comte, de Tocqueville, Marx and Spencer.[57] Attention to world affairs developed during the 1920s and 1930s to the extent that a sociologist could claim that 'Sociology . . . could legitimately compete with political science in studying international relations'.[58] In the 1960s there was a revival of interest in international politics by writers such as Talcott Parsons, Amitai Etzioni, and Johan Galtung.[59] Work on international social relations, as opposed to inter-state politics, increased from the late 1960s onwards. However, research progressed in isolation from other disciplines.

Mansbach and Vasquez describe values as 'subjective constructs that express human aspirations for improving their existence'.[60] They suggest that there are a limited number of values that people pursue: 'some of those which have been identified and sought through time and across space are wealth, physical security, order, freedom/autonomy, peace, status, health, equality, justice, knowledge, beauty, honesty and love'.[61] Values, according to Mansbach and Vasquez, serve *intrinsic* needs – that is, they are sought for themselves – but they also say that satisfaction of one value, in order to satisfy another, can also be seen as *instrumental*, that is, serving an end.[62] Mansbach and Vasquez recognise this difference as central to understanding the political stances of different actors by means of the nature of the values that they are aiming to satisfy.

To return to the definition of politics by David Easton in *A Framework*, politics is described as the authoritative allocation of values: 'the authoritative allocations distribute valued *things* among persons or groups'.[63] (Italics by current author.) As Mansbach and Vasquez expand,

> Politics involves efforts to allocate values. Since values are abstract and intangible ends, they cannot be attained directly and must be sought through access to and acquisition of, objects that are seen as possessing or representing values. These objects are then regarded as stakes for which actors contend.[64]

That is, values are abstract and intangible and are represented by objects or stakes representing the values. Mansbach and Vasquez make a distinction between *concrete* and *transcendental* stakes. Concrete stakes represent a means of directly satisfying a value since 'the value is inseparable from the object itself', whereas transcendental stakes are 'entirely abstract and nonspecific, and which concern beliefs, prescriptions, or norms about how people should live or behave'.[65] Mansbach and Vasquez also describe stakes is terms of their *intrinsic* or *instrumental* value, that is, valuable for their own sake, for the values they represent, or necessary for acquiring other values that are actually associated with other stakes.[66]

However, the work of Mansbach and Vasquez on values is unnecessarily confusing. They talk about both intrinsic and instrumental values and intrinsic and instrumental stakes, suggesting there is a corresponding relationship between them. Nevertheless it is clear that, since values are abstract and cannot be attained directly of themselves, all values must be intrinsic. When satisfaction of one value enhances the prospects for satisfying another, preferred value, then a stake must be involved. Stakes are not values, but the concrete goals of action based on the values being allocated. It follows, therefore, since stakes are the objects with which value satisfaction can be achieved, that all stakes are instrumental: a way of satisfying value preferences. Values can be seen to belong in a hierarchy, so it is possible to make choices among stakes embodying different values. Some stakes are pursued directly for the values they embody, whereas others are pursued in order to obtain other stakes. In this way, 'self-interest' can still be understood as value-guided behaviour, contrary to the traditional Realist approach to international politics. The United States government supported the public health and morality campaigns against opium use, because opium control represented a stake for the achievement of free trade. The missionaries' and Quaker groups' support for the anti-opium campaign can be seen to have derived from the desire to avoid human suffering.

In this way the terminology of Mansbach and Vasquez is simplified and clarified and aids in the redefining of power. All values are intrinsic, as and of themselves. No distinction is needed therefore between power as capability and power as interest. Power, another central tenet of the Realist approach to International Relations, can be understood as instrumental and not intrinsic, contrary to Realist assertions. Interests can be seen as a particular type of value. Furthermore since all stakes are instrumental, this lends itself to the 'power as influence' concept central to the Global Politics paradigm.

In the nineteenth century, drug control was seen as a stake for acquiring free trade. This is emphasised by the attempts to include cocaine and morphine on the international regulation agenda. The second meeting dealing with opium control, the Hague Conference, was called in 1911 by the United States, which was by then preparing its list of demands on China (e.g. currency reform), in repayment for all the help the United States had provided on the opium issue. Britain's introduction of cocaine into the regulation discussions of the second meeting reflected its interests not in curbing cocaine use, but in delaying international control over opium and protecting its trade monopoly with China. The necessity of acquiring statistics on the drugs would delay further measures on the restriction of opium. This action produced conflict with Germany, which was the leading drug manufacturer at the time. The German pharmaceutical company Bayer introduced the diamorphine alkaloid, (later to be given the brand name 'Heroin', from the German word *heroisch*, meaning of supernatural power) into the United States and Britain in 1898: the same company also manufactured cocaine. The German government supported Bayer, opposed the control of cocaine and engineered a unique ratification procedure, which required unanimous ratification by all 46 states in the system, ensuring that control became fully international.[67] Therefore, implementation was successfully delayed until after the First World War, when countries which ratified the Versailles Treaty automatically became parties to the Hague Convention. The Hague Convention therefore established drug control on a truly global dimension. Germany was able to protect its economic interests against the interests of Britain and the United States, so that later, as the British delegates reported: 'it [the Convention] has, for the first time, laid down as a principle of international morality that the various countries concerned cannot stand alone in these measures'.[68]

After the First World War the newly established League of Nations was given 'general supervision over agreements with regard to the traffic in opium and other dangerous drugs'.[69] Its Advisory Committee on Traffic in Opium and Other Dangerous Substances, created to carry out these responsibilities, was dominated by the colonial powers, with their opium monopolies in their Far Eastern colonies, and the drug manufacturing countries. The Committee was nicknamed 'The Old Opium Bloc'. There was no agreement on the value that drugs were immoral, evil and dangerous, but the stake of drug control was used to achieve free trade; therefore the Committee acquired the value that drugs are immoral, evil and dangerous in order to satisfy the stake of free trade with China.

One of the dominant questions for international regime theorists is why we have regimes in some areas and not in others. To answer why opium and cocaine were controlled, and not other substances, such as alcohol and tobacco, we are again back to stakes:

> Stakes that are initially beyond anyone's control are likely to reach the agenda, because this may be the only acceptable manner to allocate them. Conversely, when a stake is initially under some actor's control, that actor will oppose its inclusion on the agenda, unless its loss appears inevitable.[70]

This is clearly applicable to nineteenth-century drug control and aids understanding of why, amongst other factors, substances such as tobacco and alcohol were not treated in the same way as opium. The stake of trade in tobacco and alcohol was not contested and there was no consensus on the value that tobacco and alcohol use was immoral, evil and dangerous. As Easton also states, writing nearly two decades earlier:

> Briefly, authoritative allocations distribute valued things among persons or groups in one or more of three possible ways. An allocation may deprive a person of a valued thing already possessed; it may obstruct the attainment of values which would otherwise have been obtained; or it may give some persons access to values and deny them to others.[71]

The concept of salience, as explained in the previous chapter, can explain why actors rank values and stakes in the way that they do. The salience of an issue to an actor can be due to either its direct or its indirect potential for value satisfaction.

Since values are not stakes, but the criteria by which we choose stakes, the evolution of conceptions of the preferable, which is why we have certain expectations and not others, needs to be explored. According to Emanuel Adler and Peter Haas, expectations in international politics come from interpretive processes, involving political and cultural structures, as well as from institutions 'dedicated to defining and modifying values and the meaning of action'.[72]

EPISTEMIC COMMUNITIES

John Ruggie introduced the term *epistemic communities* in his 1975 article 'International responses to technology', in which epistemic communities were described by Ruggie as 'interrelated roles which grow up around an episteme'.[73] The sociological term *episteme* referred to 'a dominant way of looking at social reality, a set of shared symbols and references, mutual expectations and a mutual predictability of intention'.[74] In his article Ruggie differentiated three levels of what he termed 'institutionalization', that is, as the sociologists define it, the co-ordination and patterning of behaviour, setting the boundaries which channel behaviour in one direction as against another. Ruggie saw epistemic communities as the first level of institutionalisation – as the purely cognitive level. He described international regimes as the second level of institutionalisation 'consisting of sets of mutual expectations, generally agreed to rules, regulations and plans, in accordance with which organizational energies and financial commitments are allocated'.[75] The third level Ruggie refers to is that of international organizations.

A special issue on international regimes was published in 1982 by the journal *International Organization*, followed a decade later by a special issue edited by Peter Haas exploring the development of interest in the concept of epistemic communities.[76] However, a volume analysing the relationship between the two concepts is still lacking. The inter-relationship between the first two levels of institutionalisation can be understood by utilising the role of value and norm evolution in international relations. Ruggie's introduction of the concept of epistemic communities and international regimes can be seen as an attempt to go beyond institutions or organisations and the behaviour typically analysed by Realist theorists, to explain international co-operation and conflict with a focus on the actual dynamics of change.

An understanding of epistemic communities is necessary for understanding what Krasner calls actors' converging expectations. Although Haas goes into great detail about the nature of epistemic communities in the introduction to the 1992 volume, it is in an earlier work on epistemic communities that we have what is seen as the authoritative definition of the concept:

> Epistemic communities are transnational networks of knowledge based communities that are both politically empowered through

their claims to exercise authoritative knowledge and motivated by shared causal and principled beliefs.[77]

The fact that epistemic communities are described as (1) politically empowered through their claims to exercise authoritative knowledge, and (2) motivated by shared causal and principled beliefs is illustrated in Chapter 6 with the work of the Basle Committee on Banking Regulations and Supervisory Practices.

The normative aspects to international relations, lacking development in the rule-orientated, state-centred work on international regimes, is emphasised in the literature on epistemic communities. The literature on epistemic communities focuses on 'shared causal and principled beliefs', which affect the decision-making procedures around which actors' expectations converge, a topic which is not fully developed by Krasner.[78] As with the literature on regimes, however, much of the later work on epistemic communities has concentrated on states as the actors in the system and has been restricted to 'helping states identify their interests'.[79] But the epistemic community literature does not equate interests solely with power. The literature suggests that it is possible to perceive interests in terms of values, rather than in terms of power as it is currently understood. The concept of change, therefore, unlike in much of the work on international regimes, has not been limited to changes in state power. As Haas explains, epistemic communities identify 'a dynamic for persistent co-operation independent of the distribution of international power'.[80] The literature on epistemic communities also emphasises that there is no distinction between domestic and international politics, a point that is significant for an understanding of the drug phenomenon. As Adler and Haas state,

> to study the ideas of epistemic communities and their impact on policy making is to immerse oneself in the inner world of international relations theory and to erase the artificial boundaries between international and domestic politics so that the dynamic between structure and choice can be illuminated.[81]

Epistemic communities help define and modify values in a society by their claim to authoritative knowledge, and can be one way of identifying where expectations come from in international politics. Both beliefs and values contribute to the epistemic community in an attempt by its members to establish a consensus of knowledge or norm. Since epistemic communities are set in a social context and not divorced from society, there is a danger of beliefs being established as authoritative knowledge, as has been previously stated in the case of nineteenth-century drug control, where 'moral judgements were given some form of spurious scientific respectability, simply by being transferred to a medical context'.[82] Furthermore, by helping to define and modify values epistemic communities also develop the context for establishing norms and creating a climate favourable to the further acceptance and diffusion of their beliefs. This can aid in an understanding of why some substances and not others are controlled by the international community. That is, epistemic communities institutionalise values by evolving norms.

The epistemic communities literature highlights the relationship between the role of experts and the providers of knowledge and the role of political actors. The literature focuses attention on the process by which consensus is reached in international politics and directs our attention to the impact this consensual knowledge (norms) has on the evolution of international regimes, as will be explored in Chapter 5.

CONCLUSION

To conclude, drug control became a question on the international agenda at the beginning of the twentieth century due to the value of free trade coming under contention. The Far-Eastern focus of the Shanghai meeting widened, to produce a world-wide system of control at the Hague Conferences (see next chapter). Although attitudes were changing in the United Kingdom and the United States regarding the dangers associated with domestic opium use, and particularly with the more potent derivatives, heroin and morphine, and moral questions were being raised by the missionaries returning from the Far East, the question generated conflict only when the parties involved began to disagree on the distribution of the benefits of trade and commerce with China. It was necessary to regulate their interdependence, if they wished to continue collaborating despite the conflict. As E. B. Haas states, 'an international issue arises when the terms of interdependence are questioned'.[83]

A global drug-prohibition regime was set up as a weak regime in the first half of the nineteenth century, because it was based on the stake of trade with China rather than on an anti-drugs value.

During this period there were two values under contention, namely the value of free trade and the value that drugs were evil, immoral and dangerous, represented by the two stakes of trade in opium with China and general trade in other commodities. The value of free trade was more salient than the anti-drugs value for governments, merchants and pharmaceutical companies, but the same stake was under contention: general trade with China (whether supporting the status quo or opening up to a free market) was instrumental in achieving both value preferences. Supporters of the free-trade value made a value-linkage to the anti-drug position in order to achieve their objectives. Hostility to drugs and support for the free-trade position were both satisfied. In this way, the goal of the end of the opium trade with China was achieved. The drugs trade was not controlled due to the support of the value that drugs were evil, immoral and dangerous but due to the salience of the free-trade value for the actors concerned and the fact that the same allocation of stakes – suppression of opium trade and opening up general trade – was necessary for the satisfaction of both values. A strong regime, however, needs to be based on an intrinsic value which can be *authoritatively allocated*. Therefore, a regime can be seen to have emerged to control the licit trade in drugs, based on the free-trade value, as the next chapter will explore further, but only a weak regime emerged to control drug use.

The concept of an international regime focuses our attention on the source and role of values in international relations. However, the limiting strait-jacket of the dominant hegemonic power-theory of regime creation, change and decline has denied the concept any independent impact on change in international relations. The creation and maintenance of international regimes is described as dependent on the rules and decision-making procedures of powerful states. In this sense current regime analysis over-emphasises the static, as Susan Strange criticises, rather than emphasising the dynamic nature of international relations. By focusing on changing values, however, as illustrated by the complex value shifts in nineteenth-century drug control, and understanding where 'convergent expectations' come from, regime analysis can be seen to challenge this criticism.

4 The United Nations and International Drug Control

INTRODUCTION

This chapter will consider the fact that despite eight decades of international co-operation on drug control, firstly by the League of Nations and then by its successor, the United Nations, the production, distribution and demand for illicit drugs has increased dramatically in the last decade and shows no sign of decreasing. Furthermore, the threat to domestic and international security brought about by drug-related activity, as explained in Chapter 2, has forced the concern to the forefront of the international political agenda. This chapter will look at the history of drug control in this century, beginning with the League of Nations. The central part played by the United Nations in the establishment of various bodies and organs with the mandate to control drugs, and the formation of rules and decision-making procedures with regard to global drug control, will be discussed. The preoccupation of the United Nations with the development of rules and decision-making procedures will be seen to be ineffective, both in controlling illicit drug use and in understanding the nature of the phenomenon.

Regime theory emphasises the normative nature of international politics lacking in much of the state-centric, rule-orientated work on international organisations. However, the preoccupation of much of the literature on international regimes with rules and structures, repeats the path taken by those writing on international organisations and therefore has similar limitations, as the second part of this chapter will demonstrate. A theory of international regimes encompassing an understanding of international organisations and formal rules and decision-making procedures, but also emphasising an understanding of the nature of issues, value consensus and norm emergence, is necessary for understanding the drug phenomenon.

An understanding of the values and the norms evoked by issues explains why international drug control to date has been unsuccessful and why no single regime to regulate drug use is possible. As the last chapter has demonstrated, the values evoked by nineteenth-century drug use were dominated by the value of free trade. This can be seen to have continued into the twentieth century and the establishment of the League of Nations.

THE LEAGUE OF NATIONS PERIOD

As the last chapter has demonstrated, international action on drug control began as early as the 1909 Shanghai Conference. The Shanghai Conference in turn led to the Hague Conference and the drafting of the 1912 International Opium Convention, the first international agreement to regulate trade in, and abuse of, opium and other related substances, including cocaine.[1] The Convention provided for the control of the export and import of raw opium, but did not prepare for any preventative action to restrict it, the responsibility being mainly given to customs officials. The trade in prepared opium was to be suppressed gradually, but the responsibility for this lay with the states party to the Convention.[2] They were free to decide as to how to take action towards the gradual suppression of the manufacture, internal trade in, and use of prepared opium. The Covenant of the League of Nations empowered the League to control both licit and illicit manufacture of, and trade and traffic in, opium and other dangerous drugs, with the League Assembly establishing at its first session in 1920 an Advisory Committee on Traffic in Opium and Other Dangerous Drugs (later replaced by the Commission on Narcotic Drugs) to carry out these responsibilities. During the League period, three Conventions were completed focusing on control of the trade in licit and illicit substances: the International Opium Convention of 1925; the Convention for Limiting the Manufacture and Regulating the Distribution of Narcotic Drugs of 1931; and the Convention for the Suppression of Illicit Traffic in Dangerous Drugs of 1936. These Conventions established various procedures and bodies, and also established various values and principles which were carried over into the United Nations period, and are therefore worth noting.

The 1925 Convention devised the procedure for establishing whether or not a drug should be categorised as a dangerous drug for international control. This would be the responsibility of the Health Committee of the League in consultation with the Permanent Committee of the Office International d'Hygiène Publique in Paris. Under the Convention, coca leaves, crude cocaine and Indian hemp, substances not covered by the Hague Convention, were brought under control. The Convention also established an intricate system of import and export certificates to control the international trade in drugs. The Permanent Control Board, the forerunner of the International Narcotics Control Board (see later), was set up to receive and disseminate information concerning the trade. The Board had no power to prevent the accumulation of excessive quantities of drugs, but Article 24 of the Convention authorised the Board to report to the Secretary-General of the League if any country was accumulating a controlled drug. If the Secretary-General received no adequate response from the country concerned on inquiry, the Board could recommend to the Contracting Parties to the Convention and the Council of the League that no further Convention substances should be made available to the country concerned. The Board was composed of eight experts, independent of their governments, elected on the basis of their impartiality, competence and disinterestedness. Although established by treaty, the Board's status lay somewhere between an inter-governmental organisation and a non-governmental organisation.

The Convention for Limiting the Manufacture and Regulating the Distribution of Narcotic Drugs of 1931 was unique from a legal point of view in that 'it applied the principles of a controlled economy to a group of commodities by international agreement'.[3] As its title describes, the Convention's aim was to limit the manufacture and trade in narcotic drugs, and to regulate their distribution by a system of estimates in order to limit manufacture to the requirements of medicine and science. One of the special features of the Convention was with regard to Non-Contracting Parties. They were also expected to provide estimates of their drug requirements. A Supervisory Board, created by the Convention to monitor the operations of the estimates system, would, in the absence of any estimate from a Non-Contracting Party, submit an estimate for that country to the Permanent Control Board established by the 1925 Convention.

Neither the 1925 nor the 1931 Convention directly defined traffic in illicit drugs as being a criminal offence. The Convention for the Suppression of Illicit Traffic in Dangerous Drugs of 1936 was the first international convention to make the offence punishable. Unfortunately, the conditions necessary for strengthening 'the measures intended to penalise offences' were not in existence at the time the Convention was concluded. Although some of the contemporary international conventions dealt with criminal offences, such as the Convention on the Suppression of the Traffic in Women and Children of 1921, the Convention on the Suppression of the Traffic in Obscene Publications of 1923, the Slavery Convention of 1926, and the Convention on the Suppression of Counterfeiting Currency of 1929, the Contracting States abstained from incurring obligations which went beyond what was seen as 'the necessities of the situation'.[4] However, in attempting to encourage closer co-operation in respect of drug offences between the police authorities of different countries, the Convention raised issues to do with international enforcement and drug trafficking which remain just as pertinent to international drug control today (indeed the initiative to conclude the Convention was taken by the International Criminal Police Commission, which later changed its name to the International Criminal Police Organization – Interpol). Despite this, the concerns with trafficking, for all intents and purposes, remained dormant until the 1980s, as the United Nations focused on supply-reduction programmes. The 1936 Convention's direct recognition of illicit traffic as a criminal offence would not be the focus of United Nations drug-control policy again until the 1988 Convention Against Illicit Traffic in Narcotic Drugs and Psychotropic Substances.

As has already been illustrated in the previous chapter, the concern of the inter-war period, as in the late nineteenth century, was in the economic benefits to be achieved through free trade. The conventions concluded during the League period were generally 'promotive' to licit trade rather than 'preventive' against illicit trade. This was also to be the focus of the work of the United Nations, until recent developments, with the International Opium Convention of 1925 and the International Convention of 1931 forming the basis, to a considerable extent, of the Single Convention on Narcotic Drugs three decades later.

THE UNITED NATIONS PERIOD

In 1946 the United Nations took over the functions of the League of Nations in the narcotics field. In the pre-war years, the number of products considered to be a danger, and therefore subject to control, was largely limited to those relating to the opium poppy, the coca bush and the cannabis plant. The period just before the

Second World War saw many other compounds being synthesised. A desire to control those substances led to emerging new problems for international control. By 1960 six different drug-control treaties, plus three amending protocols, were in force.[5] The main impact of the 1961 Single Convention on Narcotic Drugs, (hereinafter, the Single Convention), was to consolidate the nine instruments into a single one, thereby simplifying and strengthening United Nations drug-control activities. Like the focus of much of the work of the League, the initial work of the United Nations in the field of drug control aimed primarily to limit the supply of narcotic drugs and psychotropic substances to amounts required by states for scientific and medical purposes, so as to prevent their diversion into illicit traffic. Article 4 of the Convention states the general obligation 'to limit exclusively to medical and scientific purposes the production, manufacture, export, import, distribution of, trade in, use, and possession of drugs'.[6]

The United Nations bodies, and the conventions ratified, had little effect on controlling illicit drug use during the first two decades of drug-control activities, and no international regime to regulate the recreational use of illicit drugs or to deal with the problem of addiction can be seen to have emerged. The work of the League and the work of the various United Nations bodies had focused on limiting the supply of narcotic drugs and psychotropic substances. The dominant stake for the actors for whom drug control was salient was the importance of controlling effective trade of licit drugs for medical and scientific purposes. The importance of the 'medical use of narcotic drugs . . . for the relief of pain and suffering'[7] was the value utilised to allow for the effective trade to continue, and superseded the value that drug use and drug addiction was evil and immoral. Therefore no regime to control illicit drug use can be seen to have emerged. The value position that drugs were evil and immoral was not represented by a salient stake. Instead, an international regime for the control of the licit manufacture and trade in dangerous drugs for scientific and medical purposes can be seen to have emerged, centred around the International Narcotics Control Board.

The lack of salience of the concerns surrounding illicit drug use to the actors participating in the drug-control regime was emphasised by the lack of attention given to drug addicts or drug abuse in the Single Convention. Despite the reference, in the preamble to the convention, to the dangers of drug addiction, the article in the convention concerned with the treatment and after-care of addicts was one of the briefest. Article 38 of the 1961 Single Convention requires that parties 'give special attention to the provision of facilities for the medical treatment, care, and rehabilitation of drug addicts' and that if a party's 'economic resources permit, it is desirable that it establish adequate facilities for the effective treatment of drug addicts'.[8] No further detail was given, emphasising the point made by Stein that 'much of the history of national and international narcotics control can be written without reference to addicts or addiction'.[9]

Drug use and addiction were seen as a social problem for national, and not international, concern during this period. Furthermore, the level of drug use and addiction were seen as relatively minor and unimportant in this period before the arrival of the 'sixties drug culture'. The belief that drugs were evil and dangerous was also not salient to actors in producer countries, as was emphasised in Chapter 2. The trade in licit drugs was seen as an inter-state concern, addiction an internal social problem, and therefore there was no possibility of a global regime emerging to control drugs in their supply, distribution and demand side.

STRUCTURE FOR UN DRUG CONTROL ACTIVITIES, PRE-SPECIAL SESSION

Until the recent restructuring of United Nations drug-control activities, initiated by a Special Session of the General Assembly in 1990 (see later), there were five United Nations organs concerned wholly with drugs. They were two committee bodies and three Secretariat units: the Commission on Narcotic Drugs (CND), a functional commission of the Economic and Social Council (ECOSOC); the International Narcotics Control Board (INCB), an autonomous body of independent experts; and three units staffed by members of the Secretariat, the Division of Narcotic Drugs (DND), the secretariat to the INCB, and the United Nations Fund for Drug Abuse Control (UNFDAC). There were, furthermore, numerous other programmes, agencies and entities which took part in drug-control activities (see Figure 4.1).

The Commission on Narcotic Drugs (CND) is one of the six functional commissions of the Economic and Social Council, and was established in 1946. It is the successor of the Advisory Com-

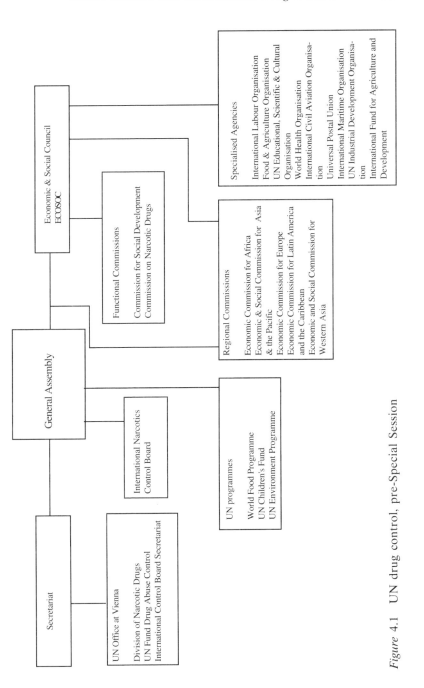

Figure 4.1 UN drug control, pre-Special Session

mittee on the Traffic in Opium and Other Dangerous Drugs, which was set up by the first Assembly of the League of Nations. The Commission is the central policy-making body in the United Nations system for drug control. The main functions of the Commission are defined in the Single Convention (Articles 3 and 8), the 1971 Convention on Psychotropic Substances (Articles 2, 3 and 17) and the 1988 Convention Against Illicit Traffic in Narcotic Drugs and Psychotropic Substances (Articles 12, 20, 21 and 22). The Commission assists the Economic and Social Council in supervising the application of international drug conventions; prepares drafts for international conventions; considers changes to the existing machinery for international control; and receives recommendations from the World Health Organization for changes in the substances under control. The Commission meets annually and its members are elected by ECOSOC. The sessions are also attended by many observer governments (including states not members of the United Nations, such as the Holy See and the Republic of Korea), specialised agencies (such as the ILO, UNESCO and the WHO), inter-governmental organisations (such as the Commission of the European Communities, the Commonwealth Secretariat, the Council of Europe, the Customs Co-operation Council and Interpol) and non-governmental organisations in consultative status with the Economic and Social Council, for example, the International Alliance of Women, the International Pharmaceutical Federation, the International Catholic Child Bureau, the International Road Transport Union and the Association for the Study of the World Refugee Problem. Membership of the Commission was enlarged in February 1992 from 40 to 53 representatives of Member States.

The Commission has established subsidiary bodies to co-ordinate the mechanisms for drug law enforcement at the regional level: The Sub-Commission on Illicit Traffic and Related Matters in the Near and Middle East, and regional meetings of the operational Heads of National Drug Law Enforcement Agencies (HONLEA). The Asian and Pacific HONLEA dates back to the 1970s; the Latin America and the Caribbean, and the African HONLEA were both established in 1987 and a European HONLEA was established in 1990.

The International Narcotics Control Board was established by the Single Convention of 1961 to help simplify and unify international narcotics regulation by the merger of the various supervisory mechanisms into a unified body.[10] The Board replaced the

Permanent Control Board. The most important functions of the Board (outlined in Articles 12, 13, 14, 19 and 20 of the Single Convention, Article 2 of the 1972 Protocol which amended Article 9 of the Single Convention, and Article 19 of the 1971 Convention on Psychotropic Substances) are to administer the estimates system and a statistical returns system for the monitoring of international licit trade in drugs and to take measures to ensure the execution of the conventions. The Board consists of 13 members who are elected for a period of five years by the Economic and Social Council. Three are elected from candidates nominated by the World Health Organization and ten from a list of persons nominated by members of the United Nations and by non-member States Parties to the 1961 Convention. These members serve in their personal capacity rather than as representatives of their governments and are 'persons who, by their competence, impartiality and disinterestedness, will command general confidence'.[11] Furthermore, as Article 9(3) states, ECOSOC 'shall give consideration to the importance of including on the Board, in equitable proportion, persons possessing a knowledge of the drug situation in the producing, manufacturing, and consuming countries, and connected with such countries'.[12]

In order to ensure the maintenance of the 'technical independence' of the Board as specified in Article 9(2) of the Single Convention, the Board, like its predecessor body, has a separate staff responsible exclusively to the Board. This stems from the responsibilities assigned by the international drug-control treaties, including 'quasi-judicial functions' as described above. However, the Board's Secretary and secretariat (described below) were an integral part of the Secretariat of the United Nations and were under the full administrative control of the Secretary-General, confusing the position of the Board in the United Nations drug-control structure. Being primarily responsible for supervising the licit supply of drugs for legitimate medical and scientific uses, and in so doing preventing the diversion of licit drugs into illicit channels, the Board has a very limited mandate in the control of illicit drugs.

As already mentioned, previous to the restructuring of United Nations drug-control activities, there were three secretarial units concerned wholly with drug control. The Division of Narcotic Drugs (DND) served as secretariat to the Commission on Narcotic Drugs. The functions of the DND were specified by the international drug-control treaties and specific mandates of the General Assembly,

ECOSOC and the Commission. The Division advised and assisted governments and the specialised agencies on the application of the international drug-control treaties and provided governments with information on supply and demand reduction. It collected data and reported on the extent, patterns and trends of drug abuse worldwide. It analysed and published data on illicit-drug traffic, seizures, counter measures and trends. In addition, the Division organised training seminars and workshops for expert groups on technical subjects such as the use of drug-scenting dogs, detecting illicit cultivation through satellite remote sensing and aerial photography, and environmentally sound methods to eradicate drug crops. The Division was also the technical centre of the drug-control bodies and provided a variety of technical services to developing countries. The work of the Division was extremely varied and overlaps inevitably occurred with the other two secretariat units. For example, statistical data monitoring the trade in narcotic drugs and psychotropic substances was also collected by the INCB secretariat.

The second secretariat unit, the INCB secretariat, took its instructions exclusively from the International Control Board itself on substantive matters. However, on administrative matters and those concerning overall co-ordination of the United Nations drug-control activities the INCB secretariat reported directly to the chief executive designated by the Secretary-General, being an integral part of the United Nations Secretariat. Its work was carried out under five sub-programmes: the Office of the Secretary of the Board; the Narcotics Control Unit; the Estimates Unit; the Psychotropic Control Unit; and the Precursors Control Unit. The secretariat represented the Board at meetings of United Nations organs, specialised agencies and international, regional or inter-governmental bodies.

Finally, the United Nations Fund for Drug Abuse Control was established in 1971 by General Assembly Resolution 2719 (XXV) on the initiative of the Secretary-General. The specific primary purpose of the Fund was to finance actions in developing countries in order to ensure their full participation in the global drug-control effort. Funded entirely from voluntary contributions, and headed by an Executive Director, it reported directly to the United Nations Secretary-General. During its first decade UNFDAC was the principal 'operational arm' of United Nations drug-control activities, most clearly illustrated in the 'master plan' projects. In 1982, the Fund developed its country and regional 'master plans', which were a key element in the organisation of its activities, thoroughly analysing the drug problems within a country or region and implementing cohesive, integrated projects. In Colombia, the country where the Fund was most involved, there were 20 projects in operation in 1990. These projects included four rural development programmes featuring crop substitution; education and public information programmes through the mass media; two training programmes for educators; and special programmes on AIDS and for street children in Bogota.

The *ad hoc* emergence of bodies, and the development of the bodies established by the League of Nations to deal with the evolving new concerns of unprecedented scale, complexity and gravity, has been a significant problem in effective, co-ordinated international control. The diversity and multiplicity of United Nations drug-control mechanisms has handicapped effective action. In addition, most of them were established at a time when international action was principally concerned with the control of licit drugs for medical and scientific purposes. The diverse origins of the two main bodies, the CND and the INCB, and the *ad hoc* way in which their responsibilities have evolved, add to the complexity of co-ordinating international drug control, which the 1988 Vienna Convention confused further (see later). The complex, overlapping structure of the United Nations drug-control secretariat further complicated the decision-making and co-ordinating process. Confusion over overlapping mandates and lines of reporting led to calls for restructuring. Before the restructuring of the drug-control units, the three Secretariats were each responsible to the United Nations Secretary-General. However, they had markedly different structures and lines of reporting. The Director of the Division of Narcotic Drugs was immediately responsible to the Director-General of the United Nations Office in Vienna (who was in turn responsible to the Secretary-General). The Secretary of the INCB reported on administrative matters to the chief executive for drug-control activities as designated by the Secretary-General and on policy questions to the Board itself. The Executive Director of the United Nations Fund for Drug Abuse Control reported directly to the Secretary-General. This led to problems of co-ordination. Recognition of the problem of co-ordination led to the Secretary-General transferring co-ordination to the Director-General of the United Nations Office at Vienna in 1987 from the previous co-ordinator, the Under-Secretary-General for Political and General Assembly Affairs (appointed in 1984), who had to travel back and forth to Vienna for meetings.

The number of United Nations bodies, programmes and agencies which took part in drug-control activities before the restructuring illustrated the complexity involved in co-ordinating activities. In the field of prevention and reduction of the illicit demand for narcotic drugs, the Centre for Social Development and Humanitarian Affairs through its committee of experts, the Committee on Crime Prevention and Control, considered various issues relating to drug trafficking and drug control including the formulation of technical co-operation projects in co-operation with UNFDAC, focusing on measures against organised crime, with emphasis on drug trafficking, and the treatment of HIV-infected prisoners. Drug-control activities carried out by the International Labour Organization (ILO), related to the question of employment and the well-being of workers, focusing on drug-related problems in the workplace. Drug-control projects were often carried out with the assistance and/or funding of the WHO, UNFDAC, and the United Nations Development Programme (UNDP). From 1987 the United Nations Development Programme and UNFDAC operated under a co-operative agreement in which UNDP provided administrative and liaison services and field support and monitoring of UNFDAC projects. The United Nations Educational, Scientific and Cultural Organization (UNESCO) was involved with the prevention of drug abuse through public education and awareness programmes. It also became increasingly active in professional training programmes. The United Nations Children's Fund (UNICEF) was involved with drug abuse as it related to the estimated 100 million 'street children' world-wide. The Food and Agriculture Organization of the United Nations (FAO), and the United Nations Industrial Development Organization (UNIDO) were both involved in the elimination of the supply of drugs from illicit sources. The World Food Programme (WFP) was involved with drug-control programmes through integrated rural development schemes aimed at substituting other agricultural products for illicitly-grown opium poppy. It also provided food assistance for farmers and their families in areas where crop substitution was under way. United Nations entities involved in the suppression of illicit drug-traffic besides the DND and the INCB included the Centre for Social Development and Humanitarian Affairs, the United Nations Interregional Crime and Justice Research Institute, the International Civil Aviation Organization (ICAO), the Universal Postal Union (UPU) and the International Maritime Organization (IMO). A major concern of the IMO related to the increasing amounts of illicit drugs being transported by ship.

An examination of international co-operation in the drugs field shows clearly the multiplicity of functions and responsibilities and also the diversity of their origins. The *ad hoc* way in which organs and mandates evolved emphasised the lack of co-ordination of the United Nations structures for drug control. An understanding of this complexity, as well as an understanding of the need to reconsider the supply-reduction focus, led to the recent reforms and restructuring of United Nations drug-control activities which will be looked at in the next sections. As we have seen, for the greater part of this century drug legislation focused primarily on controlling the manufacture and movement of licit drugs and in preventing their diversion into illicit channels, thereby curtailing the supply of illicit drugs. During the 1980s, an opposing view emerged, that drug control efforts should concentrate equally on demand reduction and on controlling the movement of illicit drugs.

DRUG CONTROL IN THE 1980s

The increasing complexity of the drug phenomenon throughout the 1980s was mirrored by the increasing complexity of the evolving drug-control structures and activities. Three major UN events during the 1980s emphasised this expanded approach to drug control by the United Nations: the 1987 International Conference on Drug Abuse and Illicit Trafficking, the 1988 United Nations Convention Against Illicit Traffic in Narcotic Drugs and Psychotropic Substances, and the 1990 Seventeenth Special Session of the General Assembly, devoted to the question of international co-operation against illicit production, supply, demand, trafficking and distribution of narcotic drugs and psychotropic substances.

Initial calls for a specialised conference to focus on the fight against drug trafficking began as early as December 1984 in paragraph 9 of resolution 39/141, in which the General Assembly requested the Economic and Social Council, through the Commission on Narcotic Drugs, to consider the possibility of convening a specialised conference. Mr Javier Perez de Cuellar, then Secretary-General of the United Nations, on his own initiative, proposed to the Economic and Social Council in May 1985 that a world conference at the ministerial level to deal with all aspects of drug abuse should be held in 1987.[13]

The International Conference on Drug Abuse and Illicit Trafficking (ICDAIT), held in Vienna in June 1987, led to the adoption of the

Comprehensive Multidisciplinary Outline of Future Activities in Drug Abuse Control (CMO).[14] As the title suggests, the document introduced a major expansion in focus of United Nations drug-control activities. The CMO states that both the supply *and* demand for illicit drugs should be reduced, and that action must be taken to break the link between demand and supply, that is, illicit traffic.[15] The CMO contains four chapters, dealing with preventing and reducing illicit demand, controlling supply, illicit trafficking, and treatment and rehabilitation. The four chapters contain 35 targets which are meant as recommendations to governments and to non-governmental organisations suggesting practical measures, 'realistically attainable' over the next 10–15 years, which can contribute to the fight against drug trafficking (the targets are listed in Appendix A of this work). The important role of NGOs is specifically emphasised in paragraph 24 of the document. The document also disaggregates the state into numerous branches involved with drug control such as: legislative organs; the authorities concerned with public health, education, social welfare; the judiciary; law enforcement; and economic affairs – significant for an understanding of the state which does not conform to the unitary state actor envisaged by the orthodox approach to International Relations.

The CMO, adopted by the ICDAIT, recognised the importance of effective international co-operation on law enforcement in order to reduce the availabilty of illicit drugs, stating that co-ordination of activities and co-operation among national agencies within each country and between countries was vital for the achievement of the objective.[16] The two pillars of international drug control, the 1961 Single Convention on Narcotic Drugs and the 1971 Convention on Psychotropic Substances, were seen as inadequate to deal with modern international drug trafficking, focusing as they did on controlling the production of licit drugs and the prevention of their diversion into the illicit market-place. They made little provision for effective law enforcement.

As the opening paragraph of the document notes, 'it is not and was not designed to be a formal legal instrument'.[17] The significance of the CMO was that it was a move away from the treaty-based supply-side approach to international drug control, inherited from the League and pursued during the first three and a half decades of United Nations involvement in international drug control. The CMO entails no binding legal commitments of states, but was a move towards recognising the complexity and multi-faceted nature of the phenomenon and a move towards consensus-building. However, the CMO was followed instead by the adoption of the 1988 United Nations Convention Against Illicit Traffic in Narcotic Drugs and Psychotropic Substances and a return to the treaty-based approach to international co-operation.

United Nations General Assembly resolution 39/141 in December 1984, following an initiative from the government of Venezuela, expressed the conviction that the wide scope of illicit drug trafficking and its consequences made it necessary to prepare a convention which considered the various aspects of the problem as a whole, and, in particular, those not envisaged in existing international instruments. The Commission on Narcotic Drugs was requested by the Economic and Social Council to initiate the preparation of a draft convention and adopted by consensus on February 1986 a resolution in which it identified 14 elements for inclusion in a draft convention, which after debate and discussion culminated in the holding of the United Nations Plenipotentiary Conference for the Adoption of a Convention Against Illicit Traffic in Narcotic Drugs and Psychotropic Substances in Vienna from 25 November to 20 December 1988.[18] The Conference was attended by 106 countries and a variety of observers and adopted, again by consensus, a treaty text of 34 articles and one annex. The United Nations Convention Against Illicit Traffic in Narcotic Drugs and Psychotropic Substances was adopted on 19 December 1988 (hereinafter the Vienna Convention).[19] The next day, 96 states signed the Convention's Final Act, 44 of which signed the Convention itself. The adoption of the convention marked only a two-year negotiation process, the speed of which emphasises that the drug phenomenon, as understood by Chapter 2 of this research, had achieved 'a certain level of opprobrium in the commonly shared values of mankind'.[20]

The preamble to the Vienna Convention explicitly recognises illicit trafficking as 'an international criminal activity' and calls upon party states to take specific law-enforcement measures to improve their ability to identify, arrest, prosecute and convict drug traffickers. The Vienna Convention attempts to give force to the illicit trafficking recommendations of the CMO, in recognition of the changing nature of the drug phenomenon and the increase in trafficking since the 1970s. It requires that signatory states establish as criminal offences under their domestic law a comprehensive list of activities involved in or related to international drug trafficking, such as the production, manufacture, distribution or sale of any narcotic drug or psychotropic substance, money laundering, and the trade in chemicals, materials and equipment used in the manufacture of controlled substances. However, although the Convention does not permit parties to escape their obligations by arguing that they are inconsistent with domestic law (as Article 36(2) of the Single Convention, as amended, does allow), the principle of state sovereignty as defined by international law remains.

Although David Stewart states that 'The Convention is one of the most detailed and far-reaching instruments ever adopted in the field of international criminal law, and if widely adopted and effectively implemented, will be a major force in harmonizing national laws and enforcement actions around the world',[21] there is little of great innovation in its provisions for policy-makers in North America and Western Europe. Efforts to address the problems associated with the extremely large profits generated by illicit traffickers by the 'confiscation' (i.e. freezing, seizing and forfeiting) of traffickers' assets provided for in Article 5 of the Convention are familiar to European and American policy-makers. United States law already permits the forfeiture of property located in the United States 'which represents the proceeds of an offence against a foreign nation involving the manufacture, importation, sale or distribution of a controlled substance', if such offence would have been punishable by imprisonment for one year or more had it occurred in the United States.[22] In reference to Article 6 concerning the extradition of narcotics traffickers, the Vienna Convention simply supplements older bilateral treaties already established, but which did not cover drug offences. In the area of mutual legal assistance covered by Article 7, assistance was already provided for on a regional basis in Europe and on a bilateral basis in the United States through 'MLATs' (mutual legal assistance treaties). In addition to the mutual legal assistance provided for by Article 7, states party to the Convention are required by Article 9 to provide other, less formal types of law-enforcement assistance, co-operation and training. These less formal activities are, however, already provided for to a great extent by the work of the International Criminal Police Organization (Interpol). Under Article 11, states party are required to take the necessary measures to allow for 'controlled delivery', widely used by United States authorities, to monitor the passage of an illicit consignment without arrest or seizure in order to trace the further movement of the consignment and to identify higher levels of the trafficking organisation. Furthermore, the insertion of safeguard

clauses in many articles, and the weakness of monitoring and supervisory mechanisms, allows for parties to avoid obligations under
the convention with relative impunity. A further criticism of the
Vienna Convention and of the law-making treaties of the United
Nations in general, is that they often reflect the lowest common
denominator of consensus; if they were more than that, states could
simply refuse to ratify them.

The growing complexity of the nature of the drug phenomenon
and the increasing recognition of its threat to international order
and stability during the 1980s paralleled a period of increasing
activity in United Nations drug-control activities, as has been described. However, developments necessitated by the more comprehensive understanding of the nature of the phenomenon emphasised
by the Comprehensive Multidisciplinary Outline of Future Activities in Drug Abuse Control can be seen to have complicated an
already complex structure, rather than to have achieved the aim of
greater co-ordination among the various United Nations bodies,
units and programmes involved in drug control. Confusion over
mandates in drug-control activities was added to by the Vienna
Convention. The Vienna Convention partly blurred the legislative
and policy-making functions entrusted to the Commission and the
technical supervisory and control functions entrusted to the International Narcotics Control Board. Comparison of the articles of
the Vienna Convention on the respective functions of the Commission and the Board with the corresponding articles of the previous treaties reveals that the supervision of the application of some
provisions of the 1988 Convention were entrusted to the Commission instead of the Board.[23] At the same time, the responsibility
for the control of the implementation of the provisions on precursors and chemicals used for the manufacture of illicit drugs described in Articles 12, 13 and 16 rests with the INCB.[24]

As has already been referred to, problems of co-ordination of
the drug-control units at Vienna led to the appointment in 1984 of
the Under-Secretary-General for Political and General Assembly
Affairs to act as overall co-ordinator. However, the Under-Secretary-
General being based in New York complicated rather than promoted co-ordination. In 1987, the Director-General of the United
Nations Office at Vienna became co-ordinator for the drug
programmes. This decision was not so much based on the necessity of having those involved in drug control in the same location,
but rather in the context of budget reform and rationalisation.

However, the responsibilities of the Director-General of the United Nations Office at Vienna were already substantial and had increased further in the 1980s. The need of the drug units was not so much for co-ordination, but for direction and integration, which were not achieved.

Throughout the 1980s, the issues involved in drug control had been discussed in a large number of meetings of heads of government, for example, the 1989 summit of the Non-Aligned Movement, the Group of Seven industrialised nations, the European Council and the Commonwealth. In order for the United Nations to remain the focus for multi-lateral action in view of the changing nature of the drug phenomenon, a Special Session of the General Assembly was called.

THE RESTRUCTURING PROCESS

The Seventeenth Special Session of the General Assembly was held in New York in February 1990, to enhance the role of the United Nations in the field of drug control. The decision to hold a Special Session of the General Assembly was taken in resolution 44/16 of 1 November 1989 (initiated by the President of Colombia), in response to the issues involved receiving increasing attention in other international meetings of heads of governments, and to growing official concern over the expanding dimensions of the drug phenomenon, reflected in a number of United Nations inter-governmental forums, including the Second Interregional Meeting of Heads of National Drug Law Enforcement Agencies (Vienna, 11–15 September 1989),[25] and the Forty-Fourth Session of the General Assembly (New York, September to December 1989). A Political Declaration and Global Programme of Action were adopted in an acknowledgment of the importance of the changing nature of the drug phenomenon, recognised not only as a threat to health, but as a 'grave and persistent threat . . . to the stability of nations, [and] the political, economic, social and cultural structures of all societies'.[26] The Global Programme of Action emphasises demand reduction, with the Comprehensive Multidisciplinary Outline of Future Activities in Drug Abuse Control (outlined above) as its reference. The emphasis on demand reduction is stressed as being necessary to break the distribution link between supply and demand, and in so doing to diminish the increasing financial power of the drug traffickers that the previous focus on supply had failed to achieve. The Political Declaration affirms the need for comprehensive and multi-disciplinary strategies to eliminate illicit demand for narcotic drugs and psychotropic substances, cultivation of illicit crops and illicit drug trafficking and to prevent the misuse of the financial and banking systems. It also promotes effective treatment, rehabilitation and social reintegration.[27]

The Programme of Action calls for states to enhance the role of the United Nations as an 'advisory centre' for collecting, analysing and disseminating information on drug control. It also outlines specific efforts to address the treatment, rehabilitation and social reintegration of drug addicts, the strengthening of judicial and legal systems, measures to be taken against the diversion of arms and explosives, and additional resources for United Nations drug-control units, as well as the measures outlined above.

The emphasis on demand reduction during the Special Session reaffirmed the change in United Nations' focus from the previous supply reduction focus, and an expanded conceptualisation of the drug problem. As the representative from Colombia stated: 'We are witnessing an evolution towards a comprehensive, concerted, and joint confrontation of the problem, with recognition of the effects of demand and consumer abuse as the determining factors in this complex area.'[28] Despite these optimistic words and the fact that the Political Declaration did recognise the importance of viable alternative income schemes for developing countries, implementation was not forthcoming. Instead the Special Session decided to investigate restructuring options. Paragraph 94(a) of the Global Programme of Action expresses the need for coherence of activities within the drug-related units, co-ordination, complementarity, and non-duplication of all drug-related activities across the United Nations system. A Group of Experts was established to investigate the efficiency of the United Nations structure for drug-abuse control.

THE UNITED NATIONS INTERNATIONAL DRUG CONTROL PROGRAMME

A group of fifteen experts, selected by the Secretary-General from both developed and developing countries, was set up to develop a plan to integrate and upgrade the drug-control activities of the Vienna-based drug-control secretariats. The Group held a number of meetings during three sessions in Vienna in May, June and July 1990 and submitted their report to the Secretary-General. In December 1990 the General Assembly approved the recommendation for a United Nations International Drug Control Programme (UNDCP) to replace the drug control organs described above.

The United Nations International Drug Control Programme integrates the structures and the functions of the three main secretariat bodies, the International Narcotics Control Board's Secretariat, the Division of Narcotic Drugs and the United Nations Fund for Drug Abuse Control, with the objective of enhancing the effectiveness and efficiency of drug-control activities. The Programme is headed by an Executive Director at the level of Assistant Secretary-General with the exclusive responsibility for co-ordinating and providing effective leadership for drug-control activities, appointed by the Secretary-General and reporting directly to the Secretary-General. The Programme provides secretariat services to the Commission on Narcotic Drugs and the International Narcotics Control Board. Despite the recommendation of the expert group that the Commission be given a greater policy-making role, the roles of both the Commission and the Board remain unchanged by the creation of a drug control programme.[29]

In respect of the secretariat, a unified unit has been created at Vienna with responsibilities for (a) treaty implementation; (b) policy implementation and research; and (c) operational activities. The unit is headed by an Assistant Secretary-General. As regards treaty implementation there are two services: the secretariat of the INCB and the secretariat of the CND. The secretariat of the INCB continues to be responsible to the INCB for substantive matters in order to ensure the full technical independence of the INCB, as described earlier (see Figure 4.2).

The United Nations International Drug Control Programme is an organisational unit within the United Nations Secretariat, accountable to the Secretary-General. The Programme's work covers a wide range of activities, including demand reduction, suppression of illicit traffic, integrated rural development and crop substitution, law enforcement, legal assistance, treatment and rehabilitation and social reintegration of drug addicts in its role of carrying out the mandates and recommendations of the Comprehensive Multidisciplinary Outline of Future Activities in Drug Abuse Control and the Global Programme of Action.[30] The Programme's financial resources come from two sources: the United Nations'

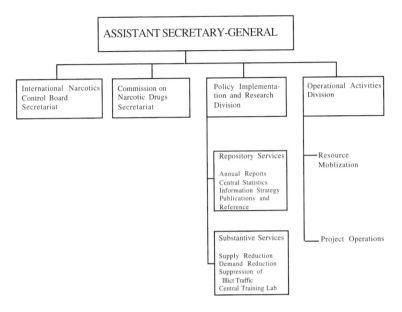

Figure 4.2   United Nations International Drug Control Programme

Source: *Enhancement of the efficiency of the United Nations structure for drug abuse control. Report of the Secretary General*, 23 October 1990. United Nations document A/45/652, Annex, p. 6.

regular budget and voluntary contributions. In the latter respect it is supported by the Fund of the United Nations International Drug Control Programme, established by the General Assembly in 1992. The budget for UNDCP in 1992 and 1993 totalled $183 million.[31] The Fund is the successor to the United Nations Fund for Drug Abuse Control; like its predecessor it is supported entirely from voluntary contributions of member governments and private organisations and is responsible for financing operational activities mainly in developing countries.

In addition to co-ordinating UN drug-related activities, UNDCP has encouraged parties outside the UN, especially financial institutions such as the World Bank, to include the drug dimension in their own policies and programmes. The World Bank has recently incorporated drug-related considerations in reports on Bolivia and Peru.[32] The more structured approach of the programme in its co-operation with organisations such as Interpol and the Customs

Cooperation Council has the aim of avoiding overlap and duplication of work. Significantly, however, the restructuring of United Nations drug-related activities has seen minimal change to the role of the two committee bodies, the Commission on Narcotic Drugs and the International Narcotics Control Board.

THE FUTURE ROLE OF THE UN IN INTERNATIONAL DRUG CONTROL

The problems associated with the United Nations drug-control structure reflect the problems associated with the expansion in scope, range and volume of work of the United Nations in the last 40 years. The increase in the number of issues on the international agenda that are truly global in nature has led to an increase in inter-governmental machinery, a growth in institutions, subsequent overlap of agendas and duplication of work in the United Nations itself and its affiliated bodies and Specialised Agencies. The United Nations structures have become too complex, leading to dispersion of responsibility and a diffusion of lines of authority, accountability and communication. Furthermore, the emergence of other organisations with terms of reference similar to its own has led to an inefficient duplication of work. This is particularly illustrated by drug-control efforts.

On the question of law enforcement and policing there was unnecessary overlap in Europe between the work of the DND, and now the work of the UNDCP and the Co-operation Group to Combat Drug Abuse and Illicit Trafficking in Drugs (the Pompidou Group), the Trevi Group of EC Ministers of the Interior and Justice (Terrorism, Radicalism, Extremism and International Violence)[33] and the International Criminal Police Organization ICPO/Interpol, where the work of the Drugs Intelligence Unit of the DND came close to police operations. Member countries reported drug seizures to the DND and exactly the same information went to Interpol. The DND also sponsored meetings of the Heads of National Law Enforcement Agencies (HONLEA). The DND was here involved in an activity in which Interpol has long specialised. Since the creation of the Drugs Sub-Division in 1930, Interpol has concerned itself with controlling drug trafficking, first working with the League of Nations and later with the United Nations drug control bodies. This co-operation culminated in Resolution 1579 (L) adopted in

1971 by the United Nations Economic and Social Council, which made it obligatory for the Secretariats of the two organisations to exchange information and documents concerning matters of mutual interest, to consult each other, and to set up a system of technical co-operation for independent projects. Furthermore, following a meeting of Trevi ministers in The Hague on 2–3 December 1991 to discuss the 1992 Programme of Action, a formal agreement was made to establish a European Police Organisation or 'Europol', whose purpose is to collect and analyse information on cross-border crime, including crime that extends beyond the Community. The first stage in this process was the establishment of a European Drugs Unit (EDU).[34] Title VI of the Maastricht Treaty for the first time brought 'combating drug addiction' and 'preventing and combating unlawful drug trafficking' within the scope of the Council of Ministers, the Commission and the European Parliament. This and other work of the Trevi Group still remains outside the European Community but is part of the wider European Union.[35] The work of the United Nations, in many areas, can be seen to be superseded by numerous other multi-national and regional initiatives.

The importance of achieving direction and integration of the drug programme reflects the same problems facing the United Nations system in general, as numerous inquiries into the need for reform of the United Nations have pointed out. Various calls for reform of the United Nations system, such as the 1969 Jackson Report, the 1975 Report of the Secretary-General's Experts, the 1985 Bertrand Report and the 1986 Report of the Committee of Eighteen have each emphasised different areas for reform, whether managerial, structural or financial, but have added more sub-headings to the agenda of reform rather than improving and streamlining the system itself. According to Maurice Bertrand this has led to a preoccupation in the way in which the mill operates becoming more important than the quality of the flour it produces.[36]

The decade-old Bertrand Report, often quoted by scholars writing about the United Nations, still reads as a relevant critique of the system today, and the major criticisms made are particularly relevant to United Nations drug-control activities and structures. The structural complexity leads to lack of co-ordination and definition of priorities. The *ad hoc* emergence of bodies and programmes reflects the development of drug-control activities as the organisation fought to keep up with events in the outside world. Indeed, this sectoralisation and fragmentation of the United Nations has

meant that the Specialised Agencies have become, in various re-
spects, detached from the real world, and are not therefore able to
identify global problems properly.

The view that the United Nations should have the capacity to
deal with global problems, co-ordinating the international response,
was emphasised by the Roundtable on 'The Future Role of the
United Nations in an Interdependent World' held in Moscow in
September 1988 on the initiative of the United Nations Institute
for Training and Research (UNITAR) and the USSR United Nations Association.[37] A new structure for the United Nations was
called for in order to enable it to deal with what were termed 'global watch issues'; issues on which convergence of interests exists.
It was suggested that global watch would be appropriate for such
issues as natural disasters, the global biosphere, international debt,
disease control (such as AIDS), refugees, illegal capital flight and
international narcotics trafficking. However, the inability of the United
Nations drug-control bodies to control the expansion in the production, distribution and demand for illicit drugs can be seen to
reflect its limitations as a formal organisation to manage the new
global concerns on the international agenda.

The restructuring and reorganisation of the Secretariat units called
for by the Global Programme of Action, unless the roles of the
Commission and the Board are also clearly defined, are not sufficient to have an effect on the United Nations' impact on global
drug control. It is the involvement of the Specialised Agencies and
other United Nations programmes, whose activities were numerous but lacked co-ordination, which requires fundamental and far-
reaching analysis. The United Nations International Drug Control
Programme is still at a relatively early stage in 'generating the necessary momentum for a globally coordinated drug effort'.[38] The UNDCP
has begun the process of developing effective co-ordination and
co-operation arrangements not only with other United Nations
entities, but with those outside the United Nations system as well.
However, as shown by Chapter 2, the phenomenon is too complex
and multi-faceted to be viewed as a single issue, despite the expanded conceptualisation of the drug phenomenon by the UNDCP.
The creation of a drug-control programme perpetuates the view of
the phenomenon as a single issue. The structural approach adopted
by international organisations is, alone, incapable of understanding the nature of the drug phenomenon. International regimes, in
encompassing an understanding of international organisations and

ormal rules and decision-making procedures, but also in encompassing an understanding of the nature of issues, values and norms, can more clearly explain the phenomenon.

INTERNATIONAL COLLABORATION AND INTERNATIONAL REGIMES

The study of international organisations has declined since the Second World War as scholars have turned their attention away from the study of formal international institutions and the perspective that international governance was whatever international organisations did, towards interest in broader forms of international institution-alized behaviour and the problem of international governance.[39] As Kratochwil and Ruggie state: 'When the presumed identity between international organizations and international governance was explicitly rejected, the precise roles of organizations *in* international governance became a central concern.'[40] This has led to increasing interest in the concept of international regimes, as expressing 'the parameters and the perimeters of international governance',[41] which can be seen to have culminated in the 1982 conference on international regimes in the United States, and a more recent European conference in Tubingen, Germany in 1991.[42]

However, concern with the nature of international governance, the role of international organisations and the role of international regimes has not been developed in any systematic fashion, so as to lead to an enhancement of our understanding of the nature of the relationship between international organisations, such as the United Nations and its drug-control activities, and the possible evolution of an international drug-control regime. This is because, to date, the dominant work on international regimes, as with international organisations, has concentrated on structural models to explain the nature of both regimes and international organisations, within a Realist hegemonic framework.

In the introduction to his book, Krasner identifies three distinct models for understanding international regimes: structuralist or Realist, modified structuralist or modified Realist, and Grotian. The structuralist model assumes a world of unitary state actors engaged in power maximisation. According to this model, the concept of international regimes is useless since they have no independent impact on international outcomes, and as Kenneth Waltz states can be seen

as only one small step removed from the underlying power capabilities that sustain them.[43] It was the work of Keohane and Nye,
already mentioned in earlier chapters, that first linked regime emergence and decline with rise and fall of the power of a hegemon.
They proposed a more disaggregated structural model, or 'issue-
structural' model, that emphasised states as the dominant actors in
international affairs, but that, in certain restrictive conditions, accepted states may have to give up a certain degree of independence in order to reach the optimum outcome. In this situation,
they say, regimes may arise. For modified structuralists, regimes
'constitute the general obligations and rights that are a guide to
states' behaviour' and must be viewed as 'something more than
temporary arrangements that change with every shift in power or
interests'.[44] The above approach, which has been labelled 'conventional structuralism', and its modification, 'modified structuralism',
both emphasise 'states' as the dominant actors, and inter-state
behaviour as the dominant concern for study. In this way international regimes can have no independent impact on global change
and are therefore not analytically useful.

Although the structural approach has dominated much of the
work on international regimes to date, an alternative, what has been
termed the 'Grotian approach', has been offered by writers such as
Donald Puchala, Raymond Hopkins and Oran Young, which emphasises the existence of regimes in 'every substantive issue-area
where there is discernibly patterned behaviour'.[45] Indeed, Oran Young
begins one of his articles, 'We live in a world of international regimes.'[46] The Grotian approach to international regimes is in contrast to both conventional and modified structuralism, in accepting
regimes as a fundamental part of the international system. The
international system is not seen as composed only of sovereign states,
with the only issue being one of power and security. The concept
of state sovereignty is challenged by this approach. The ability of
states to maintain dominance over all aspects of the system is seen
as limited, as is the use of force. For Puchala and Hopkins, élites
are the 'practical actors' in international regimes: 'bureaucratic units
or individuals who operate as parts of the 'government' of an international subsystem by creating, enforcing or otherwise acting in
compliance with norms'.[47] In this approach a regime is defined as
'a set of principles, norms, rules, and procedures around which actors'
expectations converge. These serve to channel political action within
a system and give it meaning.'[48]

The Grotian approach has been criticised by writers such as Arthur Stein for being so broad 'as to constitute either all international relations or all interactions within a given issue-area', and that 'Such use of the term regime does no more than signify a disaggregated issue-area approach to the study of international relations'.[49] And as such, as Jack Donnelly comments, 'regime' means little more than 'issue-area or political subsystem' and 'pointlessly adds to our already overstocked store of jargon'.[50] However, Stein also criticises current regime analysis for the other extreme, in that 'regimes are defined as international institutions. In this sense, they equal the formal rules of behaviour specified by charters of such institutions . . . This formulation reduces the new international political economy to the old study of international organizations . . .'[51]

The Puchala and Hopkins definition of an international regime, outlined above, draws upon the work of David Easton.[52] Indeed, this explanation of the nature of international regimes can be seen as synonymous with David Easton's definition of a political system as 'any set of variables selected for description and explanation'.[53] However, an exploration of the relationship between regimes and systems can lead to a more satisfactory explanation of regime dynamics. As has already been stated in Chapter 2, two key concepts emerged from the literature of interdependence: the concept of regimes, and the concept of issues forming distinct issue-systems governing behaviour within a state of interdependence. Chapter 2 has already looked at the nature of issues in international politics and Chapter 3 developed a theory of the emergence of issues onto the international agenda through a focus on values. The emphasis on understanding the nature of issues through an understanding of values is central to systems analysis and gives a firmer theoretical footing for exploring the normative nature of international regimes which is lacking in the dominant structural approach to regime creation.

The linking of systems theory with regime theory is not divorced from the intellectual progression of the discipline as described earlier. Indeed, in David Easton's 1965 volume of political theory, *A Systems Analysis of Political Life*, his description of a regime, as an 'object of support' between a constitutional order and a political community, introduces concepts utilised by the later regime theorists.[54] A regime is described as a set of constraints on political interaction which can be broken down into three components: values (described as goals and principles), norms, and structures of authority.

The values are described as 'broad limits with regard to what can be taken for granted in the guidance of day-to-day policy without violating deep feelings of important segments of the community'; norms are described as specifying 'the kinds of procedures that are expected and acceptable in the processing and implementation of demands'; and the structures of authority 'designate the formal and informal patterns in which power is distributed and organized with regard to the authoritative making and implementing of decisions – the roles and their relationships through which authority is distributed and exercised.'[55] Easton goes on to say that 'The regime also includes, however, those parts of the established expectations in political life that may seldom be envisaged as part of a constitution . . .'.[56] The work of Easton parallels the later Krasner definition of a regime as 'sets of implicit or explicit principles, norms, rules and decision-making procedures around which actors' expectations converge in a given area of international relations'.[57]

Although critics of regimes believe that regime theory is simply a new disguise for systems theory, this research claims that international regimes and issue-systems can be seen as different stages in the same process of agenda-formation. As already explained in Chapter 2, an issue-system is a set of actors for whom a single issue is salient. The extent to which the actors in the issue-system regulate the issue, by authoritatively allocating the values at stake (Easton), is variable. Where regulation occurs the phenomenon of an international regime emerges. A regime can be seen as a subset of an issue-system. Regulation occurs when the values under contention lead to the acceptance of a norm on which the regime is based. A focus on norms as more specific values can explain the relationship between issue-systems and regimes. Issue-systems form norms through the process of contention over values, leading to consensus around a norm, and regimes enforce and regulate norms in the policy-system.

Despite the criticisms of regime theory as a 'passing fad . . . an American academic fashion' by Susan Strange,[58] as we have seen, regime theory is part of the intellectual progression of the discipline of International Relations. Another criticism of regimes levied by Susan Strange in her article is that regimes were invented by social scientists. On the contrary, the concept of regimes has a long history in international law which the next chapter, on the norms of international drug control, will explore further.

CONCLUSION

This chapter has attempted to show how, despite eight decades of international action by the League of Nations and the United Nations in the field of international drug control, the problems associated with all aspects of the drug phenomenon, as described in Chapters 1 and 2, have increased. The ineffectiveness of the United Nations in this area can be seen to be due to the fact that the structural approach to global change adopted by international organisations, that concentrates on bargaining and negotiating procedures and legal rules, has not allowed the United Nations to recognise the diversity of issues involved. Therefore there has been no movement towards consensus on the issues and no agreement on norms by consensus. As Bertrand stated in his 1985 report, the United Nations needs to return to the aims of its Charter as a focus for international consensus-building. The drug phenomenon reflects this necessity. As the Executive Summary of the report on the *Enhancement of the Efficiency of the United Nations Structure for Drug Abuse Control* states, the drug problem 'involves the use that Governments wish to make of the United Nations and how they wish to confront a challenge that endangers the survival of human civilisation'.[59] The recent changes to United Nations drug-control activities, as well as the numerous efforts at reforming the United Nations system, have concentrated on administrative and co-ordination changes. Consensus-building on the issues involved in the drug phenomenon has taken second place.

During the 1980s, however, consensus was reached on the need to 'break the link between demand and supply, that is, the illicit traffic'.[60] The adoption by consensus in Vienna in December 1988 of the United Nations Convention Against Illicit Traffic in Narcotic Drugs and Psychotropic Substances can be seen to be an example of the willingness of states to attempt to control an activity which had 'attained a certain level of opprobrium in the commonly shared values of mankind'.[61] However, this focus on trafficking by the United Nations cannot be seen to have produced an effective global regime to control the activity. Implementation of the norm has proved to be impossible due to the nature of the drugs themselves and the ease with which they can be transported, as outlined in Chapter 2. Furthermore, the drug-control bodies of the United Nations, despite the restructuring, have clearly not evolved into an authoritative decision-making focus, necessary for regime creation and norm implementation. Whether the United Nations International Drug Control Programme can evolve into a global decision-making focus remains to be seen. The regionalisation of trafficking control, as demonstrated by the work of the European Community, suggests not. Attempts to control drug trafficking can be seen to have led at best to the emergence of a 'declaratory regime', to use Jack Donnelly's regime classification.[62] This will be discussed further in Chapter 7.

The expansion of illicit drug production, trafficking and consumption has outpaced the United Nation's efforts to contain it. Furthermore, some of the economic, political and social developments that have occurred throughout the early 1990s can be seen as potential harbingers of crisis for countries that have so far been relatively free of drug-related problems. Alternative forms of co-operation, such as the creation of several different international regimes for the various drug-related problems, is urgently needed. In order to understand regime creation, we need to understand the nature and role of norms in international relations. This will be the subject of the next chapter.

5 Keep off the Grass: Drug Norms and International Relations

INTRODUCTION

The inclusion of norms and principles in Krasner's definition of an international regime emphasises one of the earlier attractions of regime theory, in that it included patterns of co-operation that were not embodied in specific sets of legal rules or international organisations and so highlighted the normative area for exploration by regime theorists. Yet despite this, as the previous chapter has emphasised, structural explanations of regime dynamics, with a concentration on the rules and decision-making procedures of regimes, have predominated. The concept of hegemony, with powerful actors writing the rules in their own interests, has been used to explain regime creation, change and decline. However, as Donald Puchala and Raymond Hopkins write, international regimes 'exist primarily as participants' understandings, expectations or convictions about *legitimate, appropriate* or *moral* behaviour'[1] (emphasis by current author), which suggests that state-centric power theory cannot alone adequately explain regime creation. Despite the obvious need, therefore, to understand the nature and role of norms in regime analysis, very little work has been done in this area.

One reason why regime norms have been neglected is the dominance of American literature on regime theory, with its preoccupation with the concept of hegemonic stability and, until recently, the lack of development of regime theory within a European context and its broader tradition of thought on the role of the individual, the state, and the existence of various conceptions of an 'international society'. One of the few International Relations scholars to have focused on the importance of norms in international affairs, Friedrich Kratochwil, talks about the 'premature fascination' of regime scholars with regime change as failing to develop criteria by which regime adaption (changes to rules and decision-making procedures, in the Krasner definition) can be distinguished from regime change itself (changes to norms and principles, in the Krasner definition) or from regime decline, since regime change was originally identified with regime decay and associated with reflections of hegemonic power. If regimes are simply to be associated with notions of hegemonic power then they can have no independent impact on international affairs, and so the answer to Stephen Haggard's and Beth Simmons' cry, in their 1987 overview of regime literature, 'Do regimes "matter"?' would have to be a negative one.[2] As Oran Young states, one of the most surprising features of the emerging literature on regimes is the relative absence of sustained discussions of the significance of regimes as determinants of collective outcomes at the international level. Indeed, as Young asks, why bother to study regimes, if you give them no impact on institutional behaviour? But as Young states, the proposition that regimes do matter and affect behaviour 'is relegated to the realm of assumptions rather than brought to the forefront as a focus for analytical and empirical investigations'.[3] Whether regimes matter depends on the role allotted to norms in international affairs. Many analysts agree that norms are a central feature of international regimes. However, recent regime literature can be seen to have moved even further away from an understanding of the importance of norms and principles in regime creation. A recent description of regimes by Robert Keohane as 'institutions with explicit rules, agreed upon by governments, which pertain to particular sets of issues in International Relations',[4] makes no reference to norms. In this he makes little distinction between regime theory and work on international institutions. With this approach the concept adds little to our understanding of global politics.

Krasner states that norms and principles, and not rules and decision-making procedures, are fundamental for understanding regime change and therefore by implication regime creation and decline. In this sense the phenomenon of regime continuation after the removal of hegemonic support (of interest to several regime theorists) can be explained. But the Krasner volume fails to develop this side of the definition and to explain the nature of norms, with 'norms' and 'rules' not clearly distinguished from each other in much of the volume. Research into international regimes has concentrated on hegemonic power explanations of regimes, which dismiss totally, or sideline, the importance of norms. In this way regimes are denied any independent impact in world politics and cannot, as Haggard and Simmons ponder, 'matter'. This work has based itself on the premise that regimes do matter, and therefore we need a clearer understanding of the nature, role and impact of norms in International Relations, as this chapter will demonstrate. Again, problems over terminology highlighted in previous chapters will be addressed. Problems concerning the use of the term 'norm' strike at the heart of the concerns over regime theory, that there is still no fundamental answer to Krasner's first question, 'What is a regime?', because, as Haas points out, 'theorists of regimes disagree widely because the words they use ... come from different normative and philosophical traditions'.[5] These traditions therefore have to be explored.

ISSUE-SYSTEMS, NORMS AND INTERNATIONAL REGIMES

The last chapter referred to the relationship between the concept of issue-systems and international regimes as different stages in the same process of agenda-formation. However, critics of regime theory have attacked international regimes for simply being systems in disguise. This writer believes the two concepts to be analytically distinct, and this distinction can be comprehended by an understanding of the concept of norms.

As Chapter 3 explained, values are abstract aspirations for improving the human condition that can only be pursued indirectly by the acquisition of concrete objects, or stakes. As Mansbach and Ferguson write, 'Abstract values are sought as consummatory ends with intrinsic worth, while the stakes that represent them are merely instrumental in terms of their satisfaction.'[6] When a high level of consensus is reached over the disposition of stakes, we can see norm emergence. Issue-systems can be seen to generate norms if and when the process of contention over values leads to consensus around a norm. Then regimes can be seen to enforce and regulate norms (see Figure 5.1).

The norm-regulated rules of a regime are implemented in what can be seen as a drugs policy-system, as referred to in Chapter 2. A policy-system can be seen as a set of issues conceptually different but behaviourally linked. The issue of money laundering, for example, involves contention among actors for whom the issue is salient, forming an issue-system. The issue-system generates a norm, which is implemented within the banking and finance policy-system,

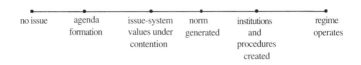

Figure 5.1   Regime Creation

as the next chapter will explain further.

As the previous chapter on the changing attitudes towards drug use in the nineteenth century demonstrated, contention among actors over values led to the formation of various issue-systems, with economic efficiency and economic welfare, as values, overriding anti-drug values. There was no agreement on the value position that drugs were evil and dangerous and therefore no norm emerged to be enforced and regulated by a drug-control regime. With the decline in the relative salience of the economic welfare value, for the actors concerned during the first half of the twentieth century, the anti-drug value position increased in importance. As a result a number of anti-drug norms were formed along with a weak drug-control regime. In this sense issue-systems and regimes can be seen as producing the same process of behaviour modification, with norms forming the link in understanding both the conceptual world of issues and the behavioural world of policy formation. It is therefore necessary to identify norms in the present-day politics of drugs in order to understand regime creation and regime absence. To identify the norms concerned with drug-related activity, and to understand the role norms play in regime creation and significance, it is necessary to reach a suitable definition of a norm.

As has already been emphasised in this work and in the work of others, the apparently haphazard aggregation of disparate phenomena in the Krasner definition of an international regime, such as implicit rules, principles and norms, adds to the confusion in understanding the nature of international regimes. The difficulty of distinguishing an 'implicit rule' from a 'norm' or from a 'principle' has led to the role of norms not being explicitly explored by regime theorists. A clearer understanding of the role of norms in international regimes is needed, distinct from rules and decision-making procedures.

THE NATURE OF NORMS

The concept of a norm is not expanded in the Krasner work beyond the initial description as outlined above, despite the emphasis on the importance of norms in the introduction to the book. Neither does Kratochwil present us with a definitive understanding of the concept. He states, 'Norms are used to make demands, rally support, justify actions, ascribe responsibility, and assess the praiseworthy or blameworthy character of an action.'[7] This is an extensive list of characteristics that will be refined later in the chapter. But Kratochwil emphasises that his purpose is not to understand the nature of norms: 'I shall use the terms "norms" and "rules" interchangeably, since I am mainly concerned with the *force* of prescriptions'.[8] One of the difficulties involved in understanding norms is that the term is often used interchangeably with both 'rules', as the work of Kratochwil emphasises, and 'values'.

As Kratochwil states, he is not interested in distinguishing between rules and norms. The sociologist Ullmann-Margalit, in *The Emergence of Norms*, hypothesises that a lack of clarity over the two terms may be due to the different backgrounds of writers: that the term 'norm' tends to be used by Continental authors, whereas the terms 'rule' and 'law' are preferred by Anglo-Saxons to cover more or less the same domain of discourse.[9] Although the Krasner definition does blur the two by talking about 'implicit rules' and 'explicit norms', and although, at the margin, they can be seen to merge into one another, it is clear that there is a difference between the two. As will be shown, it is important to distinguish between the two for an understanding of the importance of norms for international regimes. In order to understand the impact of regimes, we need to separate out the norms from the rules and from the actual behaviour. That is, in asking whether regimes matter we need to know if norms change an actor's behaviour.

Norms are often used interchangeably with values in International Relations literature, with little methodological consistency. This can be seen to be due to the dominance in the discipline of the Realist paradigm, which dismisses norms and values as of little importance in international affairs, concentrating instead on notions of power and status. It is, however, common to find both terms in the disciplines of anthropology, sociology and political science with the study of comparative politics. However, as James Rosenau states in *The Scientific Study of Foreign Policy*, neither students of comparative politics nor those in international politics are 'drawn by conceptual necessity to find a theoretical home for the external behaviour of societies'.[10] Students of comparative politics, concerned with political functions, goal attainment and political culture, focus primarily on processes *within* societies. As such, they have generally not accounted for the penetration of national societies by international systems. This penetration is clearly demonstrated by international drug control, where international legislation at the turn of the century preceded national legislation in many cases. Similarly, one reason many national governments now give as to why the legalisation of cannabis cannot be considered is their commitment to international control. Students of the traditional approach to International Relations have focused on processes of interactions that occur *between* national systems. However, in the Globalist paradigm, adopted by this work, the boundary between the national and the international is challenged. An exploration of recent literature in the discipline of sociology, beginning with the work of Amitai Etzioni (as referred to in Chapter 3), can be seen to have begun to illuminate the relationship between the national and the international, and the discipline of Sociology generally can be used to illuminate the concept of norms.

The Krasner description of norms as 'standards of behaviour defined in terms of rights and obligations' and Milton Rokeach's description of values as 'an enduring belief that a specific mode of conduct or end-state of existence is personally or socially preferable to an opposite or converse mode of conduct or end-state of existence'[11] obviously share some common ground. But it is important to differentiate between them. Norms are not the same as values. Values are abstract: they can exist independently of a specific situation. In contrast norms are role-specific and context-specific modes of behaviour. When norms are used in general terms, detached from specific issues and circumstances, they can be difficult to distinguish from values, adding to the confusion. Values, however, can be seen as more general, and norms as more specific. A single value can be translated into and codified into a great number and variety of different norms. As the sociologist Robin Williams describes it, 'The same value may be a point of reference for a great many specific norms; a particular norm may represent the simultaneous application of several separable values ... Values as standards (criteria) for establishing what should be regarded as desirable, provide the grounds for accepting or rejecting particular norms.'[12]

A fundamental difficulty with reaching an understanding of a norm is that the concept has different meanings in the literature of different fields, as suggested above. In the discipline of International Relations, the term would appear to be naturally associated with 'normative theory', which has become increasingly popular in the last decade, in the same period that the concept of international regimes has also become popular. Normative theory asks of world politics a question that political theory has asked of politics in domestic societies for centuries, 'What is the good life?' In this sense, it stands in the tradition of ethical political philosophy and seeks to warrant or justify alternative ethical positions. Therefore, although it concerns itself with values and norms, as do those studying comparative politics, the current debate between 'cosmopolitanism and communitarianism'[13] in asking whether present structures of the international system promote or detract from the living of 'the good life', does little to explain behaviour and impact on decision-making, but rather restricts itself to philosophical considerations, and works in isolation from regime theorists. For normative theorists, norms are seen as standards of behaviour that are considered 'right', and are a standard by which behaviour can be considered and judged.

The term 'legal norm' is widely understood to refer to those norms embodied in formal documents such as written constitutions or legal codes in what is known as International Law. Legal norms are therefore often institutionalised and can be seen as instruments for the joint pursuit of shared purposes by states. The concept of a norm however is not clarified by its use in International Law, since the discipline of law also makes a sharp distinction between the domestic and the international. In the theory of law there are two broad schools of thought about the nature of law, and therefore of norms. On the one hand, there are those, especially within the Anglo-American legal tradition, who see all law as positive, as direct commands from someone or something to enforce them. This school clearly differentiates between law and morality. They also deny the status of 'law' to non-enforceable rules, such as norms making up the body of conventions and expectations known as 'International' law. On the other hand, there is the 'Natural Law' school which sees law as somehow representing binding obligations arising from a prior moral sphere, to which the actual positive laws merely give effect (or ought to). Therefore, norms play a significant role. Until quite recently the 'positive law' tradition was dominant in American

and English legal thinking and most common amongst practition-
ers of law, if not theorists, everywhere, but this position is increasingly challenged, especially by writers in the new liberal tradition
following philosophers such as John Rawls, whose influence will
be discussed later.

Kratochwil, in writing about the role of norms in international
life, refers a great deal to concepts from international law. In talking about the concept of 'rights', used by Krasner to define norms,
along with the idea of 'obligations', Kratochwil makes a distinction
between rights as 'it is right that' and as 'having rights'. As Kratochwil
argues in his book, international law has been clearly divorced from
conceptions of morality. In writing about the wars of religion he
states that 'it was no accident that a legal conceptualization of international relations attained importance when attempts to use "the
right way of life" as an organizing principle of political life had to
be abandoned.'[14] Norms as morals can be seen to have been replaced by norms as rules in modern political thinking.

In sociology the general reference to 'cultural norms' or 'social
norms', as the general conceptions about right and wrong ways of
behaving in political life, shade off into 'technical or cognitive norms'
(how to boil an egg, the most effective way to manufacture a car)
to 'moral' norms (Thou shalt not kill). Between these, as Williams
points out, come others such as 'conventional' norms ('custom',
'etiquette', etc.) and aesthetic norms (standards of taste, beauty,
etc.),[15] adding a further element to our understanding of the concept. As Williams states, norms always carry some prescriptive or
proscriptive quality, although there is an enormous variation in the
kind of normative emphasis. He cites as examples the difference
between the conformity accompanying fashions and the most deeply
ingrained taboos.

Analysis of regime norms can draw on all three disciplines, as
described above, and further emphasise the connections between
these various artificially separated areas. Writers on regimes, however, have for the most part avoided exploring the notion of 'justice and fairness', as emphasised by normative theory. More attention
could be paid to this, as the current interests within International
Relations theory demonstrate. The concept of values, evoking as it
does domestic social, cultural and political factors, necessitates some
accounting for concepts of fairness and equity, since values are
closely related to distinct domestic histories and cultures. From
the legal tradition, we can see that international regimes also in-

volve the idea of commonly accepted behaviour in order to reached shared goals, or to use Terry Nardin's phrase, of 'purposive associations'.[16] The 1990 Keohane definition of a regime, already mentioned, stresses the explicit, persistent and connected sets of rules rather than implicit rules or norms. In so doing, regime theory and international law are brought very closely together. Kratochwil has emphasised what he sees as the neglect of the legal bases of the regime concept, among those from an international politics perspective.[17] For regimes there is overlap between these different uses. Many international conventions provide the framework of legal norms under which international regimes may develop. From the discipline of sociology, we can see that norms can be understood as commonly accepted types of behaviour outside an institutionalised context. This is an important modification to the use of the term by many regime theorists and international lawyers. Sociology also shows us that there is an enormous difference in types of norms. As Kratochwil stresses it is important to make the distinction between 'norms which are clear and whose duty-imposing character is easily established and other norms such as "comity" or tacit understandings which carry no such obligations'.[18] This distinction is necessary for understanding regime norms or 'norms of obligation', as will be explained later.

As the previous chapter has illustrated, the concept of regimes can be traced back to David Easton. His work can also be used to give a clearer understanding of the nature of regime norms. For Easton, normative theory means the adoption of a value as an objective and the evolution of an explanation in terms of the conditions necessary to maximise the selected value, rather than an understanding of the 'good life' as in the tradition of ethical philosophy. The concept of a norm therefore can be see to mean different things for different disciplines, but a widely acceptable definition of the concept comes from the sociologist Robin Williams. Norms are described as 'rules of conduct; they specify what should and should not be done by various kinds of social actors in various kinds of situations'.[19]

These 'norms of obligation' are described by the sociologist Edna Ullmann-Margalit as a 'sub-class' of 'social norm'.[20] Ullmann-Margalit describes a 'social norm' as a 'prescribed guide for conduct or action which is generally complied with by the members of a society'.[21] This broad definition, which emphasises the idea of collective consensus, is then refined by focusing on a sub-class of social norms.

For this purpose she utilises H. L. A. Hart's *The Concept of Law*,[22] in which Hart describes 'social norms' as 'rules of obligation'. In order to maintain uniform terminology, Ullmann-Margalit substitutes norms for rules in utilising Hart's description. This sub-class of norms is characterised as follows:

1. '[Norms] are conceived and spoken of as imposing obligations when the general demand for conformity is insistent and the social pressure brought to bear upon those who deviate or threaten to deviate is great.'
2. 'The [norms] supported by [a] serious pressure are thought important because they are believed to be necessary to the maintenance of social life or some highly prized feature of it'.
3. 'It is generally recognized that the conduct required by these [norms] may, while benefitting others, conflict with what the person who owes the duty may wish to do'.[23]

These features, however, are not intended to provide the necessary conditions for norms of obligation. As Ullmann-Margalit writes, 'examples can be found of norms of obligation to which one, or more, of these features does not apply'.[24]

It is the third characteristic which highlights the fact that actors do not necessarily act in their own interests, contrary to Realist understanding of regime creation and change. The first characteristic, concerned with the process of 'socialisation', shows that power as force cannot adequately explain actor behaviour. United Kingdom drug-control policy emphasises the importance of norms for actors' decision-making: 'In all instances, UK drug law has been strengthened to comply with international treaty obligations rather than to combat British drug problems'.[25]

This diversity over the concept of 'norm' in normative theory, international law and sociology is significant when we consider the question of what impact norms have: that is, whether they do change the behaviour of actors, as suggested by the features above. Whether actions are guided solely by self-interest or whether values and/or morality also play a part is a central question for political philosophy. It also must be a central question for regime theorists, as highlighted by the use of the term 'norm' in the Krasner definition.

THE ROLE OF NORMS

There are several contending schools of thought on the role of norms in international affairs which can be broadly viewed in relation to the inter-paradigm debate in International Relations: that is, the debate between Realism and Globalism as explained in this work. These approaches in turn relate clearly to the philosophical debate which underpins much of International Relations, as to whether the 'rules of conduct' described above by Robin Williams are derived from the interests of the actors or have an independent influence and constrain such interests. The former position was espoused by the nineteenth-century philosopher Jeremy Bentham, who considered moral truths 'nonsense on stilts', while the latter was adopted by John Locke in the seventeenth century and in this century by John Rawls. The contending schools of thought are reflected in the debate amongst regime theorists over why states obey rules of a regime that are usually unenforced and mostly unenforceable: that is, explanations of power, coercion, egoistic self-interest and reciprocal benefits contrasted with the role of values, morality, and a sense of justice.

The dominant approach to International Relations, Realism, has traditionally been seen as exemplified by the work of Thomas Hobbes, writing more than 300 years ago. His philosophy on the nature of life as a struggle for power in an anarchic world underlines much Realist thought. Hobbes argued that before governments existed, the state of nature was dominated by the problem of selfish individuals who competed on such ruthless terms that life was 'solitary, poor, nasty, brutish, and short'.[26] In his view, states could not function without a central authority, and consequently a strong government (a Leviathan/Hegemon) was necessary. All the people commit themselves to transfer authority to the sovereign by a 'social contract' or covenant and in so doing the sovereign becomes possessed of unlimited right of sanction. His word is then the law and therefore there is no higher moral authority. This philosophy makes the assumption that international life is almost norm-free. States are condemned to anarchy and the constant threat of war; there is no escape from the struggle for power.

A variation on this theme acknowledges the existence of norms, but argues that they are the servants and not the masters of national interest. For Realists such as E. H. Carr, norms are merely 'the unconscious reflections of national policy based on a particular interpretation of national interests at a particular time'.[27] There can be no norms, guaranteeing stability and order. David Hume's description of the emergence of convention and co-operation within domestic society illustrates this:

> I observe, that it will be for my interest to leave another in possession of his goods, provided he will act in the same manner with regard to me. He is sensible of a like interest in the regulation of his conduct. When this common sense of interest is mutually expressed, and is known to both, it produces a suitable resolution and behaviour.[28]

A modification of this approach views norm compliance, not in terms of hegemonic power, but in terms of the long-term calculations of actors' interests. This approach, developed by the philosopher Jeremy Bentham from the work of Hobbes and Hume, has been termed utilitarianism.[29] Bentham's work covered many areas, but his utilitarian position was most fully developed in his political theory and moral philosophy. His general argument was that pleasure and pain were the two driving forces of mankind and that moral or political values had to be translated into these terms. Treating man as selfish, Bentham argued that the only way to judge any policy, choice or decision was to discover whether it produced a positive or negative balance of pleasure over pain. Whatever maximises the positive balance of pleasure over pain across a group or for a single individual, if only one person is concerned, is what is 'good' and therefore 'right'. There have of course been many adjustments and refinements to this basic approach. One problem has been that what tends to maximise the interests or happiness of a single individual might, were everyone to act in the same way, be disastrous as a public policy. Therefore there has come about a distinction between 'Rule' versus 'Act' utilitarianism. An act-utilitarian requires that each individual ensures that his every act maximises his own utility, whereas a rule-utilitarian requires that laws and regulations be decided so that, on balance, the rule maximises the sum of individual utilities, even though in particular cases individuals would not, as selfish utility maximisers, choose to act as the rule requires. Utilitarianism is a further move away from relying on any source of moral authority or 'natural law', appealing instead to rational self-interest.

An alternative approach to norms, and a challenge to the utilitarianism of Bentham, has been the functionalist school in sociology from Durkheim to Parsons, which contrasts with the above approaches in seeing norms as 'givens' in any social system, including the international system, and stresses the *consensus-generating and order-maintaining* functions of norms – a direct challenge to the Hobbesian–Realist anarchic world. As Talcott Parsons writes,

> In most current sociological theory, order is conceived as the existence of normative control over a range of the action of acting units, whether these be individuals or collectives, so that, on the one hand, their action is kept within limits which are compatible with at least the minimum stability of the system as a whole and, on the other hand, there is a basis for at least certain types of concerted action when the occasion requires.[30]

Durkheim contrasts with both Hobbes and Hume, in conceptualising norms and rules as 'social facts' existing objectively and constraining individual choices. In other words, as Durkheim and Parsons and others have argued, it is norms rather than 'social contracts' which should be proposed as primitives in explaining how international co-operation comes about. According to Durkheim and Parsons, interaction presupposes convergent expectations based on some sort of common value orientation. The increase in interactions under conditions of interdependence also fosters the convergence of value orientations, which allows for further institutionalisation of co-operation. This is in contrast to the 'rationalist approach' of Bentham. Interactions do not presuppose, yet create a demand for normative institutions which can reduce the probability of undesirable outcomes.

This view influenced the philosophy of John Rawls. His major book, *A Theory of Justice*, published at the beginning of the 1970s, was a major attack on the prevailing utilitarian theories of political obligation and social order and attempted to revivify the 'social contract' approach to political theory.[31] The essential points of Rawls' work are two-fold. He argued for the re-establishment of some form of 'natural rights' so that there would be some values to be held as absolute, principally the right to liberty, and developed the 'justice as fairness' argument in challenge to the cost-accounting approach of the utilitarians.

Rawls developed his ideas from the political theory of John Locke, who was the contemporary of Hobbes, whose work he opposed. Despite the work of Locke, there has been very little opposition to the idea of utilitarianism since its inception (dominating Western political parties and governments, most economic theory, policy analysis and until recently law and jurisprudence). Only in the 1970s did political theorists of a non-Marxist kind even begin to develop non-utilitarian general political philosophies, so total was the hold of the Benthamite tradition over Western intellectuals.

The role of norms in decision-making presents no problem for the Realist, since his or her conception of the world is state-centric and power political. The Hobbesian–Realist decision-maker acts in a rational self-interested manner. Given that society is composed of extremely self-interested individuals, co-operation is based on the concept of social covenant. As Hobbes writes, individuals are driven to covenant/contract with each other by the dominant element of fear common to them all. However, for the Globalist, understanding decision-making is more complex. Rosenau's work, already referred to, has gone some way in showing just how complex.

Kratochwil challenges the Hobbesian–Realist notion of rationality outlined above. As Kratochwil states, the problem with the modified structuralist (or Utilitarian) approach is that norms are conceived 'largely in instrumental terms' and as such the approach does not take into account the other important functions served by norms. Norms define social settings within which actors operate: they 'simplify choices and impart "rationality" to situations by delineating the factors that a decision-maker has to take into account'.[32] The 'rational' choice of the modified structuralist actor is possible only after the actor has interpreted the situation, and as Kratochwil states, the interpretations themselves are largely governed by the actor's attitudes, which are informed by general social values. Kratochwil illustrates this with the Prisoner's Dilemma game. The dilemma of whether to give evidence against the other prisoner is caused by the attitude of the two players towards each other, derived from a lack of trust. As Kratochwil states, where mutual trust exists it would be 'rational' to co-operate, and 'irrational' to defect. Therefore, values can be seen as establishing a 'general medium which makes co-ordination of choices and co-operation possible'.[33]

As has been suggested, the different approaches to norms amongst International Relations theorists have been influenced by different philosophical traditions. Hobbes's, Hume's, and Durkheim's theories of norms have been shown to be roughly identifiable with the Realist, modified Realist (or Utilitarian) and Globalist positions respectively. The domination of the Realist and Utilitarian approaches has limited the use of norms to explain international co-operation in the form of international regimes. One of the reasons for this limitation is due to the concept of a norm being firmly established in domestic politics. It is not investigated thoroughly in an international setting due to the separation of the domestic and the international by Realist writers. The understanding of the role of norms in regime theory has in the main been associated with international law by regime theorists, and therefore concern with both the nature of norms and their role has been limited. Regime norms, however, evoke both custom and law in understanding the nature of international regimes. The concept of a 'norm' encompasses both rule-like characteristics, and standards of behaviour appropriate to a particular role or situation, elaborated or codified in accordance with the value-system of international society. In this sense it is possible to imagine that there are thousands and thousands of norms in international affairs, rather than the absence of norms claimed by the Realists. Furthermore, these norms can be seen to affect the behaviour of actors in decision-making.

THE NORMS OF DRUG CONTROL

If we take on board the complexity of the concept of norms as illustrated above, we can see that norms do not come about at a definitive point in time, nor can their emergence be explained by a manageable number of discernible acts. They are the result of complex patterns of behaviour of a large number of people over an extended period of time. Such a description does not suggest that straightforward utilitarian calculations of interest can explain the existence of norms. Their emergence requires the utilisation of the concept of salience as described in this research. This concept of salience has been utilised in contrast to the Realist hegemonic-power theory of agenda-building. When actors in an issue-system reach consensus over values, they will try to realise those values by the creation of a norm.

As we have seen, norms can be seen to contain two ideas, the specification of a more general value and the formation of consensus. I will now proceed to identify the norms in the politics of drugs. I have chosen these particular norms because of the high level of consensus within the international system, over the last ten years, and the salience to many political actors of the values under threat. The following propositions would now appear to have the status of being global norms.

1. Private associations should not seek to prevent governments from exercising their authority, or to seek to exercise the authority of legitimate governments.
2. Activities should not be engaged in which lead to the corruption of the due process of government, whether by financial inducements or threats.
3. Activities should not be engaged in which would damage the emotional, mental or physical growth of a minor.
4. Banks should not profit from criminal finance.

The norm that 'Private associations should not seek to prevent governments from exercising their authority, or seek to exercise the authority of legitimate governments' can be seen to have emerged due to the alliance of terrorist and insurgency movements with drug production. The adverse effects of the drug phenomenon on political and economic dimensions of domestic and international security in an increasing number of countries throughout the 1980s has been explained in Chapter 2. Colombia in particular, throughout the 1980s, experienced 'narco-terrorism', with an open war declared by the Medellin cartel. The huge increase in organised crime of a non-drug-related nature, such as illicit arms trading, the trafficking in transplant organs, insurance fraud, etc. by groups such as the Cosa Nostra, Triads, Yakusa, Yardies and others, is seen as constituting a grave threat to public security, the rule of law and other fundamental social, economic and political institutions by nearly every country. The evolution of organised crime can be regarded as a process of rational reorganisation on an international basis of criminal 'enterprises', following the same patterns as legal enterprises. As the United Nations report on Crime Prevention and Criminal Justice states,

> This 'transnationalization' of organised crime represents a situation that is both quantitatively and qualitatively different from that which prevailed in the past and which, needless to say, complicates the implementation of effective prevention and control measures.[34]

The break-up of the former Soviet Union and the downfall of one-party regimes in Central and Eastern Europe has opened up extensive possibilities to both domestic and 'imported' organised crime, threatening the still frail political institutions. Concern was reflected in the recent International Seminar on Organised Crime, held in Moscow in October 1991.[35]

Throughout the 1980s there have been increasing examples of how the vast profits to be made from organised crime have corrupted the governments, military and judiciary of various states throughout the world. This has led to the acceptance of the norm that 'Activities should not be engaged in which lead to the corruption of the due process of government whether by financial inducements or threats'. The interface with political power is an integral part of the phenomenon of organised crime. Preventing corruption has therefore increased in importance in recent years. The assassinations of Judges Giovanni Falcone and Paolo Borsellino in Italy and numerous other senior law-enforcement figures around the world, committed to uncovering corruption, serve as an illustration of organised crime's influence and perseverance. The expansion of transnational and organised crime outlined above has led to the concern being placed higher up the political agenda. Resolution seven of the Eighth United Nations Congress on Crime Prevention and Treatment of Offenders[36] entitled 'Corruption in Government' recommended that Member States devise a variety of administrative and regulatory mechanisms to prevent corrupt practices involving the abuse of power.

The Mafia, as important actors in all areas of drug-related activity, obviously do not support the first and second norms. However, the third norm is universally accepted by all actors for whom the questions involved in drug-related activity are salient: that children and youth should not have access to potentially harmful psychoactive substances. In contrast to the attitude towards adults, the sale of all such substances, including alcohol and tobacco, to children is prohibited by law in most Western industrialised countries, while their use is prohibited by social norm in most countries.

The recognition of the importance of protecting the young in this manner is a relatively recent phenomenon. The assertion of John Ruskin in 1851 that it was 'indisputable' that the first duty of a state was to ensure the well-being of every child 'til it attain years of discretion'[37] went against nineteenth-century reality. However, as Jordan notes, 'a powerless minority, exploited and then cast aside, came to enjoy schooling and the protection of effective, enforced legislation by the end of the century'.[38] The protection of children's welfare was soon to be extended to include protection from potential harm arising from their own choices and actions.

The law passed in England at the end of the nineteenth century prohibiting the sale of liquor to children for consumption on the premises was a decisive break with the past. In America too, the restriction of 'youthful drinking' was not seen as a problem for much of the nineteenth century and the intervention of the state was seen as a major break with the past. The oft-quoted statement of justification for this action comes from John Stuart Mill's *On Liberty*, as quoted in Chapter 1. Although Mill said 'over himself, over his own body and mind, the individual is sovereign', he qualified this doctrine by adding that children 'must be protected against their own actions as well as external injury'.[39] As Chapter 3 argued, pressure to legislate over drug use in the nineteenth century came from various sources, including concern over widespread opiate use among the working classes. In particular, however, the public was outraged by a number of infant deaths from overdoses of preparations of opium soothing-syrups, commonly administered to infants.

Throughout the first half of the twentieth century the question of child drug use was of minimal concern. Drug users were seen as a criminal and sick minority of foreign elements, hoods and hookers. Then in the 1960s, it seemed that an entire generation of white, well-educated youth were smoking marijuana, 'turning on, tuning in and dropping out'. With the 1960s came a new era of 'recreational drug use', and drug users were viewed as challenging the values of society. Similarly, during the 1980s and early 1990s the increase in drug use for recreational purposes among increasingly younger groups has led to fears over law and order, strengthening the norm that activities should not be engaged in which would damage the emotional, mental or physical growth of a minor. Consensus over child drug use evokes different values from the question of adult drug use. The norm that activities should not be engaged in which would damage the emotional, mental or physical growth of a minor has emerged because there is a high level of consensus over the values that the actors share. On the other hand, there is no consensus on adult drug use. There is no agreement, within most societies, on whether adults should be free to take drugs or not.

Actors for whom the issue of adult drug use is salient disagree on the values under contention. Some believe that adults should be free to choose which drugs they do or do not take, in line with the nineteenth-century liberalism of John Stuart Mill, described in Chapter 1. A recent Colombian Supreme Court decision, to decriminalise the personal use of small amounts, found that it was unconstitutional to violate a person's freedom to decide whether to use drugs.[40] Supporters of the legalisation of cannabis argue that the drug is not harmful, despite the claims of those that advocate its continued criminalisation, and indeed emphasise the medical benefits that legalisation of the drug would bring (see Chapter 1). Supporters also emphasise that the continued criminalisation of cannabis is putting undue pressure on the forces of law and order. They also claim that the criminalisation of cannabis along with other substances such as cocaine, crack and heroin makes a mockery of law enforcement, due to its inability to control the problem, and is therefore creating a challenge to the status of enforcement authorities. There is also the view that the knowledge surrounding the dangers of certain substances is unreliable (see Chapters 1 and 3). There is no consensus on adult drug use amongst users, policy-makers and traffickers. The conflicting values can be seen to form an issue-system of actors for whom the issue of adult drug-use is salient, but no norm and therefore no regime is possible.

Because there was no consensus on the use of drugs by adults, there was no widespread direct support, until the 1980s, for an international norm that 'trade in drugs should be stopped'. It is only since drug gangs have challenged government authority and corrupted government processes of that support for a ban on trafficking has grown. However, as we will see in examination of the debate on the legalisation of drugs in the last chapter, a ban on trafficking is not the only way of promoting this norm.

Of the four norms it is the one concerned with the tracing, freezing and confiscation of traffickers' assets that can be seen most clearly to be regulated by an international regime, as the next chapter will demonstrate. The norm that banks should not profit from criminal finance concerns the problem of money laundering of traffickers' illicit funds. The norm has emerged since the increase in drug trafficking with the subsequent flourishing of organised criminal networks, explained earlier in this work, has made the issue salient to many actors who previously were not active in the area. The anti-laundering norm has gained support from many actors, for example the Swiss government, who were important for achieving results. Contested values regarding banking secrecy and the need for banking regulation not to interfere with criminal investigations in the context of international co-operation have led to the acceptance of the norm that banks should not profit from illicit funds. The next chapter will look at the emergence of a money-laundering control regime.

CONCLUSION

The answer to the question of regime significance, raised at the beginning of this chapter, depends on the behavioural assumptions that underlie the different theoretical models of International Relations. Commitment to one or other understanding of the nature and role of norms in international affairs clearly illustrates this. Despite the fact that what can be seen to distinguish regimes from other international phenomena is their specifically normative element, the nature and role of norms have been glossed over by most writers in the field. This writer believes that the Krasner definition forces us to consider norms and decision-making procedures in world politics.

The different approaches to norms among International Relations theorists have been influenced by different philosophical traditions. The dominance of the Realist rational-actor approach, stated by Krasner in his volume as regarded by the majority of writers as the most important determinant of regimes, has limited the use of norms to explain international co-operation and the creation of international regimes. Norm emergence has been explained in terms of the power of actors writing the rules in their own interests. This chapter, however, emphasises the role of values in norm emergence. Norms can be seen to evolve within a framework defined and legitimated by the value system of a group. By looking at values and norms our attention is drawn to the importance of understanding the aspect of norms as the setting of standards, in terms of the 'right' and the 'good' of current normative theory, which is lacking in current understanding of regime theory. But for this study on international drug control, perhaps more importantly, norms draw our attention to the study of how standards are set.

Regime theory to date has concerned itself with asking 'Why and how do regimes come about and vanish?' rather than 'Why and how ought they to come about in the service of a normative principle of world order?'[41] As Susan Strange says, Krasner's common question is about order – how, in an international system of territorial states claiming sovereignty within their respective territories, can order be achieved and maintained (a Hobbesian view), rather than a concern with justice or efficiency, or legitimacy, or any other moral value.[42] Strange argues that we need to answer the question 'How to achieve change?', which she sees as no less important than 'How to keep order?' This work has shown that in order to understand change we need to understand values and norms, but our understanding of the role of values and norms must not be restricted by notions of morality on the one hand, and power politics on the other.

Norms can be seen to evolve within a framework defined and legitimated by the value-system of a group. As Kim writes, 'The common political science definition of politics as described as the authoritative allocation of values indicates that societies' value system guides what social roles and functions are to be legitimated by what kind of norms.' In this way we can see international politics as a 'value-realizing, norm-setting process'.[43] Norms are real and do influence behaviour and outcomes. Furthermore, a focus on regime norms emphasises the increasingly fragmented, issue-specific character of world politics in the 1990s.

6 The International Money-Laundering Control Regime

INTRODUCTION

Money laundering is not a new phenomenon. Techniques have always been used to dispose of the proceeds of a variety of criminal offences that involve payments for contraband goods (such as during Prohibition). Historically, a variety of banking and money-laundering services outside normal banking channels have been available for the 'washing' of money from illicit activities. However, the dramatic increase in drug use in the early 1980s substantially increased money-laundering activity and brought about increased international interest and concern. Interest was first awakened to the problem of drug-money laundering in 1979 with the opening up of a suitcase containing $600,000 at Palermo airport, leading to the Italian–American 'Pizza Connection' case that came to trial in 1985. An estimated 1.6 billion dollars of illicit profits from five heroin-refining laboratories in Sicily was laundered through Mafia-run pizzerias in New York, passing through Canada and the Caribbean to Switzerland and Italy, and ending up in banks in Hong Kong, Singapore and Bangkok. The trial exposed the huge amounts of money involved, as well as demonstrating the transnationalisation of the phenomenon. As an issue, money laundering is truly international.

The increased integration of financial markets and the removal of barriers to the free movement of capital during the 1980s has led to increased activity in the world economy, enhanced the ease with which criminal money can be laundered, and complicated the tracing process. The ease with which assets can pass from one country to another has meant that an order enforceable only in the country of origin can have limited effect. The need for enhanced international co-operation in this area was thus evident to the actors for whom the issue was salient. Domestic and transnational law-enforcement strategies have increasingly emphasised the need to focus on the financial aspects of the drug trade, 'going after the money', with the object of more effectively disrupting the major trafficking networks.

Various international conferences, such as the United Nations Conference for the Adoption of a Convention Against the Illicit Traffic in Narcotic Drugs and Psychotropic Substances at Vienna in December 1988,[1] the 1990 World Ministerial Summit to Reduce Demand for Drugs and to Combat the Cocaine Threat,[2] the 9th Non-Aligned Summit, Belgrade, 1989,[3] the Commonwealth Heads of Government Meetings held in Kuala Lumpur (October 1989)[4] and Harare (October 1991),[5] and the Second Interregional Meeting of Heads of National Law Enforcement Agencies convened in Vienna in September 1989,[6] all emphasised growing awareness of the vast profits generated by this form of criminal activity and the need for international co-operation.

The accumulation of illicit profits can be seen as perhaps the most politically and economically destabilising element of the international drugs trade: it gives traffickers the means to buy arms, property, companies, political power, and protection. Estimates of the size of the drug trade vary enormously, from $76 billion to $800 billion.[7] Illegal drugs have been estimated to have overtaken oil as a source of revenue globally and to be, after armaments, the second biggest trading commodity, according to the Director-General of the United Nations Office in Vienna.[8] Profits from drugs are huge – so much so that a relatively small group of criminals was estimated to have a bigger turnover than the income of 150 of the world's 170 countries in 1989.[9] Some individuals are even believed to have a personal worth that exceeds their country's national debt. Profits from drug trafficking erode and distort the legal economies of public institutions and entire societies. Furthermore, the free circulation of untaxed funds can be seen to distort freedom of competition and undermine legitimate business.

In this sense, drug-money laundering has created problems in the financial world. Drug traffickers seek out countries and territories with weak central banks, restrictive bank secrecy practices and limited controls on foreign exchange. Experience indicates that even when jurisdictions have enacted laws to control money laundering, such laws are likely to be ineffective unless bank, corporate and official secrecy requirements are relaxed. Financial institutions have been reluctant to do this in the past. However, the salience of the money-laundering issue has increased in importance for all actors involved during the last decade, due to the recognition of the negative impact that such vast flows of 'dirty money' can have on the financial sector. As the Basle Committee on Banking Regulations and Supervisory Practices stated in December 1988:

> Public confidence in banks, and hence their stability, can be undermined by adverse publicity as a result of inadvertent association by banks with criminals. In addition, banks may lay themselves open to direct losses from fraud, either through negligence in screening undesirable customers or where the integrity of their own officers has been undermined through association with criminals.[10]

The salience of the money-laundering issue as it has emerged in the last decade arises from the amount of money being laundered due to the increase in drug trafficking. The international politics of the issue becomes complicated as the forum for debate at various times involves the Basle Committee, the United Nations, the Council of Europe, the European Community, the Group of Seven industrialised countries and a Financial Action Task Force. This chapter will look at the changing attitudes towards money laundering among actors for whom the issue is salient, and the emergence of the norm that 'Banks should not profit from illicit funds'. The fact that this norm is adhered to by the actors for whom the issue is salient (except the drug barons) has led to the emergence of an international regime to regulate the issue.

THE MONEY-LAUNDERING ISSUE

'Money laundering' is a widely used term that is difficult to define concisely. The term itself is reputed to have originated from the 1920s, when Al Capone and Bugsy Moran literally opened up laundry companies in Chicago in order to disguise their illicit earnings. The 1988 United Nations Convention Against Illicit Traffic in Narcotic Drugs and Psychotropic Substances, discussed in the previous chapter, limits the definition of money laundering solely to drug-related offences, unlike the later European Economic Community Directive which allows for any conversion or transfer of property derived from criminal activity, for the purpose of concealing or disguising the illicit origin of the property, to be a criminal offence.[11] Any attempt to counsel, facilitate or assist the commission of such actions is also an offence. The Article concludes by stating that money laundering is to be considered as such even when the activities which generated the property to be laundered were perpetrated in the territory of another Member State or third country. This somewhat long-winded description reflects the long-winded process of money laundering, which makes it difficult to control. As the *International Narcotics Control Strategy Report* of 1988 stated: 'The techniques of money laundering are innumerable, diverse, complex, subtle and secret.'[12] The broadening of the definition of money laundering to include all criminal funds and not simply drug money is a significant change in attitude among financial actors, the importance of which will be explained later.

Cash lends anonymity to many forms of criminal activity and is the normal medium of exchange in drug trafficking. This gives rise to three common factors:

– drug dealers need to *conceal* the true ownership and origin of the money;
– they need to *control* the money; and
– they need to *change* the form of the money.

Money laundering can therefore be summarised as 'the *conversion* of illicit cash to another asset, the *concealment* of the true source or ownership of the illegally acquired proceeds, and the *creation* of the perception of legitimacy of source and ownership'.[13]

There are three stages of money laundering, during which there may be numerous transactions made by money launderers that could alert a financial business to criminal activity:

(a) *Placement* – the physical disposal of cash proceeds derived from illegal activity.
(b) *Layering* – separating illicit proceeds from their source by creating complex layers of financial transactions designed to disguise the audit trail and provide anonymity.
(c) *Integration* – the provision of apparent legitimacy to criminally derived wealth.

If the layering process has succeeded, integration schemes place the laundered proceeds back into the economy in such a way that they re-enter the financial system appearing to be normal business funds.

THE SCALE OF THE PROBLEM

As has been already stated, illicit drug traffic has been estimated as generating an annual income of between $76 and $800 billion. The Financial Action Task Force (FATF), created on the recommendation of the seven major industrialised nations at the July 1989 Paris Economic Summit, estimated the sales of cocaine, heroin and cannabis to be approximately $122 billion per year in the United States and Europe. The Group estimated that as much as $85 billion per year could be available for laundering and investment.[14] Profit margins in drug trafficking are huge, and all the more so because profits are untaxed. In 1993, a single gram of heroin cost the British National Health Service £5.86, which has been estimated as about 3 per cent of the price on the illicit market.[15] Some studies claim that the street prices of drugs such as heroin and cocaine are 60–100 times higher than licit pharmaceutical prices.[16] As has already been mentioned in this study, the power that drug money bestows on the major traffickers has been seen in many Latin American countries.

The reason why it is difficult to estimate with any accuracy the amount of drug money being laundered was explored by the Financial Action Task Force. Their report points to the fact that the financial flows arising from drug trafficking might be estimated directly or indirectly. A direct estimation would involve the measuring of these flows from the international banking statistics and capital account statistics for the balance of payments. This would involve an analysis of errors and omissions and other discrepancies. The Task Force concluded, however, that this method was not viable. Although deposits covered by international banking statistics may include a substantial amount of drug money, this aspect cannot be singled out and was believed to account for only a small percentage of the totals. Instead, three indirect methods of estimation were used to assess the scale of financial flows arising from drug traffic: estimations of world drug production; consumption needs of drug users; and seizures of illicit drugs. All these methods have their weaknesses. Using the first method, estimated drug trafficking proceeds world-wide were put at $300 billion in 1987 by the United Nations, but the figure remains very uncertain. The second method also has a fundamental flaw. The consumption needs of drug abusers, obtained through surveys, are frequently of doubtful reliability since the activity is illegal: sample populations surveyed, for example, in homes or schools may miss a significant proportion of drug users. The final estimate projects the total amounts of drugs available for sale by the application of a multiplier to recorded seizures, which is estimated on the basis of a law-enforcement seizure rate. This varies between 5 per cent and 20 per cent according to the type of drug considered, and on a weighted average could be approximately 10 per cent. This approach, too, raises significant methodological problems, as the Task Force Report points out.

WASHING THE MONEY

As has already been emphasised in this work, the numerous methods drug traffickers use to transport drugs form a significant problem for enforcement authorities. Similarly, it is impossible to detail, and difficult for enforcement authorities to anticipate, the entire range of methods used to launder money. However, all the methods outlined share some common factors, regarding the role of cash domestically, of various kinds of financial institutions, of international cash transfers, and of corporate techniques.

The form of money generated through drug trafficking needs to be changed in order to shrink the huge volumes of cash generated. Because of the huge sums involved, often largely in small denomination notes, the physical volume of notes received from street dealing in heroin and cocaine has been estimated as being much larger than the volume of the drugs themselves. This accounts for the view that the proceeds from drugs should be more detectable than the drugs themselves. These large amounts of cash present drug traffickers with major difficulties. The complications involved with dealing with such large amounts of cash are illustrated by the example of drug traffickers in Colombia reportedly having regularly to dig up plastic-covered bundles of cash hidden in the Colombian jungle and dry them with battery-powered hairdryers before the money disintegrates in the humidity. The money is buried again to await its injection at some future date into the international banking system.[17] The transporting of suitcases full of money, so fundamental to the money launderers' activities in the past, has been replaced by other techniques as regulators in various countries have tried to control the problem by specifying an upper limit for a single cash transaction, leading to the use by launderers of 'smurfs' (see later) and more sophisticated techniques as the volume of money involved has become too great to handle.

Banks and other deposit-taking financial institutions are the main transmitters of money internationally. The stage of depositing money in institutions (placement) is therefore obviously a key one for money-launderers. Deposits have to be disguised to avoid the currency reporting systems in many countries, or laws that allow or require the reporting of suspicious transactions. In countries where there is cash transaction reporting, deposits have to be broken down into sizes which are lower than the threshold for that reporting ('smurfing') in order to escape attention. However, as the sums of money became larger and larger, this method proved too cumbersome for some of the larger operations and new methods have been utilised to launder their illicit funds.

One method utilised by money launderers has been the depositing of funds in the name of a company whose beneficial owners do not have to be disclosed in the country in which it is headquartered. In some countries, bank accounts were opened in the name of trustees, and the beneficiaries under the trust kept secret. Deposits could also be made by the legal profession in the name of clients, for whom the rules of attorney confidentiality may apply.

Another method often utilised by launderers is currency exchange. It is easier for the launderer if the cash in which he operates can be directly accepted abroad as a means of exchange. The US dollar is acceptable as a means of exchange in large amounts in many parts of the world. Federal Reserve Board staff estimated that adult residents in the United States held only 11–12 per cent of issued notes and coins in 1984. The remainder were held by legitimate and illegitimate business enterprises, residents of foreign countries, and persons less than eighteen years old.[18]

Formal financial institutions are of course not the only avenue open to launderers. Informal and largely unregulated financial institutions, which under the law are not supposed to accept deposits, can also be used. The first category of these are the Bureaux de Change. Bureaux de Change accept money in one currency and exchange it for another. Although still working in cash, a first transformation has taken place which makes it more difficult to detect the origin of the funds. The identity of the transactor is often not recorded. Increasing use of gambling or lottery facilities is another example. Large sums of small denomination notes can be exchanged for gambling chips or winning lottery tickets, then turned in for clean notes.

The informal system of 'hawalla' evolved and is used, perfectly legally, mainly by Indians and Pakistanis. Hawalla, which means 'reference' in Urdu, is a centuries-old banking system. It relies on a system of trust between families and ethnic groups who may be thousands of miles apart. A merchant travelling overseas would take with him a letter of credit issued by a hawalla banker in his own country which would be honoured by a hawalla banker in the other country. This tradition has continued to the present day and has been used by Asian immigrants in Europe, who have used it to transfer money to their families in Pakistan or India. Hawalla banking does not necessarily require a letter of credit: any agreed form of recognition in the form of a secret code or simple object, such as a half playing card or a bus ticket, can be a binding instrument of exchange for cash. Hawalla bankers are often involved in the gold bullion, gold jewellery or currency exchange business. The scale of their operations varies from families with similar businesses in several countries to a single trader in a street-corner confectionery shop. Hawalla banking has been utilised by the drug traffickers to launder their illicit funds.

Another method of laundering drug proceeds is the depositing of funds abroad in jurisdictions where the banking system is insufficiently regulated and where the establishment of 'letter box' companies is permitted. These jurisdictions may include countries attempting to establish a financial services industry, since the sale of banking licences can constitute a major source of revenue to the authorities, as well as countries known as tax havens. Cash is integrated into the financial systems of these countries and can then be returned by means of wire transfers for example. Offshore fiscal havens offer to the money launderer banking anonymity, unregulated financial transactions, and often judicial protection. The financial sanctuaries of the Caribbean in particular have been important centres for money laundering, since its island archipelagos are geographically well situated for cocaine transit from South America to Europe and North America. The spectacular growth of the Cayman Islands as an offshore financial centre illustrates the problem for those attempting to stem the illicit flow of drug money:

> In 1964 the Cayman Islands had two banks and no offshore business. By 1981 the Caymans had 360 branches of American and foreign banks, over 8,000 registered companies, and more telex machines per capita . . . than any other country.[19]

Fiscal havens exist within and on the periphery of Europe too. Monaco, Andorra, Luxembourg, Liechtenstein, the Channel Islands, the Isle of Man, Malta and Ireland all offer considerable tax incentives to outside investors and opportunities to the money launderer.

Various corporate techniques can also be used to launder money. Offshore companies can be used by launderers in ways other than simply as depositories for cash. Launderers can set up or buy corporations in a tax haven for example, using a local lawyer or nominee owner with an account at a local bank. They can then finance the purchase of a similar business at home through a loan from their corporation abroad (or the bank), in effect borrowing their own money and paying it back as if it were a legitimate loan.

The technique known as 'double invoicing' is another example of a corporate technique used by launderers. Goods are purchased at inflated prices by domestic companies owned by money launderers from offshore corporations which they also own. The difference between the price and the true value is then deposited offshore and paid to the offshore company and repatriated at will. For instance, researchers have found that raw cane sugar exported from Britain to America at $1,407 a kilogram, was priced 282,530 per cent higher than the average world price of 50 cents. Similarly, pine wood moulding was being shipped from England at $828 a metre, a mark-up of 176,213 per cent. Commodities fraud is not a new phenomenon. In the 1970s, Iranians sold sets of tyres for $20,000 to get their money out of Iran when the Shah was overthrown.[20]

As the Financial Action Task Force report states, all these techniques involve going through stages where detection is possible. Cash has to be exported over a territorial frontier and then deposited in a foreign financial institution; or it requires the knowing or unknowing complicity of someone at home not connected with the drug trade, or it requires convincing a domestic financial institution that a large cash deposit is legitimate. As has been discussed above, key stages for the detection of money-laundering operations are those where cash enters the domestic financial system, formally or informally, where it is sent abroad to be integrated into the financial systems of regulatory havens, and where it is repatriated in the form of transfers of legitimate appearance. Identifying these stages is quite simple, finding the money much less so and preventing the utilisation of the financial services in this way even less. The diverse methods used to launder illicit funds have made the job of enforcement agencies very difficult. This has become worse due to the changing conditions of the financial market-place.

The 1980s saw many of the boundaries between national financial markets dissolve and a truly global capital market emerge. The 'globalisation' of the world economy – expanding international trade, the growth of multi-national businesses, the rise in international joint ventures and increasing interdependence through capital flows – has led to problems for those concerned with combatting money laundering. Although the scale of this internationalisation has increased fundamentally in recent times, paralleling the expansion of multi-national corporations, banking has been international almost from the very beginning of the institution, circa AD 1000. Bankers soon settled outside their home countries to serve clients better, to simplify funds transfers, to meet the requirements of international trade that began expanding in the thirteenth century, and to profit from differences in exchange rates. The development of rules and norms from this period can be seen in the rules, norms and values of modern-day banking.

The increased integration of financial markets and the removal of barriers to the free movement of capital that we have witnessed in the second half of the 1980s and the early 1990s, such as in Europe, have enhanced the ease with which criminal money can be laundered. Money-laundering channels generally involve international operations. As the Commission of the European Communities noted:

> Internationalisation of economies and financial services are opportunities which are seized by money launderers to carry out their criminal activities, since the origin of funds can be better disguised in an international context.[21]

This enables money launderers to use differences in national laws, regulations and enforcement practices. When funds are repatriated after laundering abroad and detected, these differences in national laws, regulations and enforcement practices seriously impair the efficiency of enquiries and law-enforcement measures.

The 'globalisation' of the world economy has been driven by the forces of innovation, technology and deregulation acting together, and each multiplying the effects of the others. The links between telecommunications and technology and the foreign expansion of banks have been fundamental. When foreign branches came into existence on a wide scale, a telephone call or telex message to a branch bank could often accomplish in a few minutes what might have taken at least a day through a correspondence bank. Banks have not been slow to realise the importance of technology to banking. When the first experimental telephone exchange began operation in Boston in 1877, one of the three corporate clients was a banking firm.[22] Since the spread of telephone systems, foreign exchange dealings have come to rely heavily on telephone commitments, backed up by exchange of written documentation later. This has meant that money can be described as rushing around the world at a furious pace, where entire cycles of borrowing and depositing can take place every fifteen minutes or so.

The rise of telecommunications networks has been accompanied by a rise in computer networks. The electronic transfer of funds, not only among banks, or between banks and corporate clients, but also between banks and the general public, has added a new dimension to money laundering. And, just as with the establishment of the first telephone exchange, some of the larger banks are recognised leaders in information-processing technology, with research and development departments and database subsidiaries. The construction of these international computerised information-processing networks, such as The Society for Worldwide Interbank Financial Telecommunications (Swift), can be seen as one of the major technological developments in banking of the past twenty years. Swift was founded in May 1973 by 240 European, American and Canadian Banks, but became operational only in May 1977. There were by 1981 about 680 member banks in 26 countries, which were exchanging over 170,000 messages a day.[23] Computerisation has powered the innovations in techniques that, with rapid communication networks, make for an unstoppable combination: 'Securitization is driven by the IT revolution, and each new payments system introduces an almost new form of money as a transactions vehicle.'[24] However, a disadvantage of this technology has been that launderers have been able to use the systems without giving names and addresses of recipients, making it impossible for investigators to trace the money. Traffickers have also been able to utilise this technology in avoiding some of the problems of dealing in large sums of cash, as described above.

The skill and speed with which large-scale traffickers are able to launder their profits using this new technology is a problem for judicial and law-enforcement authorities. The global nature of financial markets, the new communications and new computer technologies mean that assets derived from trafficking in one country can readily be transferred to another, in contrast to the central Realist axiom of state sovereignty. New communications and new computer technologies are together altering the dimensions of markets, the relative importance of location and the organisation of firms, and destroying the barriers that hitherto have been synonymous with specific geographical co-ordinates. As Jackson states:

> The international flowing of funds information electronically has, according to some, resulted in the phenomena of *money without a country* and a supranational banking system.[25] [Emphasis by current author.]

On the other hand, money launderers are able to exploit the rigidities of state sovereignty that limit enforcement agencies and regulators, moving money from one country to another less-regulated country with strong bank secrecy laws where their funds will be protected. Money is 'a creature of regulation' but it is also adept at finding its way around regulation. As O'Brien states, 'Whatever efforts are made to maintain barriers in financial services or to help define the role of money and the rules governing it, the job is almost impossible.'[26] Attempts to 'control' illicit funds are complicated by the fact that property and funds for drug trafficking are often intermingled with, or converted into, legitimate property and funds, hence posing a problem for judicial and law-enforcement officials. It is all too easy for illicit funds to be converted into licit funds.

Another significant problem in attempting to control the money involved in laundering is that individual countries have different cultures and values with regard to cash. As has been discussed above, traffickers, at the first stage of their operations, must deal in cash. Control of the amount of cash transactions by financial institutions has been shown to limit fraud, and could be utilised by regulators attempting to control drug-money laundering. However, some economies are very cash-centred. In Italy, for example, credit cards are still relatively rare compared with some other European countries. Banks do not formally accept responsibility for customer losses incurred when cheques are stolen or forged, even within the clearing system. Therefore cash or cash instruments are frequently the preferred option for payment of wages, professional services, and a wide variety of commercial transactions. In general, therefore, substantial cash movements are not likely to arouse suspicion in Italy.

Another problem for regulators, therefore, is the sheer volume of financial activities and the impossibility of verifying every transaction. The cost of registering every large cash transaction over a given sum would signify major cost and resource implications for the banks. Every large Currency Transaction Report (CTR) in the United States costs seventeen dollars, and there are approximately 6 million of them per year.[27] Therefore, attempts at moves towards mandatory reporting of cash transactions over a certain amount have faced a great deal of opposition (see later).

The number and diversity of financial institutions also aid the money launderer. Money laundering is not limited to banks and building societies alone. Once illicit funds are in the financial system, they can readily be switched into different types of assets and between institutions (the layering and integration stages). Some of those utilised by money launderers have been mentioned above, such as bureaux de change, cheque cashers, money transmission services, casinos and lotteries. Therefore other types of financial institutions need to accept regulation.

Money laundering is a very sophisticated crime. The increased use of complex corporate structures and intricate business transactions involving banks, trust companies, firms dealing in real estate and other financial institutions has added to the difficulties of the enforcement agencies. Some countries do not have sophisticated enough financial institutions to attempt to deal with the problem. It is these countries, often dealing predominantly in cash, which are most at risk generally. For more developed financial systems, the banking secrecy rule, which has governed banking for the greater part of this decade, meant that bankers could not report their suspicions even if they wanted to. In order to avoid any involvement in money-laundering activities they would simply deny assistance and the funds would go elsewhere, moving the problem on rather than dealing with it.

Money laundering has been described as 'Financial AIDS'; once the money reaches the system nothing can remove it. Furthermore, as with AIDS, the problem is spreading dramatically. Once in the financial system, illicit funds can at best be diverted. If money is diverted in its course, as described in the example above of financial institutions denying assistance to suspicious transactions, it can simply return to the financial flow further down stream. Therefore the only ways to control money laundering are to prevent the money entering the financial system in the first place by truly international co-operation, or to make illicit money licit by legalising drug trafficking. The legalisation debate will be looked at in the concluding chapter to this study.

There is a great deal of national legislation in place to combat money laundering. The United States pioneered legislation to prevent the flow of illicit profits with the requirement from 1971 for documentation of all financial transactions over $10,000 by means of a Currency Transaction Report (CTR). That legislation, commonly known as the Bank Secrecy Act (BSA), mandated a series of reporting and record-keeping requirements designed to help track down money-laundering activity and to prevent the veil of secrecy surrounding offshore bank accounts. However, implementation of the Act was delayed due to a number of factors. Bankers challenged the constitutionality of the law, claiming that the BSA reporting requirements violated the search and seizure provisions of the Fourth Amendment. This issue was not settled until 1974, when the Supreme Court ruled against the bankers. This unsuccessful challenge was followed by a period of massive non-compliance with BSA reporting requirements by banks and other financial institutions. The non-compliance problem was aggravated by a lack of concern and interest by bank regulatory agencies towards BSA compliance issues. It was not seen as a priority issue for the regulators and consequently enforcement was minimal between 1974 and 1984. The increase in drug use and the increase in funds available for laundering challenged this position.

In 1979, the Federal Reserve Bank conducted a study that showed that there was a $4.3 billion surplus of currency in Florida while the rest of the country was for the most part showing currency deficits.[28] This led to increased enforcement activity against money laundering.[29] In the years that followed there were several amendments to the law, including the inclusion of non-bank financial institutions and foreign banks (including foreign subsidiaries) in the currency reporting requirements. These amendments were incorporated into the Money Laundering Control Act of 1986, establishing the crime of money laundering where previously no such crime had existed. The Act also provided for an amendment to the Right to Financial Privacy Act that made it easier for banks to report suspicious transactions information to federal enforcement agencies without running the risk of being sued by customers. In 1989, a federal law was introduced which permits the government to track and to claim ownership of laundered drug money. The pre-trial freezing of assets of suspected drug traffickers pending judicial forfeiture procedures is also permissible.

In the United Kingdom a different path was taken to control money laundering. The Drug Trafficking Offences Act 1986 (DTOA) obliged anyone handling finances on behalf of a third party – solicitors and accountants as well as banks and financial institutions – to disclose suspicious transactions, overriding any confidentiality imposed by contract. However, unlike in the United States, there was no obligation to report transactions above a certain amount and it was left to the banks' discretion as to what constituted a suspicious transaction.

INTERNATIONAL CO-OPERATION

It is generally accepted that in order to combat the financial aspects of drug trafficking and other forms of criminal activity, preventative strategies and not just penal measures, as has been the approach, for example, of the Vienna Convention (see previous chapter and below), can play a significant and positive role. This belief lay at the heart of the Recommendations by the Committee of Ministers of the Council of Europe of 27 June 1980 on measures against the transfer and the safekeeping of funds of criminal origin.[30] However, this initiative, prompted in the main by concern over a growing number of acts of criminal violence such as kidnapping, did not see its recommendations generally implemented. It was not until the late 1980s, with the dramatic increase in drug-money laundering, that attitudes had changed sufficiently to consider the measures put forward by this earlier initiative.

The Statement of Principles for the guidance of bank supervisors issued on 12 December 1988 by the Basle Committee on Banking Regulations and Supervisory Practices encourages the banking sector to adopt a common position in order to ensure that banks are not used to hide or launder funds acquired through criminal activities and, in particular, through drug trafficking (see Appendix B). Although the Statement refers throughout to 'banks' it is applicable to all financial institutions. The document consists of 'a general statement of ethical principles' to encourage a bank's management to properly identify persons conducting business with their banks, to discourage transactions that do not appear legitimate and to co-operate with law-enforcement agencies.[31]

The Statement sets out the following basic principles:

(a) *Customer identification* – when establishing a relationship by opening an account or providing any other service, including safe deposit box facilities, reasonable effort should be taken to determine the true identity of the customer requesting the service.

(b) *Compliance with legislation and law-enforcement agencies* – business should be conducted in conformity with high ethical standards and local laws and regulations pertaining to financial transactions. Institutions should co-operate fully with national law-enforcement authorities to the extent permitted without breaching customer confidentiality.

(c) *Record keeping and systems* – institutions should implement specific procedures for retaining internal records of transactions and establish an effective means of testing for general compliance with the Statement.

(d) *Staff training* – attention should be given to staff training and their on-going education in the institution's procedures to facilitate the recognition and reporting of money laundering.

The Basle Statement of Principles is not a treaty in terms of public international law and has no direct legal effect in the domestic law of any country. However, as the Financial Action Task Force Report pointed out:

> Although it is not itself a legally binding document, various formulas have been used to make its principles an obligation, notably a formal agreement among banks that commits them explicitly (Austria, Italy, Switzerland), a formal indication by bank regulators that failure to comply with these principles could lead to administrative sanctions (France, United Kingdom), or legally binding texts with a reference to these principles (Luxembourg).[32]

In spite of its relatively recent nature, the FATF was able to report that practical measures towards implementation 'have already been taken in many countries'.[33]

The first treaty in terms of public international law to attempt to control money laundering came with the conclusion in Vienna in December 1988 of the United Nations Convention Against Illicit Traffic in Narcotic Drugs and Psychotropic Substances.[34] The Convention recognised the need to define with care the specific elements which the notion of the effective control of illicit traffic encompasses. Article 3(1) of the final text, frequently described as the cornerstone of the Convention, requires parties to legislate as necessary to establish a modern code of criminal offences relating to illicit trafficking in all its different aspects. To that end Article 3(1)(a) requires that each state party shall 'establish as criminal offences under its domestic law, when committed intentionally' a fairly comprehensive list of activities which have a major international impact. This includes, in Article 3(1)(b), requiring the criminalisation of drug-related money laundering by each state party. They are required to establish as criminal offences:

(i) The conversion or transfer of property, knowing that such property is derived from any offence or offences established in accordance with subparagraph (a) of this paragraph, or from an act of participation in such offence or offences, for the purpose of concealing or disguising the illicit origin of the property or of assisting any person who is involved in the commission of such offence or offences to evade the legal consequences of his actions;

(ii) The concealment or disguise of the true nature, source, location, disposition, movement, rights with respect to, or ownership of property, knowing that such property is derived from an offence or offences established in accordance with subparagraph (a) of this paragraph or from an act of participation in such an offence or offences.

Also of relevance in this context is Article 3(1)(c)(i), which requires parties to take measures to render criminal 'The acquisition, possession or use of property, knowing, at the time of receipt, that such property was derived from an offence or offences established in accordance with subparagraph (a) of this paragraph or from an act of participation in such offence or offences.' However, the obligation on parties is qualified by the constitutional principles and the basic concepts of parties' legal systems. The Convention created an obligation to criminalise the laundering of money derived from drug trafficking, thereby facilitating judicial co-operation and extradition, which was seen as hampered by the fact that many countries had not criminalised money laundering.

Article 5, paragraph 3 of the Convention requires that each state party empowers its courts or other relevant authorities to order that bank, financial or commercial records be made available for the investigation of drug-related offences; and that 'A Party shall not decline to act under the provisions of this paragraph on the ground of bank secrecy'. The inclusion of this affirmative obligation to act can be seen as a major breakthrough in combatting money laundering.

The 1990 Council of Europe Convention represented the final product of an initiative taken by European Ministers of Justice in 1986 in order to combat the problems in the financial area posed by drug trafficking. A Select Committee of Experts was established by the European Committee on Crime Problems, with fairly wide terms of reference. In particular, it was not obliged to restrict its focus to the proceeds derived from drug trafficking alone. Although the Committee of Experts made direct reference to the relevant provisions of the 1988 United Nations Convention in their study, the Council of Europe can be seen to have gone beyond the United Nations Convention in its much wider scope. The Council of Europe Convention promotes international co-operation on all types of criminality and specifies co-operation on arms dealing, terrorist offences, trafficking in children and young women as well as drug offences and other 'offences which generate large profits'.[35] Article 2 of the Convention illustrates the nature of, and limits to, its ambition. It addresses confiscation measures to be taken at the national level. In essence, Article 2(1) obliges states to enact legislation to permit the confiscation of the proceeds of crime and contains an implicit invitation for such legislation to be as broad as possible. However, the article did not impose an obligation to require confiscation in relation to all forms of criminal conduct, which is not supported by certain participating states' existing legislation.

A further indication of the Council of Europe's intention to go beyond the 1988 Convention can be seen in Article 6. The basic approach has been summarised in a House of Lords Select Committee report as follows:

> Article 6 of the Convention requires States Parties to establish an offence of international money laundering. The property involved in any conversion or transfer could be proceeds not only of drug trafficking or terrorism but of any criminal offence (described as the 'predicate offence') and the State Party prosecuting need not have criminal jurisdiction over the predicate offence. Although this constitutes a very wide definition of money laundering, it is open to States on signature or ratification to limit the definition for themselves to more limited categories of predicate offence.[36]

This definition therefore expands money laundering beyond the association with drug trafficking as described above, and finds support in the existing legislative practice of certain states such as Switzerland.[37] This development has the backing of the Financial Action Task Force, which recommended in its 1990 Report that countries should consider extending the scope of the offence of money laundering to reach any other crime for which there is a link to drugs, or to all serious offences. This approach signals the awareness of many experts of the disadvantages associated with drug-specific definitions of money laundering. As Levi points out in the context of the United Kingdom Drug Trafficking Offences Act of 1986: 'Sometimes – particularly in the laundering sphere and in the case of organised crime groups – the same people are involved in drug trafficking, fraud and terrorism.'[38]

As with the Vienna Convention, the Council of Europe Convention concentrates mainly on penal means to combat money laundering within the framework of international co-operation among judicial and law-enforcement authorities. The European Economic Community Directive of 10 June 1991 recognises that the financial system, and actors not associated with law enforcement, can play a highly effective role in preventing the use of the financial system for money laundering. The first paragraph of the preamble to the Directive lays out its essential objective, emphasising that when credit and financial institutions are used to launder money 'the soundness and stability of the particular institution concerned and confidence in the financial system as a whole could be seriously jeopardised, thereby losing the trust of the public'.[39] The Directive is primarily a pro-active tool in the sense that it deals with measures to be taken before any crime has taken place. This is a deliberate approach since the explanatory memorandum states that repressive measures are dealt with by the 1988 United Nations Convention, described above. The recognition of the importance of prevention is central to the work of the European Communities. Community action in this area has been prompted by the perceived need to ensure 'the integrity and cleanliness of the financial system'[40] in the light of moves towards the creation of a single financial market. As the House of Lords Select Committee observed, the free movement of capital and of financial services 'offers great scope for organised crime as well as for legitimate enterprise'.[41] Also, it was felt that inaction by the Community against money laundering could lead Member States, for the purpose of protecting their financial systems, to adopt measures which could be inconsistent with completion of the single market. Like the 1990 Council of Europe Convention mentioned above, the Directive recognises the fact that money laundering occurs in relation to the proceeds of other criminal activities such as organised crime and terrorism and not only in relation to the proceeds of drug trafficking. Thus, while the definition of money laundering contained in Article 1 is derived from that used in the 1988 United Nations Convention, it relates to 'criminal activity' rather than merely to serious drug-trafficking offences. The Directive also recognised the importance of including the whole financial system, including, for example, the insurance industry and other types of professions and undertakings (Articles 12 and 13(1)(d)), since partial coverage could lead to a shift in money laundering from one kind of financial institution to another. The Directive states that scrutiny of the non-banking sector remains one of the major problems facing efforts to combat money laundering.

The Directive imposes a number of specific obligations. Firstly, it requires the identification of customers and beneficial owners, particularly when opening an account or when offering safe-custody facilities (Article 3(1)). This requirement also applies when transacting business at or above 15,000 ECUs. Secondly, provision is made to ensure the due diligence of credit and financial institutions (Article 5). Thirdly, obligations are imposed on financial institutions to ensure co-operation with the relevant institutions and authorities responsible for combatting money laundering. In particular, the financial institutions must 'on their own initiative' inform such authorities of any fact that might be an indication of money laundering. Furthermore, on request, they must furnish those authorities with all necessary information (Articles 6 and 10), without informing the customer concerned or any other third parties (Article 8). The Directive also provides for the legal immunity of institutions under such conditions (Article 9). The Directive calls for the establishment of procedures of internal control by credit and financial institutions and the creation by them of appropriate training programmes (Article 11).

In contrast to both the 1988 and 1990 Conventions, the Directive has as a primary objective 'preventing abuse of the financial system and detecting laundering, rather than increasing international co-operation in regard to punishment of offenders and confiscation of the proceeds of their crimes'.[42] Furthermore, it recognises the importance of the participation of non-state actors – banks, insurance companies, investment businesses, etc. – in controlling money laundering.

NORM EMERGENCE

As has been emphasised above, in order successfully to prevent illicit funds from entering the financial system, and thereby to control money laundering, the co-operation of banks and other financial institutions is crucial. Up until the 1980s banks for the most part did not see money laundering as their concern. The old maxim of 'see no evil, hear no evil' was prevalent in the financial world. As Brian Quinn, Executive Director of the Bank of England, said as recently as February 1991 in a conference speech, the idea that money laundering is a concern of banks is a recent occurrence: 'At first sight it may not be obvious that a Central Bank has an important role to play in combatting money laundering.'[43] But during the 1980s banking values, such as support for the free market, the dominance of economic efficiency, customer confidentiality and the importance of maintaining banking soundness and stability, came into conflict with each other.

Support for the free market meant that financial institutions had been reluctant for free capital movements to be disrupted in any way. Support for economic efficiency and profit meant that banks were not primarily concerned with whether the business offered to them was legitimate or not. This reflected the role of banking supervision, the primary function of which, as the Basle Statement of Principles states, was to 'maintain the overall financial stability and soundness of banks rather than to ensure that individual transactions conducted by bank customers are legitimate'.[44] Furthermore, it was difficult to separate 'dirty' money from 'grey' or 'hot' money, that is, capital in flight for fiscal reasons – speculation, tax evasion or tax avoidance. Banks in Switzerland, for example, had an estimated 150 billion Swiss Francs of tax evaders' money in 1989.[45] The difficulty of separating drug money from other illicit funds led to an awareness in the 1980s that it was necessary to legislate for all illicit funds.

It has always been the duty of our bankers to keep our banking affairs secret. Customer confidentiality has been the holiest of holies for the financial sector since its creation. Enshrined in banking tradition, the basic principles were accepted and restated by the Court of Appeal in the case of *Tournier* in 1924. In the United Kingdom, for example, until the Drug Trafficking Offences Act of 1986, statutory disclosure was permitted only rarely and then with strict safeguards. Drug trafficking was seen to be a special case where there was a clear need to track down offenders and prevent money laundering. The Act made it an offence for a bank official to handle a transaction he or she regarded as suspicious without reporting it to the police.

The Financial Action Task Force, reporting in 1990, called for banks and other types of depository institutions such as savings banks and building societies to improve their monitoring of money transactions. The report says this can best be done with a 'suspicion-based' system by which banks are required to report cash movements which they suspected might be drug-related.

Conflict arose in the financial world between those who wanted the adoption of an American system of mandatory reporting of all cash movements above a certain amount, in the American case $10,000, and those who thought this was inefficient and costly. As Quinn stated in his speech:

> While we wish to see effective measures taken against money laundering on a global basis, it is also important to try to avoid recommendations being brought forward that could involve unnecessary cost and complexity for financial institutions or be unduly disruptive to the efficiency of their operation.[46]

There was also conflict between those who felt that the suspicion-based system would lead to banking confidentiality becoming a sham, as officials, facing prosecution for failing to report suspicions, would report every irregularity that might conceivably relate to crime of any kind, leading to the financial affairs of many innocent people being investigated needlessly. The American mandatory reporting system was also rejected by the Bank of England.

The Bank of England opposed the so-called Kerry Amendment, whereby Section 4702 of the 1988 United States' Anti-Drug Abuse Act instructs the Secretary of the United States Treasury to negotiate with other countries whose financial institutions do business in US currency, to ensure that they maintain records of their large US currency transactions and to establish a mechanism whereby such records may be made available to US law-enforcement officials. The Bank of England stated that: 'In our view, this legislation was both extra-territorial in nature and an unnecessary erosion of customer/banker confidentiality'.[47]

Mandatory reporting of transactions was also a problem for the emerging financial sectors of former Eastern bloc countries. In beginning to build up their financial systems, it was important that these countries participated in money-laundering initiatives. Some countries, however, have reservations regarding the declarations of suspicious transactions. It was felt that strong bank secrecy laws were essential to obtain the confidence of the population in the new financial system, because in the old system, a general obligation existed to report any suspicion of illegal activity. A balance between the different views was struck, with consensus reached that the mandatory reporting of all cash movements above a certain amount was too cumbersome and inefficient and that a suspicion-based system would be more appropriate.

A change in opinion also came about that measures to deter money laundering through 'know your customer' provisions were helpful in the fight against fraud, which was seen as a growing cause of loss by banks. Concerns over the costs of implementing reporting systems (the cost in the United States has already been mentioned) by the major financial centres is balanced by the view that every centre will have to do the same to avoid their competitive position being damaged and to keep their reputation for financial honesty and integrity.

The shift in value salience for the financial institutions is due to a number of factors. As has already been mentioned, the increase in money laundering due to an increase in crime, particularly trafficking in illicit drugs, has meant that it has become an issue that financial institutions have not been able to ignore or dismiss as unimportant. Furthermore, the idea of society consciously sustaining norms through socialisation, as described in the previous chapter, led to bankers responding to the general concern outside the banking world about a 'major social evil'.[48] The Basle Statement describes itself as 'a general statement of ethical principles' to prevent institutions becoming associated with criminals. Efficiency, profits and secrecy had been of higher salience than honesty and stability for financial institutions. This had to change for a regime to form on money laundering.

Financial deregulation and the fierce battle fought for new accounts that developed in the early 1980s led to the erosion of customer identification procedures and, in particular, the provision of bankers' references. This has led to an increase in fraud and losses for the banks. Financial shocks and scandals, the fallout after the Big Bang in the UK, the costs of the developing countries' debt crisis, the savings and loans crisis in the United States, problems with the United States insurance industry, the stock market crashes of 1987, and the failure of banking supervisors to prevent the collapse of the Bank of Credit and Commerce International (BCCI), have all undermined public confidence in banks and hence threatened their stability. As Richard O'Brien states in *Global Financial Integration: The End of Geography*: 'The most worrying aspect of the 1990s for many observers is the apparent "financial fragility" of markets'. These crises have led to increasing efforts to develop more global rules and more global co-operation in the market:

> In the financial marketplace, the trend towards some sort of global governance is best represented by the efforts of banking supervisors under the aegis of the Bank for International Settlements in Basle to impose common minimum capital requirements on banks, and, in conjunction with supervisors and regulators, in other financial sectors (security and insurance), to integrate and coordinate the supervision of banking, securities markets and insurance.[49]

This increase in international co-operation and action included a focus on efforts to combat money laundering and the emergence of an international regime based on the Financial Action Task Force.

THE FATF: A MONEY-LAUNDERING CONTROL REGIME

On a number of occasions, mention has been made of the work of the Financial Action Task Force on Money Laundering. The FATF must be seen as the decision-making focus of an international regime on money laundering. Various international organisations or groups, including the Council of Europe, the Fonds provenant des activités criminelles (FOPAC), a division of Interpol, and among EEC members, the Mutual Assistance Group (MAG) between customs administrations, and the Trevi Group of ministers in charge of security, as well as the Customs Co-operation Council (CCC), have already devoted much attention to the money-laundering problem. But none of these organisations deal exclusively with the problem of money laundering, concerned as they are with other aspects of the drug phenomenon.

The Task Force was established by the Heads of State or Government of the seven major industrial nations (Group of Seven), and the President of the Commission of the European Communities, at their fifteenth annual summit in Paris in July 1989. The resulting Economic Declaration stressed the importance of dealing with the financial aspects of drug trafficking and decided on the creation of a task force from summit participants and other countries for whom the issue was salient. Its mandate was to assess existing co-operation to prevent the use of the banking system and financial institutions for money laundering and to consider other preventative efforts in this field, including the adaptation of the legal and regulatory systems, in order to enhance multi-lateral judicial assistance.[50]

In addition to summit participants (United States, Japan, Germany, France, United Kingdom, Italy, Canada, and the Commission of the European Communities) eight other countries (Sweden, Netherlands, Belgium, Luxembourg, Switzerland, Spain and Austria) were invited to take part in this initiative. More than 130 experts from various ministries, law-enforcement authorities and bank supervisory and regulatory agencies participated in the production of a report containing 40 recommendations for action, in February 1990. These recommendations were viewed as constituting a minimum standard in the fight against money laundering, although some of the recommendations failed to attract unanimous support.

The recommendations focused on three central areas: improvements to national legal systems; the enhancement of the role of financial systems; and the strengthening of international co-operation. Within these broad areas the report identified three measures which were unanimously regarded as constituting the overall general framework for its many specific proposals. These were:

(1) Each country should take steps to ratify the Vienna Convention and proceed to implement it;
(2) Secrecy laws for financial institutions should not inhibit implementation of the recommendations of the group;
(3) Increased multi-lateral co-operation and mutual legal assistance, in investigations, prosecutions and extradition, is necessary for an effective enforcement programme.

At the Houston Summit in July 1990 it was agreed that the FATF process should continue in order to 'assess and facilitate the implementation of the forty recommendations, and to complement

them where appropriate'.[51] All Organization for Economic Cooperation and Development (OECD) countries and financial centre
countries were invited to subscribe to the recommendations and to
participate in the preparation of the second FATF report.

The FATF saw its membership enlarged, with Denmark, Fin-
land, Greece, Ireland, New Zealand, Norway, Portugal, Turkey, Hong
Kong and the Gulf Cooperation Council, together with law-enforcement specialists of Interpol and the Customs Cooperation Council
joining the process. With the involvement of Hong Kong and the
Gulf, two of the three most important offshore banking centres
were now participating. Singapore, the third most important offshore financial centre in relation to controlling money laundering,
eventually joined the Task Force at the outset of the third session.[52] The most important accomplishment of FATF-2 was the agreement reached to move from self-reporting of progress towards the
implementation of Task Force recommendations, to a system in
which mutual assessment or evaluation plays a major role.

In its second report, the Task Force made special note of the
need for its regulations to cover not just banks but non-traditional
financial institutions or professions that might be involved in money-
laundering practices. As it becomes harder for money launderers
to work in established financial centres, the Task Force highlighted
the importance of looking at businesses that have not traditionally
been associated with money laundering. These included special
mention of bureaux de change, casinos, lotteries, precious-metal
and gem dealers, auction houses, real estate agents, automobile,
aeroplane and boat dealers and professionals who, in the course of
providing their professional services, offer, in some countries, cli-
ent account facilities (for example lawyers, accountants, notaries
and certain travel agents).

In FATF-2 it was agreed that the FATF process should continue
for a further five years, when it would be reviewed again. A Secretariat was established within the OECD. In its most recent report, published on 16 June 1994, the Task Force noted that its
recommendations now form the basis of anti-money-laundering laws
in all its member states.[53]

As explained in Chapter 2, where an issue-system features a high
degree of consensus over its central norm and a high rate of actor
compliance with rules and decisions designed to uphold that norm,
then an international regime can be seen to have emerged, regulating
the issue. This can be seen to be the case with a high degree of

consensus over the norm that 'Banks should not profit from illicit funds' and the formation of the Financial Action Task Force to regulate the issue.

CONCLUSION

As has been mentioned earlier in this work, the drug phenomenon can be seen as a number of separate, identifiable issues which can be isolated into distinct issue-systems composed of actors in contention over related values. For the actors in the financial issue-system only one of the drug issues is salient, that of the problem of money laundering.

The adherence of the actors to the global norm can be seen to be determined, firstly, by how salient they perceive the norm to be to them in allocating stakes to satisfy a particular value by which they are guided. As has been explained, banking stability and soundness was threatened by the increase in drug-money laundering and therefore rules such as 'know your customer' and 'report suspicious transactions' have replaced 'see no evil, hear no evil' in the pursuit of efficiency and profit, which seemed so prevalent in the past. Secondly, an actor may be influenced by other actors into adhering to a particular norm. This process of socialisation, explained in the previous chapter, can be seen to have influenced the banks and financial institutions into accepting the 'ethical principles' of the Basle Committee and is fundamental to the work of the Financial Action Task Force.

Krasner's definition of a regime as featuring 'principles, norms, rules and decision-making procedures' is met by the Financial Action Task Force in this 'given area of international relations'.[54] The norm that banks should not profit from illicit funds is nearly universally accepted. The norms and the principles of the regime can be seen to have been developed by the Basle Committee and the work of the United Nations. The Council of Europe, the European Economic Community and the United States can be seen to have started to develop regional regimes for the control of money laundering. However, the Financial Action Task Force is the only global body whose focus is exclusively on money laundering. The emergence of the Task Force can be seen as the decision-making focus of a global money-laundering control regime.

7 International Regimes and Drug Control in the 1990s

INTRODUCTION

The 1980s saw the wider availability and growing consumption of illicit drugs. It also saw the emergence of an international consensus against drug trafficking by the international community. The increase in drug trafficking has occurred despite increasing international action through the main international control body, the United Nations, and other international institutions, to prevent it. This work has shown that there are many difficulties involved in attempts by legal structures to control an illegal activity, especially one which is as multi-faceted and multi-dimensional as the drug phenomenon. Suppression of one source of supply, one method of transportation and one pattern of abuse has often simply led to the emergence of other forms. This work has attempted to set the 'drug problem', as it has become known, into a theoretical framework which aids our understanding of the phenomenon, by further developing theories of regime creation. Because the drug phenomenon is complex and multi-faceted, it requires precisely the issue-specific approach of international regimes as understood by this research.

REGIME CREATION

It has become clear through the course of this study that the prevailing literature on international regimes has concentrated on structural models of regimes – the rules and decision-making procedures – within a Realist hegemonic-stability framework. Hegemonic-stability theory incorporates the central Realist axiom, of states rationally aiming to secure themselves through maximising their power, in the face of growing interdependence between countries. This view has been expounded by writers such as Kindleberger (1973), Gilpin (1975), Krasner (1976) and Keohane (1984), principally as an explanation of patterns of international economic co-operation. In this area, the theory might be seen to have some descriptive utility. The dominance of the United States in the post-war international economic and military order until the 1970s, exemplified by security institutions such as the North Atlantic Treaty Organization (NATO), and economically by the Bretton Woods system, illustrates this. The other classic example of hegemonic-stability advanced by the Realists is the international trade system of the second half of the nineteenth century, which was dominated by Great Britain by virtue of her vast Empire and naval strength. However, as we have seen in Chapter 3, at the turn of the century, the United States, which was not then a military power on a par with the global empires, was able to put the question of drug control onto the international agenda and Britain was forced to accept international legislation.

While accepting that Great Britain and the United States were often able to utilise their capabilities to secure international co-operation to suit their interests in the nineteenth and twentieth century respectively, hegemonic-stability theory does not help to explain the many international institutions and agreements in the form of regimes that have survived the decline of the hegemon or been created in the absence of one. Despite the decline of US hegemony in the 1970s, most international arrangements can be seen to have continued to function, including the General Agreement on Tariffs and Trade (GATT).

Critics of hegemonic-stability theory have also been able to point to the many examples of regime creation in the last 30 years, despite the decline of the US as a hegemon, as a challenge to the usefulness of the theory. Much of their work has been concerned with environmental and conservation regimes: Oran Young writing about the North Pacific fur seals regime and the Svalbard Archipelago;[1] Peter Haas writing about the development of a regional regime regulating marine pollution in the Mediterranean known as the Mediterranean Action Plan[2] and the issue of ozone depletion and the emergence of an international regime curbing CFC use and production,[3] and recently Oran Young and Gail Osherenko detailing the example of the creation of a regime to conserve polar bears in the Arctic.[4] A regime to conserve polar bears was set up in 1973 and included both superpowers. The regime can be seen to have represented a common (non-security) concern which transcended ideological differences, without apparently advancing the economic or military interests of any of the participating governments, in contrast to the hegemonic-stability argument.

Various explanations have been offered by regime theorists for the failure of international institutions and regimes created in the late 1940s to collapse in the absence of continued American hegemony. One argument is that, although American power can be judged to have declined, the United States still maintains an important position and can continue to direct international arrangements in a way which favours her interests. Roger Tooze links what can be seen as the continuation of American hegemony under a new guise to the predominantly American discourse of regime theory:

> ... regime analysis allows for the continued articulation of interest by a dominant political and economic power. In other words, the concept of regime, and its widespread adoption not only changes the way that we think about international cooperation, but also enables and legitimises a continuation of American power within the 'new' regime framework.[5]

This is what Cox refers to as the 'process of institutionalization of hegemony', where there is continued acceptance of the values underlying the structure of the world political economy.[6]

An alternative but related position accepts that American hegemony has declined but sees a new hegemon in the form of a trilateral power structure formed by the United States, Japan and the European Community. Since both Japan and the EC are in broad agreement with the ideology of the post-war economy, the values, beliefs and goals of the new hegemonic coalition broadly reflect those of the old.

Finally, to return to the work of Stephen Krasner, an alternative explanation comes from the idea that there is a time-lag between the rise and fall of a regime and the underlying changes in the structure of power. Therefore, regimes can be seen to continue and 'assume a life of their own'[7] despite a realignment of power in international society. This phenomenon, or time-lag, can be explained as being a result of custom and usage, uncertainty and cognitive failing. States which are party to a regime may continue to adhere to its rules and principles through habit, and can be reluctant to defect in order to maximise short-term interests through fear of incurring long-term costs. Although unhappy with the regime to which they are a party, states may not wish to bear the costs of constructing an alternative regime. Therefore, a regime can be seen to be able to survive the decline of the hegemon through these 'feedback mechanisms', whose preponderant position had created the conditions for the regime's creation.[8]

The above explanations are not, however, useful for understanding the setting up of regimes such as that described for polar bear or fur seal conservation or the protection of the ozone layer, or indeed the money laundering control regime described in the previous chapter. The polar bear regime cannot be seen to advance the economic or military interests of any of the participating governments. In the case of the creation of the money-laundering control regime, although the world's largest banks are based in the United States, they were not able to force the acceptance of a mandatory reporting system for all financial transactions over a certain amount on the other actors in the system.

Supporters of hegemonic-stability theory would say that its lack of application to environmental regimes does not matter, since they concern what Realist writers would term 'low politics' issues and therefore do not challenge the validity of the theory. Opponents of hegemonic-stability arguments for regime creation have often been criticised for concentrating efforts on areas where their hypotheses are, in the words of Jonsson, 'doomed to success', that is, these 'low politics', non-contentious issues.[9] However, as Chapter 1 has demonstrated, the drug phenomenon challenges the Realist approach to international relations since a social problem, drug-related activity, is seen as a threat to national and international security by many governments and could therefore be described as a 'high politics' issue. This work has shown the lack of theoretical applicability of the Realist high/low politics distinction to current developments in international relations. An alternative view, advocated by the Globalists, is that in principle any issue may affect security, involve the highest decision-makers, produce crises and be dominated by governments. The drug phenomenon clearly demonstrates that while the hegemon may be a factor in regime creation, especially in economic issues as described above, it is not the single overriding determinant that the hegemonic-stability theorists would have us believe. This study has focused on the importance of understanding the nature of the principles and norms and their dynamics for regime creation, rather than the narrower focus on the rules and decision-making procedures favoured by hegemonic-stability theory. The literature on international regimes suggests that a regime must have an issue that it seeks to regulate. The concept of an issue, however, suffers from lack of clarification in current International Relations literature.

This book has pointed out that the concept of issues forming distinct issue-systems, and the concept of international regimes which emerged from the literature on interdependence in the 1970s, developed principally in isolation from each other, the former within the Globalist paradigm and the latter within the Realist approach to International Relations as a response to the challenge of interdependence. Both concepts can be seen to have suffered from lack of clarification in the discipline. Important to both approaches is the concept of an issue. The concept is central to the Global Politics paradigm in the acceptance that there is not a single international system, but instead there are multiple issue-based systems, with each system featuring a unique cast of actors for whom the issue is salient. However, as we have seen, an authoritative theoretical literature on the nature of issues is lacking. The use of the term 'issue-area' in the work of Rosenau, Mansbach and Vasquez and Keohane and Nye has generated a great deal of confusion. The use of systems analysis in political science pioneered by David Easton defines a political system as wherever one can identify behaviour modification in any given area, which is in keeping with Mansbach's and Vasquez' description of an issue as consisting of 'a cluster of values that are to be allocated'. The concept of an 'issue-system' can be seen as more analytically useful than issue-area, because it need not evoke the behavioural processes that Rosenau associated with the term issue-area. Therefore we can concentrate attention on the contention over values of the actors concerned. This understanding of the nature of issues, in terms of contention over values being central to the study of politics, described by Easton as 'the authoritative allocation of values', is quite distinct from the Realist understanding of the nature of issues and of politics as the struggle for power in an anarchic world. According to the Realist perspective, state power and 'state interests' explain which issues come on to the agenda (and form international regimes) and which remain on the periphery.

Work on agenda-formation has not been taken up in International Relations literature. This can be seen to be partly due to the dominance of the Realist paradigm in the discipline, and the emphasis on the anarchy of the global system, rather than viewing world politics as co-operation and conflict of actors over efforts to allocate values authoritatively in multiple systems. Mansbach's and Vasquez' 'issue cycle' and crisis stage, as discussed in Chapter 2, although useful, do not claim to have general application. This study believes that the concept of salience, developed by the Globalist paradigm, is a more fundamentally useful theoretical concept for understanding issue formation and evolution because it shifts the 'critical' property from the issue to the actor. Using the concept of salience we can understand how one issue can be more salient than another for a specific actor at a specific time if it optimises the actor's own set of value preferences at that time. The concept of salience suggests a dynamic to change lacking in the emphasis on stability in the state-centric approach of Realism.

Salience can explain the emergence of issue-systems, when actors seek to generate support for particular values and to allocate them authoritatively. The extent to which the actors in an issue-system regulate the issue (by authoritatively allocating the value at stake) is variable. A regime is formed if the issue-system can successfully translate values into the form of an agreed norm and if there is a high rate of actor compliance with the rules and decisions designed to uphold that norm. Therefore the formation of issue-systems and the creation of regimes can be seen as different stages in the same process of global change. This emphasis on understanding the nature of issues through an understanding of values is central to systems analysis and has been shown in this study to give a firmer theoretical footing for explaining the normative nature of international regimes, lacking in the dominant hegemonic approach to regime creation.

A clearer understanding of values and norms and their evolution and role in international decision-making has been explored in order to develop a theory of international regimes that gave them an independent impact in international relations and not simply a role as a reflection of hegemonic interests. Developing theories of value and norm emergence can also be seen as central to understanding change in world politics.

THE DYNAMICS OF CHANGE

For the traditional Realist school, change in world politics is defined in terms of changes in state power, and the emergence of regimes is similarly defined. An alternative approach to the emergence and role of international regimes challenges this established belief by asserting that agendas are determined by the attempt of actors individually to maximise the achievement of their preferred values and collectively to *allocate values authoritatively* on specific issues.

How values emerge, change and influence decision-making in international politics has received very little attention in International Relations literature and specifically in relation to the field of regimes. The standard Krasner definition of an international regime implicitly contains the concept of values, with his definition of 'principles' and 'norms'. The concept of 'values' is evoked with the use of 'principles', defined as 'beliefs of fact causation and rectitude', and 'norms', defined as 'standards of behaviour defined in terms of rights and obligations' and further developed in this work.

In Chapter 3, this study explained the changing attitudes towards drug use in the nineteenth century and emphasised the importance of taking into account the advances and concepts from alternative disciplines, such as sociology, philosophy and history, in our understanding of change. This chapter helps to illustrate how the Realists' preoccupation with the 'struggle for power' does not explain the fact that there are a variety of values and stakes for which actors both co-operate and compete. Rapid industrialisation, urbanisation and technological advances, with corresponding social and economic transformation and increasing social unrest; a rising economic group in the form of the medical profession and their attempts to establish monopolistic restrictive practices; the attempts by traders to destroy the British monopoly of trade with China and to promote free trade; the values of the religious movements and the missionaries promoting the end of the opium trade with China – all illustrate that power, as understood by the Realist approach to International Relations, was not the sole variable for change in the nineteenth century in relation to drug use.

Chapter 3 illustrated the mix of social and technological change, competing domestic interests, changing religious values and competing trade interests which all promoted changing norms about drug use. Nineteenth-century society also illustrates how the norm towards drug use was sustained through the process of socialisation. By the end of the nineteenth century there was widespread consensus that the non-medical use of opium in particular and of its derivatives (heroin, morphine, methadone) was evil, immoral and dangerous. Although contemporary scientific evidence demonstrated that opium had no particularly harmful effects other than addiction (see the Report of the Royal Commission on Opium, 1894–95 in Chapter 3), there were few moral or political issues which were so strongly condemned by public opinion at the time. This was despite the fact that opiate use had been quite widespread earlier in the nineteenth century. In the twentieth century, anti-opium attitudes can be seen to have been institutionalised by national and international agreements, again despite conflicting scientific evidence as detailed in Chapter 1.

An authoritative literature on the source and role of values in the discipline of International Relations has been shown to be lacking. The work of Mansbach and Vasquez is one of the few examples of an attempt by International Relations writers to present an analysis of the nature of values.[10] Mansbach and Vasquez illuminate the nature of values, which they say are abstract and intangible, by proposing that they are represented by objects or stakes representing the values. However, their work is unnecessarily confusing. Confusion arises since values are also talked about as either intrinsic or instrumental, suggesting that there is a corresponding relationship between intrinsic and instrumental stakes and intrinsic and instrumental values. This work has put forward the view that since values are abstract and cannot be attained directly, all values must be intrinsic. Since stakes are the objects with which value satisfaction can be achieved, all stakes can be seen as instrumental, a way of satisfying preferences. As we have seen in this work, actors do not always continue to support stakes in a static manner, but for the value that supporting the stake may satisfy at the time, or for the satisfaction of an alternative stake. Similarly, different actors may contest the same stake for the satisfaction of different values.

In this sense, acting in your self-interest can still be understood as value-guided behaviour, a fact commonly overlooked in the traditional Realist approach to international politics. As Easton states:

> Interests is itself a conceptually ambiguous term in political research. It might be used to refer to the fundamental value system of an individual or group, his basic goals, hopes and aspirations in life. To use it so broadly is to destroy any specific analytic significance it may have. It is more helpful to abandon this possible meaning and retain 'basic goals' or 'fundamental values' as concepts for this purpose.[11]

Easton goes on to clarify that in this way 'Interests can then be more narrowly defined to refer to instrumental values' (or stakes as described by this author), those means through which a person or group seeks to implement what may be considered to be his or its fundamental goals.[12]

The United States government supported the moral position on drug control in the nineteenth century because the British monopoly of trade with China was against their interest. On the other hand, the missionaries' position derived from the value that drugs were evil, immoral and dangerous, and the abolition of the trade with China partly satisfied this value. The norm 'Banks should not profit from illicit activity' emerged as a specific interpretation of the value that drugs were evil, immoral and dangerous, and that drug trafficking should be prevented, but has come to be salient to financial institutions for its role in realising the very different value of protecting the soundness and stability of financial institutions. As Mansbach and Vasquez state, 'actors may seek the same stake in the name of different values'.[13]

THE ROLE OF NORMS

The important of understanding values, emphasised by the work on issue-systems in political science, gives us an alternative understanding of why actors co-operate in international affairs – not for the allocation of power, but for the allocation of values. The shifting values and norms of actors must therefore be understood to play a significant role in agenda-building. Norms have received very little attention in the discipline of International Relations or in the work of regime theorists. Chapter 5 discussed how the different approaches to the nature and the role of norms have been influenced by different philosophical traditions. This was seen to have led to confusion, with the term 'norm' meaning different things in the literature of different fields. The use of the concept by regime theorists has been limited to explaining their emergence in terms of the utility for powerful actors of writing the norms and rules in their own interests. Utilitarian logic and state-of-nature concepts can be seen to have no empirical referents in the complex world of individuals who are born into a pre-existing society, have multiple objectives, possess limited information, cannot necessarily conceptualise a coherent value calculus and cannot always predict the outcome of their actions. The less-logical, less-satisfactory concept of a social norm, as explained in Chapter 5, does match the reality of a society with organised religious groups and competing political parties and subject to socialisation processes. This work has portrayed norms as central to understanding the creation of international regimes and their role and impact in international affairs. The significance of norms has been shown to be what makes the study of regime theory distinctive from any other area of International Relations, such as the study of international organisations. Fundamentally, if regimes are to have any independent impact on world affairs, they must change actors' behaviour. In order to do this they must allocate values authoritatively by enforcing norms and implementing their rules and procedures amongst state and non-state actors.

Chapter 5 described various norms that have emerged in response to drug-related activity. However, from the norms listed, only one can be seen to have formed an effective international regime. Despite strong consensus around a second norm, only a 'declaratory regime', to use Jack Donnelly's terminology, can be seen to have emerged at the present time. Why this is so will be explored in the next section.

DRUG TRAFFICKING AND MONEY LAUNDERING: THE FOCUS OF INTERNATIONAL ATTENTION

As we have explained above, norm emergence is not a guarantee of regime emergence. As Chapter 4 detailed, the emergence of a consensus against drug trafficking by the international community did not lead to the creation of an international regime that could effectively enforce the norm to prevent drug trafficking. Consensus over values can be seen to have led to the emergence of a norm, but not to international decision-making procedures. This work has shown that, in the literature on international regimes, there is a great deal of definitional confusion about what constitutes a regime.

The extent to which a regime's norms and its decision-making procedures are enforced varies. As Donnelly states,

> Regime norms may range from binding international standards that are generally accepted by states as authoritative to international guidelines that are commended in word but rarely in deed. Regime procedures likewise may range from full international decision making, including generally effective enforcement powers, to procedures that amount to little more than international verbal encouragement of sovereign national action. *International regimes thus come in an immense variety of forms.*[14] [Emphasis added by current author.]

For Donnelly, a regime's 'strength' increases according to the extent of its decision-making powers – that is, the range of activities available to relevant international institutions. Four types of regimes, based on four types of action, are identified by Donnelly: *Promotion* – encouraging national implementation of international norms by public information activities; *Assistance* – providing support for national implementation of international norms, typically through financial or technical assistance; *Implementation* – playing a direct international role in putting regime norms into practice through systems of international information exchange, policy consultation or co-ordination, or (unenforceable) international monitoring of national compliance with regime norms or recommended policies; and finally, *Enforcement* – binding and enforceable international implementation of regime norms.[15]

Within each general type, as defined in the first instance by decision-making procedures, regimes can be further differentiated by their normative scope. Donnelly identifies four types of regime norms, running from fully international or 'authoritative international norms: binding international standards, generally accepted as such by states' to entirely national, described as 'the absence of substantive international norms'. A fifth type of regime can therefore be identified, a 'declaratory regime', which involves international norms but has no international decision-making procedures (see Figure 7.1). The global trafficking regime is an example of a declaratory regime. The norms of the regime are coherent, well developed, and widely commended by state and non-state actors alike. However, implementation of the norm that trafficking must be controlled has remained the responsibility of national and not international actors. In as much as governments are beginning to co-operate in the exchange of information on trafficking, the declaratory regime may be evolving into a promotional regime.

The description of international attempts to control drug trafficking given above conforms to the approach to regime formation adopted by the European regime theorists in the late 1980s. For them the final criterion for regime formation is that the behaviour of international actors must be affected by the regime's norms, rules and decision-making procedures. Wolf and Zurn have added the appendage of 'effectiveness' to Krasner's standard definition of an international regime.[16] As Rittberger points out, this enables us to distinguish between regimes and treaties, since a regime's rules may be informal. A further distinction can therefore be made between

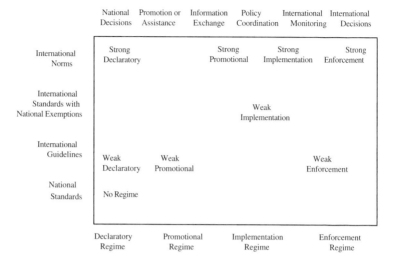

Figure 7.1   Donnelly's regime classification

Source: J. Donnelly, 'International human rights: A regime analysis', *International Organization*, Vol. 40, No. 3, Summer 1986, p. 603.

rules that are actually observed and those that exist in writing but have no discernable influence on actor behaviour. According to Rittberger, norms and rules which do not affect the behaviour of states cannot be considered prescriptions. Commenting on the research by Mendler into the issue of the working conditions of foreign journalists, where Krasner's criteria for a regime had been met, Rittberger states,

> ... norm observance and rule compliance varied so greatly over time and across countries, especially in Eastern Europe and the Soviet Union, that – using effectiveness as a criterion – it did not seem warranted to acknowledge the existence of a regime.[17]

It can be seen therefore that there is no effective trafficking regime because governments cannot implement the norm. Firstly, drug trafficking cannot be effectively controlled for practical reasons, since borders of countries have offered limited protection from smugglers throughout history, for goods for which there is a high demand. Also the nature of the drugs themselves presents practical problems: they are not a bulky commodity. Because of the demand for heroin, cocaine and marijuana, smuggling small amounts, easily disguisable about the person or in a vehicle, can generate large profits. Secondly, there is currently no regulatory body with the global authority necessary for implementation of the drug-trafficking norm. This is despite the fact that the norm is coherent, well-developed and widely commended by state and non-state actors alike. The drug-control bodies of the United Nations have shown themselves to be ineffective at implementing the norm. GATT, the main institution concerned with trade, promotes freedom of trade rather than restrictions on trade. On the other hand, the norm of the international money-laundering control regime is seen as a binding international standard that is generally accepted as authoritative, by states and non-state actors for whom the issue is salient. The regime can be seen to enforce its decision-making powers effectively through the Financial Action Task Force.

Other possible global bodies which could be the centre for a global trafficking control regime include the International Criminal Police Organization (ICPO/Interpol). However, its role has always been one of stimulating the exchange of information among national drug law-enforcement services, through the establishment of a data bank, and international bodies concerned with drug control, and in aiding the ability of national services to control illicit traffic. Its secretariat has no operational role independent of national authorities.

The lack of development of a supranational operational regulatory body for controlling drug trafficking is clearly due to the importance states give to their policing powers as a core item of their sovereignty. The lack of development of co-ordinated policing operations by the international community, despite the increase in transnational crime described earlier in this study, illustrates this. Any effective international action against drug trafficking would require relinquishing control over parts of the national law-enforcement machinery, which states are still reluctant to do. Recently there have been more examples of successful co-ordinated operations on a global level. A three-country co-operation over a drug haul was described as unprecedented by police chiefs involved. The chief of Italy's anti-drug unit described the haul as marking the end of the era of 'jealousy and territorial policing'.[18] On a regional level there have also been important developments.

The Schengen Convention drawn up in 1985 by France, Germany, Luxembourg, Holland and Belgium concerned the need for enhanced police co-operation and information exchange when Europe became frontier-free. However, the United Kingdom, the Irish

Republic and Denmark have remained outside the Schengen Group. It took until the ratification of the Maastricht Treaty in 1993 for there to be any moves towards the development of unified policing within the formal structures of the European Community. Within Europe, the activities of the Trevi Group, a forum for co-operation on law enforcement between the European Community Member States, remained separate from the work of the European Community until the ratification of the Maastricht Treaty and the creation of the European Union in November 1993.

The Declaration on Police Co-operation incorporated in the Final Act of the Maastricht conference calls for support for national criminal investigation and security authorities, in particular in the co-ordination of investigation and search operations; creation of data bases; central analysis and assessment of information in order to identify investigative approaches; collection and analysis of national prevention programmes for drawing up Europe-wide prevention strategies; measures relating to further training, research, forensic matters and criminal records departments.[19]

Co-operation on policing is viewed by member states as in the same category as co-operation on foreign policy. All decisions concerning provisions on co-operation in the fields of justice and home affairs must be decided unanimously, with Britain insisting on endorsement by Westminster of any decisions that are taken. This policy on immigration and crime is to be decided inter-governmentally and the national veto is not removed by qualified majority voting, as it is in other areas of policy, which shows the lack of willingness of Member States to surrender any sovereignty over policing. There have, however, been some recent moves towards greater co-operation over policing within Europe.

The commitment to a common police information system has led to the creation of a European Police Organization, or Europol. One of the first steps has been the creation of a Drugs Intelligence Unit (DIU), which became operational at the end of 1992. The future role of Europol is undecided. The German government, for example, want Europol to develop into a fully-fledged investigative body with powers of arrest in any country, while the British are happier with a Europol that simply exchanges information – a role that would mesh neatly with the new National Criminal Intelligence System.[20]

There are both practical problems and conflict over values involved in the establishment of a European police force and the creation of a regional drug-trafficking regime. These problems reflect the similar difficulties that would need to be overcome in establishing a global trafficking regime. British police and customs officers, unlike most of their European counterparts, are not armed, except in exceptional circumstances. Most European police forces are organised nationally and functionally and are often answerable to several ministries, whereas the UK police have no central political direction: the 52 separate forces operate a tripartite system of accountability through the Home Office, the area Chief Constable and local Police Authorities.

There are problems even at the first stage of Europol's role of data collection and information exchange. International drug trafficking has been the major rationale for broadening and intensifying international police co-operation and information-sharing. Britain's National Criminal Intelligence System (as mentioned above) is planned to co-operate with similar organisations in other countries, but there is concern that the structures through which this co-operation occurs are beyond direct democratic control at the European level. Data protection requirements may conflict with police needs for intelligence gathering and collation. Roger Birch, chair of the chief constables' International Committee stated in 1992 that 'the policing of Europe cannot wait for the total harmonisation of legislation and for the resolution of such thorny issues as data protection'.[21] Council of Europe Member States have been under an obligation since 1981 to implement the Council's Convention on Data Processing. Despite the 1984 Data Protection Act, police in the United Kingdom have reserved their right not to implement fully a critical recommendation on giving people notice that information is held on them. Furthermore, they have reserved the right to accumulate information on people not directly related to a particular investigation. Police co-operation and information-sharing therefore raises problems of responsibility and accountability in law enforcement.

The Supplementary Agreement signed at Schengen in 1990 foresaw a declaration by each signatory, at the time of ratification, to harmonise procedures for cross-border pursuit, rights of arrest, territorial and time limits, and penalties for violation of agreed procedures. However, French law has hitherto denied the possibility of arrest by a foreign policeman on French territory and hot pursuit is a particularly delicate issue in the UK, given that one EC land border is between the Irish Republic and Northern Ireland.

Nor are matters straightforward between England and Scotland, where fundamentally differing legal systems apply and there is no automatic reciprocity of powers of arrest or even validity of arrest warrants. The multi-national police apparatus that would compensate for the loss of border checks is not yet in place.

Despite all the differences in accountability, data protection regulations, issues of public order policing (such as whether British policemen should be armed) and differing judicial systems, the formal arrangements for greater police co-operation within Europe are in place. The Trevi Group discussions, the Schengen Convention, and developments within Interpol can be seen to have developed the principles and the norms of a would-be regional regime. Using Donnelly's regime types described above, the European trafficking regime can be described as a 'promotional regime'. The regime may become stronger in the future if the salience of drug trafficking, which has already led to increased centralisation of policing in the UK and increased police co-operation in Europe, reduces the commitment to national sovereignty in the field of law enforcement, or rather, if there is a shift in value salience. For the time being, the situation for trafficking is best described as being a European promotional regime operating within a global declaratory regime.

The anti-trafficking regime is also weak since, as has been shown, it has no relevant international institution to implement the regime's norms. Interpol engages in, to use Donnelly's classifications, promotional and assistance activities, providing support for national implementation of international norms, policy co-ordination, international monitoring, etc. Neither Interpol nor Trevi have any international decision-making powers. The regime will remain weak until states are willing to surrender decision-making activities to an external authority. Banking has a longer history of co-operation and more willingness to surrender sovereignty, especially in the deregulation era of Thatcherite and Reaganite economics during the 1980s. Mrs Thatcher's government abolished foreign exchange controls within days of taking office in 1979, emphasising that governmental regulation of any sort would henceforth be under attack.

If the problems associated with the creation of a regional or global anti-trafficking regime were solely of a practical nature, development of the regime's strength would seem to be forthcoming. However, the conflict over the relative value of national sovereignty in law-enforcement activities suggests that it will be much more difficult to create an effective regime. Alternatively, the norm that illicit drug trafficking should be controlled could successfully be implemented if illicit drugs were legalised.

VALUE DYNAMICS AND THE DRUG LEGALISATION DEBATE

The twentieth century has seen various massive shifts in values. Interest in environmental concerns has developed dramatically in the later half of the century in response to numerous crises – the *Torrey Canyon* disaster, the discovery of the hole in the ozone layer and Chernobyl among others – with the emergence of numerous national, international and global organisations to manage them. In the United States crisis situations have led to changing attitudes towards drug use. Concerns over the use of drugs for human health and drug-taking amongst young people have shifted to concerns for national security and increasing crime rates. The repeated declaration of the 'War on Drugs' by the American administration has seen the salience of the value shift from a health concern to a security and crime concern. The rhetorical war on drugs was militarised with the deployment of the armed forces to assist drug enforcement operations, the contribution of intelligence operations by the CIA and the involvement of NASA assisting with satellite-based surveillance of crops under cultivation. Public concern in the United States over the use of illicit drugs was critical throughout the 1980s. Regardless of political affiliation, socio-economic status and ethnicity, or geographical and occupational location, the 'drug problem' was consistently ranked by most Americans as one of the major problems facing the nation. High-profile drug convictions among prominent Americans such as the mayor of Washington, Marion Barry, have added to this public sense of urgency. That values are constantly shifting and changing is emphasised by Marion Barry successfully standing for re-election in 1994. It is necessary therefore to analyse the values people adhere to and the way they affect their approach to politics and, ultimately, why co-operation occurs in the form of international regimes. The dynamic process currently occurring concerning drug legalisation emphasises the importance of understanding the dynamics of values.

The increase in drug use and trafficking throughout the 1980s highlighted to many observers that the decades of prohibition by the international community and current drug-control strategies were a failure. Interdiction initiatives in the United States have been estimated to seize only 20 per cent of the marijuana and cocaine coming into the country. Despite the interdiction, the growing supply of drugs has resulted in increased availability and a dramatic decline in price. This pattern is also reflected in the United Kingdom.

Chapter 2 outlined how the vast profits to be made from drug trafficking, second only to the arms trade, have corrupted the governments and the military of many countries throughout the world. Throughout the 1980s, involvement in drug trafficking can be traced to the highest officials in governments in Mexico, the Bahamas, Pakistan, Argentina, Peru, Guatemala, Paraguay, Colombia and Panama. Most recently, the Colombian President, Ernesto Samper, has been at the centre of a corruption scandal that at one point threatened to bring down his government.

In the countries of the industrialised world it is the relationship between drugs and the increasing domestic and international crime rate which has added to the call for a debate over legalisation by various law-enforcement officials and members of the judiciary. Internationally, in the Lebanon, Peru, Afghanistan, Laos, Cambodia and Thailand, drug profits have fuelled insurrections. In much of Asia, South and North America and some parts of Europe the drug trade is closely associated with organised crime and terrorism. The threat of illicit funds corrupting financial institutions has also been of great concern during the 1980s, with the danger being highlighted by the collapse of the Bank of Credit and Commerce International.

It is within this context that the debate over the legalisation of drugs first emerged in the late 1980s. Drug legalisation, particularly the legalisation of marijuana, has been discussed on and off over the last twenty years. However, the range of actors involved differentiates the contemporary debate from past debates. Support for the decriminalisation of illicit drugs has traditionally come primarily from the conservative end of the political spectrum, disturbed by the infringements on individual liberty and civil rights posed by the drug laws. This view can be seen to have been reflected in the recent decision of the Colombian Supreme Court to decriminalise the possession of drugs in small amounts. The Supreme Court decided that it was unconstitutional to violate a person's freedom to decide whether to take drugs. The decision has been criticised as 'ingenuous and anachronistic, based on 19th-century liberalism' by four of the nine judges who opposed the decision.[22] A similar ruling took place in Germany in 1992 which called for the recognition of the 'constitutional right of individuals to intoxication'.[23] But there also emerged in the United States, in the later half of the 1980s an intellectual rationale for legalisation, with the work of Ethan Nadelmann and Arnold Trebach amongst others.[24] Many of the evils associated with the drug problem in the 1980s, the increase of domestic crime and international instability, were attributed to the fact that drugs were illegal. As Milton Friedman stated, 'all the atrocities associated with the illegal drug trade occur because the United States and other Western countries pass anti-drug laws which they cannot enforce'.[25] The 'drug problem', as Edward Brecher states in his influential *Licit and Illicit Drugs*, is itself a problem.[26] The advantages of legalisation have attracted a great deal of media coverage.[27] Respected intellectuals and professionals have participated in the discussions. The first elected official (a significant development) in the United States to come out in favour of broadening the debate was former prosecutor and then mayor of Baltimore, Kurt Schmoke. Speaking to the National Conference of Mayors, he asked for the merits of legalisation to be debated in congressional hearings.[28] Other prominent participants in the debate have included the head of the American Civil Liberties Union, prominent Harvard professors, lawyers, former Attorney Generals, Congressmen and prominent businessmen, who began to voice much-publicised alternatives to the drug war. Former Secretary of State George Schultz expressed the belief of many when he stated that it was necessary to 'consider and examine forms of controlled legalisation' in order to 'take the criminality out of the drug business'.[29] In the United Kingdom several judges and senior policemen (including serving police officers) have spoken on the need to reform drug laws.[30] Internationally, the Head of Interpol, Raymond Kendall, called for an end to the present drug policy and for the decriminalisation of drug use.[31] Commenting in an editorial, *The Lancet* said: 'the abject failure of prevailing policies is now so generally acknowledged that the momentum towards decriminalisation is surely becoming unstoppable'.[32]

Another group with changing attitudes has been European public health authorities, as best represented in the Netherlands. They have begun to promote a new health paradigm under the slogan of 'harm reduction'. It recognises that abstinence is not a realistic short-term goal for most dependent users. Policy therefore proceeds in a pragmatic fashion through a hierarchy of more achievable objectives. Before the discovery of Human Immunodeficiency Virus (HIV) and Acquired Immune Deficiency Syndrome (AIDS), governments were reluctant to sanction harm-reduction policies which might seem to condone drug use and require police co-operation, even though it was known that a large proportion of HIV infection was caused through needle sharing amongst drug users.[33] The realisation that AIDS posed a greater threat to public health than drug addiction removed political objections. In the United States the Surgeon-General, Dr Jocelyn Elders, identified the high murder rate (50 per cent of which is drug-related) as a major menace to public health. In December 1993, and again in January 1994, Dr Elders argued that the US administration ought at least to study legalisation as a means of reducing violent crime and other health risks.[34]

Many grass-roots non-governmental organisations have emerged which support drug-law reform: mention has already been made of Arnold Trebach's Drug Policy Foundation (DPF). Within the UK there is the National Organisation for the Reform of Marijuana Laws (NORML), and within Europe there is the European Movement for the Normalization of Drug Policy (EMNDP), The International Anti-Prohibition League and the Coordinamento Radicale Antiproibizionista (CORA), sponsored by and involved with Italy's Radical Party. The European groups have successfully lobbied for support from members of the European Parliament who now support drug-policy reform. In Italy, Marco Taradesh was elected as member to the European Parliament on an anti-prohibition ticket.

The relationship between CORA and Italy's Radical Party reflects the differences between European and American attitudes towards drug reform. The Radical Party places the social integration of marginalised people high on the agenda and looks for global and transnational solutions to problems. European arguments for drug-policy reform can be seen to be more broadly based than the American arguments, encompassing the geo-political, sociological and economic effects of prohibition. A different cultural tradition is represented by the Drug Policy Foundation which comes out of the American liberal democratic tradition, in which civil liberties arguments dominate. The difference in the political traditions of the two cultures is demonstrated in the scope of the published conference papers of the DPF and CORA.[35] These different cultural traditions and values demonstrate that for any drug policy reform strategy to succeed, it must be framed within the political traditions of that culture.

Events in countries such as Colombia and Bolivia have led to an urgent political need for radical alternatives to current policies. The decision by the Bolivian government to promote coca tea[36] and the decision by the Colombian judicial system to decriminalise personal drug use, despite opposition from the Colombian government, can be seen to reflect this momentum for change. In Europe, a group of Spanish jurists launched a campaign in February 1992 calling for a pragmatic approach to allow sales under strict conditions;[37] in May of 1994 the German courts decriminalised the possession of small amounts of marijuana and in June of the same year a decree issued in Italy repealed the prohibition of the non-medical use of drugs.

These changes in attitudes towards current drugs policy and illicit drug use can be seen in part to be due to the shift in patterns of licit drug consumption. Changing attitudes towards both licit and illicit drug use cannot be seen to be due to government legislation and law enforcement. In the United Kingdom, a recent survey for the Home Office revealed that 30 per cent of people were in favour of limited legalisation of drugs such as cannabis.[38] The Home Secretary, in recently increasing the fine for the possession of drugs five-fold to a maximum of £2,500, has faced extensive criticism from all quarters including magistrates and the police, who have criticised the decision as having little impact on the problem of drug use.[39] The use and abuse of both legal and illegal drugs have been recognised as the causes of serious health, social, and economic problems for more than 100 years. Substantial resources have been spent on trying to limit drug use and the associated crime problem created by the illegalisation of certain drugs by both the international community and states. Only the decline in the proportion of adults smoking cigarettes can be seen to have been moderately successful through education programmes. The decline in the use of licit drugs such as tobacco and alcohol is due to changing attitudes within society and the recognition of the harmful nature of the substances. This shift has occurred without any change in the law. Illicit drug consumption cannot be controlled solely by law-enforcement measures but by changes in people's attitudes towards drug use. Accurate information is therefore needed about the dangers associated with particular types of drug use, rather than the blanket condemnation under current drug policy.

The debate on reforming the drug laws outlined above is in stark contrast to the climate of the early 1980s, where there was very little resistance to the ideological orthodoxy that provided the moral weapons for the campaigns in the drug war. However, academic works such as Berridge and Edwards' *Opium and the People* and Courtwright's *Dark Paradise* have, through their analysis of drug use in early industrial society (as described in Chapter 3), provoked many into questioning whether our current drug policies ameliorate or exacerbate drug problems and led to the emergence of the legalisation rationale as described in this book.

What differentiates the debate in the latter half of the 1980s and early 1990s from previous debates has been the perception by the wide range of actors participating that the problem is critical. Previously, discussion of legalisation by policy-makers was deemed irresponsible and dismissed. However, a growing number of people in authority, including senior ministers, police officers and members of the judiciary world-wide, have come to agree that there is a case to be answered and have responded with reasoned arguments. Perhaps the current debate about drug legalisation will achieve results as impressive as the shift in values brought about in part by the British anti-opium movement of the 1890s. It is possible there will be a willingness to discard prohibitions and criminal penalties against drug users and sellers, as happened with alcohol in the 1930s. The challenge to 'law and order', 'civil rights', 'justice and fairness', etc. by current drug policies can be seen as a value challenge to the belief that 'drugs are evil and dangerous', just as in the nineteenth century the values of economic efficiency and economic welfare overrode the value position that drugs were evil and dangerous. The case for legalisation stems from the contention that prohibition is wrong in principle and does not work in practice. It is this latter functional link that can be seen to be leading to a possible successful value challenge to the current policy.

CONCLUSION

This book has attempted to show that regime analysis, which necessitates an emphasis on the role of values and norms in agenda-building, rather than concentrating on rules and decision-making procedures, is necessary for an understanding of the drug phenomenon. The drug phenomenon has been shown to be a complex phenomenon which challenges the traditional Realist approach to International Relations to explain its complexity. However, the clarification of these key terms used in international regimes literature has been necessary, due to the dominance of hegemonic-stability theory, to explain the nature and emergence of regimes.

The attempt by actors to control drug trafficking can be seen to be sub-optimal, when compared to the initial goal of the norm from which co-operation occurred. Attempts by actors to control money laundering have led to a high degree of consensus over the norm that 'Banks should not profit from illicit funds'. Unlike attempts to control drug trafficking, the fact that this norm is adhered to by the actors for whom the issue is salient has led to the emergence of a strong enforcement regime, with the Financial Action Task Force emerging as the decision-making focus of the regime. Unlike attempts to control drug trafficking, implementation of the regime's policies is not entirely in the hands of national rather than international actors. But an international drug-trafficking control regime can be seen to exist, since it can still be seen to have influenced political behaviour. By adopting this criterion for regime creation, the concept of an international regime can be distinguished from that of an issue-system, in response to criticism of much of regime theory that it is simply systems theory in disguise. An issue-system can be seen as an area of contention over proposals for the disposition of stakes that each actor perceives as being salient for the realisation of their values. An issue-system may or may not form a regime, depending on the success of translating values into the form of an agreed norm. Where regulation based on an agreed norm occurs, the phenomenon of an international regime emerges.

The norm of the international money-laundering control regime is seen as a binding international standard, accepted as authoritative by states and non-state actors. As has been explained in the previous chapter, efficiency, profits and secrecy were of higher salience than honesty and stability for financial actors during the early 1980s. However, the perceived threat to the banking system from drug money, and the response of bankers to the general concern outside the banking world about drug criminality, led to a value shift and norm emergence.

During the last two decades, there has been strong inter-governmental co-operation on the need to control illicit drug use. During the 1980s, a new focus emerged, emphasising control of demand for illicit drugs and an international consensus against drug trafficking.

However, expansion of drug trafficking continues to outpace the international communities' efforts to contain it. In response to this lack of success a shift in attitudes towards current drug policy and illicit drug use can be seen to have occurred. Either the technology for effective enforcement of the drug-trafficking norm will have to improve or the pressure towards liberalisation of current drugs policy will continue.

Appendix A: *List of Targets of the Comprehensive Multidisciplinary Outline of Future Activities in Drug Abuse Control*

I. PREVENTION AND REDUCTION OF THE ILLICIT DEMAND FOR NARCOTIC DRUGS AND PSYCHOTROPIC SUBSTANCES

1. Assessment of the extent of drug misuse and abuse.
2. Organization of comprehensive systems for the collection and evaluation of data.
3. Prevention through education.
4. Prevention of drug abuse in the workplace.
5. Prevention programmes by civic, community, and specific interest groups and law-enforcement officials.
6. Leisure-time activities in the service of the continuing campaign against drug abuse.
7. Role of the media.

II. CONTROL OF SUPPLY

8. Strengthening of the international system of control of narcotic drugs and psychotropic substances.
9. Rational use of pharmaceuticals containing narcotic drugs and psychotropic substances.
10. Strengthening the control of international movements of psychotropic substances.
11. Action related to the increase in the number of controlled psychotropic substances.
12. Control of the commercial movement of precursors, specific chemicals, and equipment.
13. Control of analogues of substances under international control.
14. Identification of illicit narcotic plant cultivation.
15. Elimination of illicit plantings.
16. Redevelopment of areas formerly under illicit drug crop cultivation.

III. SUPPRESSION OF ILLICIT TRAFFICKING

17. Disruption of major trafficking networks.
18. Promoting controlled delivery.
19. Facilitation of extradition.
20. Mutual judicial and legal assistance.
21. Admissibility in evidence of samples of bulk seizures of drugs.
22. Improved efficacy of penal provisions.
23. Forfeiture of the instruments and proceeds of illicit drug trafficking.
24. Tightening of the controls of movement through official points of entry.
25. Strengthening of external border controls and of mutual assistance machinery within economic unions of sovereign states.
26. Surveillance of land, water, and air approaches to the frontier.
27. Controls over the use of the international mails for drug trafficking.
28. Controls over ships on the high seas and aircraft in international airspace.

IV. TREATMENT AND REHABILITATION

29. Toward a policy of treatment.
30. Inventory of available modalities and techniques of treatment and rehabilitation.
31. Selection of appropriate treatment programmes.
32. Training for personnel working with drug addicts.
33. Reduction of the incidence of diseases and the number of infections transmitted through drug-using habits.
34. Care for drug-addicted offenders within the criminal justice and prison systems.
35. Social reintegration of persons who have undergone programmes for treatment and rehabilitation.

Appendix B: *Prevention of Criminal Use of the Banking System for the Purpose of Money Laundering*

Basle Committee on Banking Regulations and
Supervisory Practices
December 1988

PREAMBLE

1. Banks and other financial institutions may be unwittingly used as inter-mediaries for the transfer or deposit of funds from criminal activity. Criminals and their associates use the financial system to make payments and trans-fers of funds from one account to another; to hide the source and benefi-cial ownership of money; and to provide storage for bank-notes through a safe-deposit facility. These activities are commonly referred to as money laundering.

2. Efforts undertaken hitherto with the objective of preventing the bank-ing system from being used in this way have largely been undertaken by judicial and regulatory agencies at national level. However, the increasing international dimension of organised criminal activity, notably in relation to the narcotics trade, has prompted collaborative initiatives at the inter-national level. One of the earliest such initiatives was undertaken by the Committee of Ministers of the Council of Europe in June 1980. In its report[1] the Committee of Ministers concluded that ' . . . the banking sys-tem can play a highly effective preventive role while the co-operation of the banks also assists in the repression of such criminal acts by the judi-cial authorities and the police'. In recent years the issue of how to pre-vent criminals laundering the proceeds of crime through the financial system has attracted increasing attention from legislative authorities, law enforce-ment agencies and banking supervisors in a number of countries.

[1] *Measures against the Transfer and Safeguarding of Funds of Criminal Origin.* Recommendation No R(80)10 adopted by the committee of Ministers of the Council of Europe on 27th June 1980.

193

3. The various national banking supervisory authorities represented on the Basle Committee on Banking Regulations and Supervisory Practices[2] do not have the same roles and responsibilities in relation to the suppression of money laundering. In some countries supervisors have a specific responsibility in this field; in others they may have no direct responsibility. This reflects the role of banking supervision, the primary function of which is to maintain the overall financial stability and soundness of banks rather than to ensure that individual transactions conducted by bank customers are legitimate. Nevertheless, despite the limits in some countries on their specific responsibility, all members of the Committee firmly believe that supervisors cannot be indifferent to the use made of banks by criminals.

4. Public confidence in banks, and hence their stability, can be undermined by adverse publicity as a result of inadvertent association by banks with criminals. In addition, banks may lay themselves open to direct losses from fraud, either through negligence in screening undesirable customers or where the integrity of their own officers has been undermined through association with criminals. For these reasons the members of the Basle Committee consider that banking supervisors have a general role to encourage ethical standards of professional conduct among banks and other financial institutions.

5. The Committee believes that one way to promote this objective, consistent with differences in national supervisory practice, is to obtain international agreement to a Statement of Principles to which financial institutions should be expected to adhere.

6. The attached Statement is a general statement of ethical principles which encourages banks' management to put in place effective procedures to ensure that all persons conducting business with their institutions are properly identified; that transactions that do not appear legitimate are discouraged; and that co-operation with law enforcement agencies is achieved. The Statement is not a legal document and its implementation will depend on national practice and law. In particular, it should be noted that in some countries banks may be subject to additional more stringent legal regulations in this field and the Statement is not intended to replace or diminish those requirements. Whatever the legal position in different countries, the Committee considers that the first and most important safeguard against money-laundering is the integrity of banks' own managements and their vigilant determination to prevent their institutions becoming associated with criminals or being used as a channel for money-laundering. The Statement is intended to reinforce those standards of conduct.

7. The supervisory authorities represented on the Committee support the principles set out in the Statement. To the extent that these matters fall within the competence of supervisory authorities in different member countries, the authorities will recommend and encourage all banks to adopt

---

[2] The Committee comprises representatives of the central banks and supervisory authorities of the Group of Ten countries (Belgium, Canada, France, Germany, Italy, Japan, Netherlands, Sweden, Switzerland, United Kingdom, United States) and Luxembourg.

policies and practices consistent with the Statement. With a view to its acceptance worldwide, the Committee would also commend the Statement to supervisory authorities in other countries.

Basle, December 1988

STATEMENT OF PRINCIPLES

I. Purpose

Banks and other financial institutions may unwittingly be used as intermediaries for the transfer or deposit of money derived from criminal activity. The intention behind such transactions is often to hide the beneficial owner of funds. The use of the financial system in this way is of direct concern to police and other law enforcement agencies; it is also a matter of concern to banking supervisors and banks' managements, since public confidence in banks may be undermined through their association with criminals.

This Statement of Principles is intended to outline some basic policies and procedures that banks' managements should ensure are in place within their institutions with a view to assisting in the suppression of money-laundering through the banking system, national and international. The Statement thus sets out to reinforce existing best practices among banks and, specifically, to encourage vigilance against criminal use of the payments system, implentation by banks of effective preventive safeguards, and co-operation with law enforcement agencies.

II. Customer identification

With a view to ensuring that the financial system is not used as a channel for criminal funds, banks should make reasonable efforts to determine the true identity of all customers requesting the institution's services. Particular care should be taken to identify the ownership of all accounts and those using safe-custody facilities. All banks should institute effective procedures for obtaining identification from new customers. It should be an explicit policy that significant business transactions will not be conducted with customers who fail to provide evidence of their identity.

III. Compliance with laws

Banks' management should ensure that business is conducted in conformity with high ethical standards and that laws and regulations pertaining to financial transactions are adhered to. As regards transactions executed on behalf of customers, it is accepted that banks may have no means of knowing whether the transaction stems from or forms part of criminal activity. Similarly, in an international context it may be difficult to ensure that cross-border transactions on behalf of customers are in compliance with the regulations of another country. Nevertheless, banks should not set out to offer services or provide active assistance in transactions which they have good reason to suppose are associated with money-laundering activities.

IV. Co-operation with law-enforcement authorities

Banks should co-operate fully with national law enforcement authorities to the extent permitted by specific local regulations relating to customer confidentiality. Care should be taken to avoid providing support or assistance to customers seeking to deceive law enforcement agencies through the provision of altered, incomplete or misleading information.

Notes

1 THE GLOBAL POLITICS OF DRUG CONTROL

1. H. J. Morgenthau, *Politics Among Nations: The Struggle for Power and Peace* (Knopf, New York, 2nd edn, 1954, first pub. 1948).
2. R. Keohane and J. Nye, *Power and Interdependence: World Politics in Transition* (Little, Brown, Boston, 1977), p. 19. For the Keohane and Nye definition of interdependence, see p. 8.
3. See R. Keohane, 'The demand for international regimes', pp. 141–71 in S. D. Krasner (ed.), *International Regimes* (Cornell University Press, Ithaca, New York, 4th edn 1986, first pub. 1983), and in the same volume, Krasner, 'Structural causes and regime consequences: regimes as intervening variables', pp. 1–21.
4. A. Stein, 'Coordination and collaboration: regimes in an anarchic world', pp. 115–40 in Krasner, *op. cit.*
5. R. Keohane, 'The demand for international regimes', *op, cit.*, p. 171.
6. J. N. Rosenau, *The Study of Global Interdependence: Essays on the Transnationalization of World Affairs* (Frances Pinter, London, 1980), pp. 43–5.
7. This is despite the fact that Rosenau's work on interdependence, 'Capabilities and Control in an Interdependent World', in *International Security,* Vol. 1, 1976, pp. 32–49, pre-dates the Keohane and Nye work. It was not until the reprinting of much of his work with the 1980 publication of *The Study of Global Interdependence*, that Rosenau's theoretical contribution was acknowledged.
8. *Declaration of the International Conference on Drug Abuse and Illicit Trafficking and the Comprehensive Multidisciplinary Outline of Future Activities in Drug Abuse Control.* UN Document ST/NAR/14.
9. The designation of this body was later changed through different conventions to the Permanent Central Opium Board, Permanent Central Narcotics Board, and finally to the International Narcotics Control Board. For more information on the INCB see Chapter 4.
10. *Latin American Regional Report, Andean,* 1984, p. 4 as cited in S. B. MacDonald, *Dancing on a Volcano: The Latin American Drug Trade* (Praeger, New York, 1988), p. 36.
11. See 'French minister campaigns for British way with AIDS control', *Guardian*, 26.1.93.
12. Rosenau, *Global Interdependence, op. cit.*, p. 46.
13. *Enhancement of the Efficiency of the United Nations Structure for Drug Abuse Control. Report of the Secretary-General*, 23 October 1990, United Nations document A/45/652/Add.1, p. 7.
14. See 'Cocaine builds a bridge to the East', *Guardian*, 14.3.92.
15. Rosenau, *Global Interdependence, op. cit.*, p. 43.
16. *Ibid.*

17. See, E. Alvarez, 'Coca production in Peru', Chapter 5, pp. 72–87 in P. H. Smith (ed.), *Drug Policy in the Americas* (Westview Press, Oxford, 1992), p. 83.
18. See J. Malamud-Goti, 'Reinforcing Poverty: the Bolivian war on cocaine', Chapter 4, pp. 67–92 in A. W. McCoy and A. Block (eds), *War on Drugs. Studies in the Failure of U.S. Narcotics Policy* (Westview Press, Oxford, 1992), p. 69.
19. 'Peruvian president says cocaine blighting Amazon', *Guardian*, 7.2.91.
20. *Report of the International Narcotics Control Board for 1990*, United Nations document E/INCB/1990/1, para. 190, p. 36.
21. M. Dourojeanni, 'Impactos ambientales del cultivo de coca y la produccion de cocaina en la amazonia peruana', as quoted in E. Alvarez. Also S. B. MacDonald, *Mountain High, White Avalanche. Cocaine and Power in the Andean States and Panama* (Washington Papers 137, Praeger, New York, 1989), p. 65; *Report of the Commission on Narcotic Drugs on its Thirty-Fifth Session, Vienna, 6–15 April 1992*. United Nations document E/CN.7/1992/14, para, 33, p. 15.
22. Reported in the annual report of General Rosso Serrano, commander of Colombia's Police Narcotics Brigade, see 'Colombian drug barons open new smuggling route', *Guardian*, 3.1.92; 'Why the drug barons are talking green', *Independent*, 30.3.92; and *Report of the International Narcotics Control Board for 1992*, United Nations document E/INCB/1992/1, para. 327, p. 45.
23. *Report of the International Narcotics Control Board for 1992, op. cit.*, para, 327, p. 45.
24. In 1986 the volume of toxic waste dumped into rivers in Peru was estimated at 57 million litres of kerosene, 32 million litres of sulphuric acid, 16,000 metric tons of lime, 3,200 metric tons of carbide, 16,000 metric tons of toilet paper, 6.4 million litres of acetone and 6.4 million litres of toluene. See B. Marcelo, 'Victimas del narcotrafico', *Medio Ambiente* 23, 1987, as quoted in E. Alvarez, *op. cit.*, p. 83.
25. Rivers and streams that have been altered in such a manner that they can no longer be put to their normal uses are designated as polluted or contaminated by the WHO. See E. Alvarez, *op cit.*, p. 83.
26. B. Marcelo, 'Victimas del narcotrafico', *Medio Ambiente* 23, 1987, esp. 2, 4, as quoted in E. Alvarez, *op. cit.*, p. 83.
27. See R. del Olmo, 'Aerobiology and the war on drugs: a transnational crime', *Social Justice*, 1987, No. 30, pp. 28–44.
28. This is despite the fact that neither paraquat nor gliphosphate is used in the United States. Paraquat is banned by the courts and gliphosphate is described as economically unviable. On a visit to Colombia in 1986, the director of the US Customs Service argued that aerial spraying in the United States was not profitable because the marijuana fields were too small. See del Olmo, *op. cit.* This is despite the fact that marijuana production has been described as the United States' third-largest cash crop, with an estimated value of $14 billion in 1985. See S Wisotsky, *Breaking the Impasse* (Greenwood Press, New York, 1986) in J. A. Inciardi (ed.), *The Drug Legalization Debate* (Studies in Crime, Law and Justice Vol. 7, Sage Publications, London, 2nd edn 1991), p. 168.

29. The Bush administration in the early 1990s encouraged development of research into a caterpillar (the malumbia) that could defoliate coca plants. The plan was described by the *Washington Post National Weekly Edition* as 'dangerous, arrogant and foolish'. The administration maintained that 'neither troops nor caterpillars will go in [to Latin America] without prior request or consultation'. See 'U.S. may enlist bugs in drug war', *Montgomery Advertiser*, 21.2.90., as quoted in C. J. Johns, *Power, Ideology, and the War on Drugs* (Praeger Series in Criminology and Crime Control Policy, Praeger, New York, 1992), p. 55.
30. R. Fagan, *Forging Peace: The Challenge of Central America* (Basil Blackwell, New York, 1987), p. 49.
31. See: Commission on Narcotic Drugs, *Activities of the United Nations International Drug Control Programme. Report of the Executive Director*, United Nations document E/CN.7/1993/3, para. 80, p. 15.
32. P. Andreas and E. Bertram, 'From Cold War to Drug War', pp. 170–85 in C. Hartman and P. Vilanova (eds), *Paradigms Lost: The Post Cold War Era* (Pluto Press and TNI, London, 1992), p. 171.
33. See 'Hope that is built on heroin', *Independent*, 6.6.92.
34. 'Peru suggests way out for coca-leaf farmers', The *Financial Times*, 30.10.90.
35. See 'A Peruvian peasant fails to see Bush', *New York Times*, 16.2.90, as quoted in F. LaMond Tullis, *Beneficiaries of the Illicit Drug Trade: Political Consequences and International Policy at the Intersection of Supply and Demand*, United Nations Research Institute for Social Development, Discussion Paper 19, Geneva, March 1991, p. 11. Bush refused the meeting, which has been described as a diplomatic mistake since the need to deal not just with the drugs but with hundreds of thousands of politicised peasant growers and their development needs has since been recognised.
36. LaMond Tullis, *op. cit.*, p. 13.
37. MacDonald, *Mountain High, op. cit.*, p. 135. The UNDCP has been working on refining the concept of a 'debt-for-alternative-development swap'. In July 1992, at the Expert Group Meeting on the Conversion of Official Bilateral Assistance, sponsored by the United Nations Conference on Trade and Development, the UNDCP made a presentation on the concept.
38. Ronald MacLean, Bolivian foreign minister, as reported in 'Bolivia sees pots of profit in coca cuppa', *Financial Times*, 3.6.92. See also *INCB Report 1992, op. cit.*, Overview, Section B, 'Attempts to develop a legal international market for coca products', pp. 6–7.
39. 'High times as farmers cash in on hemp', *Guardian Weekly*, 3.9.95.
40. K. Hope, *Economic Development in the Caribbean* (Praeger Publishing, New York, 1986), pp. 62–3.
41. See F. LaMond Tullis, 'Cocaine and food: likely effects of a burgeoning transnational industry on food production in Bolivia and Peru', in W. Ladd Hollist and F. LaMond Tullis, *Pursuing Food Security. Strategies and Obstacles in Africa, Asia, Latin America, and the Middle East* (Lynne Rienner Publishers, Boulder and London, 1987), Chapter 12, pp. 247–83.

42. In his article Edward Herman claims that US aid and training to Latin American forces is closely connected to the growth of death squads in Latin America. See E. S. Herman, 'U.S. sponsorship of international terrorism: An overview', *Crime and Social Justice*, Nos. 27–28, 1987, pp. 1–31.

43. See Johns, *op. cit.*, Chapter 5, 'Latin American democracies in jeopardy', pp. 131–58; also 'The newest war', *Newsweek*, 6.1.92, pp. 18–23 and B. M. Bagley, 'Myths of militarisation: enlisting armed forces in the war on drugs', Chapter 9, pp. 129–50 in P. H. Smith, *op. cit.*

44. The report begins: 'Waving as pretext the measures adopted against drug trafficking, the military have ransacked the headquarters of grassroots organisations and the homes of political leaders, and ordered many arrests.' *Andean Newsletter*, Andean Commission of Jurists, Lima, September 1989, as quoted in N. Chomsky, *Deterring Democracy* (Verso, London, 1991), Chapter 4, 'Problems of population control', pp. 107–37, quote from pp. 128–9.

45. President Cesar Gaviria Trujillo, as quoted in B. M. Bagley, 'Myths of militarisation', *op. cit.*, p. 139.

46. *DEA Review*, December 1989, pp. 60–61, as quoted in F. LaMond Tullis, 'Cocaine and food', Chapter 12, in W. Ladd Hollist and F. LaMond Tullis, *op. cit.*, p. 248.

47. 'Drug trafficker can challenge UK profits confiscation law', *Guardian*, 16.1.92.

48. J. S. Mill, *On Liberty* (Penguin Books, Middlesex, 1986, first pub. 1859), p. 28.

49. A. W. Anderson, 'In the wake of the *Dauntless*: The background and development of maritime interdiction operations', Part 11–41 in T. A. Clingan, Jr. *The Law of the Sea: What Lies Ahead?* (The Law of the Sea Institute, William S. Richardson School of Law, University of Hawaii, Honolulu, 1988). Proceedings of the 20th Annual Conference of the Law of the Sea Institute, co-sponsored by the University of Miami School of Law, 21–24 July 1986, Miami, Florida.

50. S. D. Stein, *International Diplomacy, State Administrators and Narcotic Control. The Origins of a Social Problem* (Gower, Aldershot, 1985), p. 5.

51. P. R. Andreas and K. E. Sharpe, 'Cocaine politics in the Andes', *Current History*, 91, February 1992, p. 74.

52. For a discussion of the high/low politics distinction see the Preface by P. Willetts to A. Chetley, *The Politics of Baby Food: Successful Challenges to an International Marketing Strategy* (Frances Pinter, London, 1986).

53. The United States Attorneys and Attorney General of the United States, *Drug Trafficking, A Report to the President of the United States*, 3 August 1989, US Department of Justice, Office of the Attorney General, p. 19.

54. J. G. Ruggie, 'International responses to technology: Concepts and trends', *International Organization*, Vol. 29, No. 3, Summer 1975, pp. 557–83, quote at p. 570.

55. The definition is credited to Stephen Krasner and was first published

in a special issue of the journal *International Organization* on international regimes in Spring 1982 (*International Organization*, Vol. 36, No. 2, Spring 1982), which was later published in book form. See Krasner, *op. cit.*, p. 2 for quotation. All page references in this chapter will be to the book.

56. S. Strange, '*Cave! hic dragones*: a critique of regime analysis', pp. 337–55 in Krasner, *op. cit.*

57. Krasner, *op. cit.*, p. 3.

58. See Article 3 of the *Single Convention on Narcotic Drugs, 1961, done at New York on 30 March 1961*, in Dr S. K. Chatterjee, *A Guide to the International Drugs Conventions*, Commonwealth Secretariat, London, 1988, Appendix IV, pp. 96–137.

59. See V. P. Vatuk and S. J. Vatuk, 'Chatorpan: A culturally defined form of addiction in North India', *The International Journal of the Addictions*, Vol. 2, No. 1, Spring 1967, pp. 103–13.

60. The explorer Carletti (1574–1617) warned that 'the Spanish, and every other nation which goes to the Indies, once they have become accustomed to chocolate, its consumption becomes such a vice that they can only with difficulty leave off from drinking it every morning'. As quoted in B. Whitaker, *The Global Connection: The Crisis of Drug Addiction* (Jonathan Cape, London, 1987), p. 88. Whitaker also states, when the potato was introduced to Scotland it was sternly forbidden as unholy, because it was not mentioned in the Bible. *Op. cit.*, p. 8.

61. In 1604 James I published '*A Counterblast to Tobacco*', in which he damned it as a filthy, stinking habit which was harmful to the brain and dangerous to the lungs. As quoted in R. Rudgley, *The Alchemy of Culture. Intoxicants in Society.* (British Museum Press, London, 1993), p. 140.

62. Professor Edwards, speaking at a Ciba Foundation debate on drug addiction in Plymouth, as reported in *The Times*, 27.8.91.

63. This figure does not simply include only alcoholism and alcohol abuse treatment services. In 1986, for example, alcohol was identified as a contributing factor in 10 per cent of work-related injuries, 40 per cent of suicide attempts, and about 40 per cent of the approximately 46,000 annual traffic deaths in 1983 in the United States. An estimated 18 million Americans are reported to be either alcoholics or alcohol abusers. See *Toward a National Plan to Combat Alcohol Abuse and Alcoholism: A Report to the United States Congress* (Department of Health and Human Services, Washington, DC, September 1986) as quoted in E. A. Nadelmann, 'Drug prohibition in the United States: Costs, consequences, and alternatives', *Science*, Vol. 245, 1 September 1989, pp. 939–46 at p. 943. Another survey by Harwood reached a similarly high figure. Harwood estimated that alcohol abuse cost the United States about $80 billion in 1980. Of this, about $10 billion was for treatment services. The balance represented lost future productivity due to premature mortality ($14.5 billion), reduced productivity and lost employment due to morbidity ($54.7 billion), and the direct costs of crime ($42.5 billion), motor vehicle crashes, incarceration etc. See H. J. Harwood, et al., *Economic Costs to Society of Alcohol and Drug Abuse*

and Mental Illness: 1980 (Research Triangle Institute, Research Triangle Park, NC, 1984) as quoted in S. Jonas, 'The US drug culture: A public health solution', pp. 161–82 in J. A. Inciardi, *op. cit.*

64. Dr Peter Anderson of the WHO, speaking at the 36th Congress on Alcohol and Drug Dependency, Glasgow, 17–21 August 1992.

65. See 'Measures for Measures', a report from the charity Alcohol Concern, published 20 March 1997.

66. See *National Drug Control Strategy*, Office of National Drug Control Policy, US Government Printing Office, Washington, DC, 1989, p. 48.

67. Of this amount about $23 billion was spent for health services, the balance for lost production and premature mortality. Cigarette smoking thus appears to be the most expensive drug in terms of health care costs. See D. P. Rice, et al., 'The economic costs of the health effects of smoking, 1984', *The Millbank Quarterly*, 64, 489, 1986, as quoted in Jonas, *op. cit.*, pp. 167–8; and P. Taylor, *The Smoke Ring: Tobacco, Money and Multinational Politics* (Mentor, New York, 1985). See also Chapter 7.

68. See Chapter 7.

69. See Article 1 (n) in *United Nations Convention Against Illicit Traffic in Narcotic Drugs and Psychotropic Substances, Adopted in Vienna, on 19 December 1988*, in Dr W. Gilmore, *Combatting International Drugs Trafficking: The 1988 United Nations Convention Against Illicit Traffic in Narcotic Drugs and Psychotropic Substances*, Explanatory Documentation, Commonwealth Secretariat, London, 1991, Appendix A, pp. 59–83.

70. K. Kramer and J. Cameron (eds), *A Manual on Drug Dependence* (WHO, Geneva, 1975), p. 16.

71. National Commission on Marijuana and Drug Abuse, Second Report: *Drug Use in America: Problem in Perspective*, (US Government Printing Office, Washington DC, 1973), p. 11, as quoted in F. E. Zimring and G. Hawkins, *The Search for Rational Drug Control* (Cambridge University Press, Cambridge, 1992), p. 26.

72. WHO Bulletin No. 32, 1965, quoted in Kramer and Cameron (eds), *op. cit.*, p. 17.

73. See L. Grinspoon and J. Bakalar, *Cocaine: A Drug and Its Social Evolution* (Basic Books, New York, 1976), p. 176.

74. Office of National Drug Control Policy, *op. cit.*, p. 9.

75. See J. Kaplan, *The Hardest Drug: Heroin and Public Policy* (University of Chicago Press, Chicago, 1983); F. E. Zimring and G. Hawkins, *op. cit.*, and P. Cohen, *Drugs as a Social Construct* (University of Amsterdam, Amsterdam, 1990).

76. E. A. Nadelmann, 'The Case for Legalisation', Chapter 1, pp. 17–45, in Inciardi, *op. cit.*, p. 40.

77. A much cited work is R. Ashley, *Cocaine: Its History, Uses, and Effects* (St. Martin's Press, New York, 1975). See also, J. L. Philips and R. W. Wynne, *Cocaine: The Mystique and the Reality* (Avon Books, New York, 1980).

78. Grinspoon and Bakalar, *op. cit.*, p. 129.

79. There are many reports about marijuana's effects on the vital systems

of the body, on the brain, on immunity and resistance, and on sex and reproduction: see for example, H. C. Jones and P. W. Lovinger, *The Marijuana Question* (Dodd, Mead, New York, 1985). The recent debate concerns the damage to the lungs caused by smoking marijuana. See also *Journal of the American Medical Association*, 17.6.88, No. 259, p. 3384; and 'Marijuana more harmful than tobacco', *New Scientist*, 17.12.87, p. 15.

80. For a discussion of the 'harmless' or 'reduced risk' literature on marijuana and other drugs, see for example, J. Kaplan, 'Taking Drugs Seriously', *The Public Interest*, 92, Summer 1988, pp. 32–50.

81. Statement by the French delegate, UN document E/CN.7/SR 714, 1971 as quoted in V. Kusevic, 'Drug abuse control and international treaties', *Journal of Drug Issues*, Vol. 7, No. 1, 1977, pp. 35–53.

82. *Ibid.*, p. 47.

83. G. Arnao, 'The Semantics of Prohibition', *The International Journal on Drug Policy*, Vol. 2, No. 1, 1990, p. 33.

84. See D. Aitken and T. Mikuriya, 'The forgotten medicine. A look at the medical uses of cannabis', *Ecologist*, Vol. 10, Nos. 8/9, Oct–Nov. 1980, pp. 269–79.

85. 'Marijuana: the best medicine?', *The Times*, 4.5.93.

86. 'Turn on, tune in, get well', *New Scientist*, 15.3.97, pp. 14–15.

87. *Ibid.*, p. 14.

88. See Aitken and Mikuriya, *op. cit.*

89. See, *In the Matter of Marijuana Rescheduling Petition*, Docket No. 86–22, 6.9.88, Drug Enforcement Administration, Department of Justice, as quoted in Nadelmann, 'Drug Prohibition', *op. cit.*, p. 942.

90. 'US Resists Easing Curb on Marijuana', *New York Times*, 31.12.89, as quoted in Johns, *op. cit.*, p. 27.

91. Marijuana is made up of the dried leaves and flowering tops of the *Cannabis sativa* plant and contains 426 known chemicals, which are transformed into 2,000 chemicals when burned during the smoking process. Seventy of these chemicals are cannabinoids, substances that are found nowhere else in nature. Recently reports have been made which highlight the possibility of utilising the medical properties of cannabis without sending the patient to the 'highly illegal level of consciousness' currently achieved by cannabis use. This research involves studying cannabis receptors in species such as the puffer fish and the sea urchin. See 'Puffer fish hold secret of cannabis as medicine', *Independent*, 2.9.93 and 'Researchers putting cannabis on the right side of the law', *Guardian*, 2.9.93.

92. Zimring and Hawkins, *op. cit.*, p. 45.

2 THE SCOPE AND NATURE OF THE DRUG PHENOMENON

1. See M. E. Medina-Mora and M. del Carmen Marino, 'Drug Abuse in Latin America', in P. H. Smith (ed.) *Drug Policy in the Americas* (Westview Press, Oxford, 1992), pp. 45–56, quote at p. 46.

2. Department of State, Office of the Inspector General, 'Inspection of

the Bureau for International Narcotics Matters', January 1990, p. 5.
3. There has been a great deal of literature, both academic and governmental, on this subject. See, for example, D. Anglin and G. Speckart, 'Narcotics use and crime: A multi-method analysis', *Criminology*, Vol. 26, No. 2, 1988, pp. 197–233; J. A. Inciardi, *The Drug-Crime Connection* (Sage, Beverly Hills, 1981). See also J. A. Inciardi, 'Beyond cocaine: basuco, crack, and other coca products', *Contemporary Drug Problems*, Fall 1987, pp. 461–93.
4. See A. McCoy and A. Block (eds), *War on Drugs. Studies in the Failure of U.S. Narcotics Policy* (Westview Press, Oxford, 1992), p. 3.
5. *Report of the International Narcotics Control Board for 1990*, United Nations document E/INCB/1990/1.
6. *Ibid.*
7. *Report of the International Narcotics Control Board for 1992*, United Nations document E/INCB/1992/1, para. 287.
8. There has been a marked increase in the potency of cannabis on the illicit market in the United States, mainly because of the high tetrahydrocannabinol (THC) content of the cannabis plant varieties cultivated indoors. The average THC content of the normal 'commercial-grade' cannabis was 3.1 per cent, but the average THC content of the unpollinated and seedless female (sinsemilla) cannabis was 11.7 per cent. See *INCB Report for 1992*, *op. cit.*, para. 286, p. 40.
9. 'Designer drugs' is a term that has been used recently to describe synthetic drugs that have been specifically designed as analogues to controlled substances and yet bypass legal classification. It is not a precise scientific term and has been indiscriminately applied to a variety of contemporary drugs of abuse. One of the most infamous designer drugs is 'Ecstasy', a combination of synthetic mescaline and amphetamine that has a hallucinogenic effect. Ecstasy is known by chemists as methylenedioxymethamphetamine (MDMA).
10. By its resolution 40/122 of 13 December 1985, the General Assembly decided to convene an International Conference on Drug Abuse and Illicit Trafficking. See *Report of the International Conference on Drug Abuse and Illicit Trafficking, Vienna, 17–26 June 1987*, United Nations document A/CONF.133/12.
11. *United Nations Convention Against Illicit Traffic in Narcotic Drugs and Psychotropic Substances*, Vienna, 19 December 1988, United Nations document E/CONF.82/15, 19 December 1988. See Appendix B. The Convention was initiated by the government of Venezuela in General Assembly resolution 39/141 of December 1984. For an explanation of the Convention see Dr W. C. Gilmore, *Combatting International Drugs Trafficking: The 1988 United Nations Convention Against Illicit Traffic in Narcotic Drugs and Psychotropic Substances* (Commonwealth Secretariat, Marlborough House, London, 1991).
12. The decision to hold a Special Session of the General Assembly was taken in resolution 44/16 of 1 November 1989 (initiated by the President of Colombia). The Special Session was held in New York from 20 to 23 February 1990. See *Political Declaration and Global Programme of Action Adopted by the General Assembly at its seventeenth special*

session, devoted to the question of international co-operation against illicit production, supply, demand, trafficking and distribution of narcotic drugs and psychotropic substances, United Nations document A/RES/S–17/2, 15 March 1990.

13. See *Declaration of the World Ministerial Summit to Reduce the Demand for Drugs and to Combat the Cocaine Threat, held in London 9–11 April 1990*, UN document A/45/262.

14. See the 9th Conference of the Non-Aligned Countries, Belgrade, Yugoslavia, 1989, United Nations document A/44/551; Commonwealth Heads of Government Meeting, Malaysia 18–24 October 1989; also *World Ministerial Summit, op. cit.*; *Declaration of Cartagena*, 15 February 1990, United Nations document A/S–17/8.

15. S. B. MacDonald, *Mountain High, White Avalanche. Cocaine and Power in the Andean States and Panama* (Washington Papers 137, Praeger, New York, 1989), Chapter 2, 'Colombia: Where the Avalanche Begins', pp. 17–57.

16. B. Bullington and A. Block, 'A Trojan horse: Anti-communism and the war on drugs', *Contemporary Crises*, Vol. 14, 1990, pp. 39–55.

17. The political controversy which erupted over the Contras and links between United States officials and drug traffickers, was explored by Senator Kerry's Senate Subcommittee Report, *Drugs, Law Enforcement and Foreign Policy*. The Kerry Report shows clearly that the United States administration support for the Contras, and their corrupt supporters in the Honduran army aided cocaine smuggling operations throughout the first half of the 1980s. See P. D. Scott, 'Honduras, the Contra support networks, and cocaine: How the U.S. government has augmented America's drug crisis', in McCoy and Block, *op. cit.*; T. Draper, *A Very Thin Line: The Iran–Contra Affairs* (Hill and Wang, New York, 1991). See also US Senate Committee on Foreign Relations. Subcommittee on Terrorism, Narcotics, and International Operations, *Drugs, Law Enforcement, and Foreign Policy*. US Government Printing Office, Washington DC, 5 May 1989.

18. See R. T. Naylor, *Hot Money and the Politics of Debt* (Simon and Schuster, New York, 1987); and 'Bolivia: Coke and Black Eagles', *Newsweek*, 23.11.81.

19. Recent allegations against President Ernesto Samper have again emphasised the problem of corruption of top officials in Colombia. See 'Cartel Links Imperial Samper', *Washington Post*, as quoted in *Guardian Weekly*, 3.9.95.

20. General Manuel Noriega was implicated in drug trafficking from the early 1980s. From being considered an important asset by the Pentagon and the CIA against communist insurgency in the region, he was seized by US forces in a US invasion of Panama and forcibly extradited to the United States to face charges of drug trafficking and money laundering. See, for example, 'Panama: At the end of the avalanche', in MacDonald, *Mountain High, White Avalanche, op. cit.*, pp. 98–118.

21. See *The Fight Against the Drug Traffic in Colombia* (Office of the President of the Republic, November 1989); and B. M. Bagley, 'Co-

lombia and the war on drugs', *Foreign Affairs*, Fall 1988, No. 67105, pp. 70–92.

22. 'Colombia about to enter into "pact with devil"', *Independent*, 9.12.90; 'Colombia goes soft on drug gangs', *Independent*, 10.10.90.

23. R. W. Lee III, 'The Latin American drug connection', *Foreign Policy*, 61, Winter 1985/86, pp. 142–3.

24. World Bank, *World Development Report for 1986* (World Bank, Washington, DC, 1986), pp. 184–5.

25. 'Accused drug king [Carlos Lehder] "spoke of taking over Belize"', *Independent*, 18.11.87.

26. J. Malamud-Goti, 'Reinforcing poverty: The Bolivian war on cocaine', Chapter 4, pp. 67–92 in McCoy and Block (eds), *op. cit.*, p. 73.

27. See N. Hopkinson, *Fighting the Drug Problem* (Wilton Park Papers 15, HMSO, London, 1990), p. 11.

28. See E. Alvarez, 'Coca production in Peru', Chapter 5 in P. H. Smith (ed.), *Drug Policy in the Americas* (Westview Press, Oxford, 1992), pp. 72–88. An alternative estimate by MacDonald puts the figure as high as 15 per cent of the adult population. See MacDonald, *op. cit.*, p. 77. For Bolivia see R. W. Lee III, 'Dimensions of the South American cocaine industry', *Journal of Interamerican Studies and World Affairs*, Vol. 30, Nos. 2–3 1988, p. 89; also F. Machicados, 'Coca Production in Bolivia', Chapter 6, in P. H. Smith, *op. cit.*, pp. 88–99. For Colombia see McCoy and Block, *op. cit.*, p. 4.

29. Lee, 'Dimensions', *op. cit.*, p. 89.

30. E. Epstein, *Agency of Fear*, pp. 173–9, as quoted in J. A. Inciardi, *The Drug Legalization Debate* (Sage Publications, London, 1991), p. 103. Nixon created the DEA as the lead agency in drug enforcement and consolidating other agencies, and also built up the size and scope of the federal drug enforcement bureaucracy.

31. McCoy and Block, *op. cit.*, p. 9.

32. Office of National Drug Control Policy, *National Drug Control Strategy*, 61, as quoted in Smith, *op. cit.*, p. 7.

33. P. Andreas and E. Bertram, 'From Cold War to Drug War', Chapter 11 in C. Hartman and P. Vilanova (eds) *Paradigms Lost: The Post Cold War Era* (Pluto Press, London, 1992), p. 170.

34. For the text of the President's speech committing his administration to an increased role in the war on drugs see 'Address to the Nation on the National Drug Control Strategy', 5 September 1989, in *Public Papers of the Presidents: George Bush*, Vol. 2 (US Government Printing Office, Washington, DC, 1989), pp. 1136–40. On the Bush administration's increasing emphasis on the role of the military at home and in Latin America, see B. Trainor, 'Military's widening role in the anti-drug Effort', *New York Times*, 27.8.89; P. Grier, 'Pentagon's support role increases', *Christian Science Monitor*, 1.9.89, p. 8.

35. Dick Cheney, 'DOD and its role in the war against drugs', *Defense*, Nov–Dec 1989, pp. 2–7.

36. See 'A fatal fix of freedom', *Guardian*, 9.3.93; 'Customs braced for 1992 drugs battle', *Guardian*, 16.1.91; and 'Cocaine seizures soar in Europe', *Financial Times*, 8.10.93.

37. For more detail on the Force see Chapter 5.
38. Council of the European Communities, *Council Directive of 10 June 1991 on Prevention of the Use of the Financial System for Purpose of Money Laundering*, Brussels, Document No. 91/308/EEC.
39. See 'Swiss–Dutch drug stance: Tolerance', *New York Times*, 1.12.89; *Fact Sheet on the Netherlands. Drug Policy*, Ministry of Welfare and Cultural Affairs, Fact Sheet 19-E-1989.
40. President Cesar Gaviria of Colombia, as quoted in McCoy and Block, *op. cit.*, p. 40.
41. See J. McBeth, 'The opium laws', *Far Eastern Economic Review*, 29.3.84, pp. 40–43.
42. See *INCB Report 1992, op. cit.*
43. 'Cocaine traffickers ready for North American free trade treaty', *Guardian*, 25.5.93.
44. See *INCB Report 1990, op. cit.*, para. 75.
45. See 'Cocaine builds bridge to the East', *Guardian*, 14.3.92.
46. See 'East's freedom boosts heroin flow to West', *Independent*, 18.5.93.
47. For more on the 'French Connection' see 'Is the French Connection really dead?', *Drug Enforcement*, Summer 1981, pp. 19–21 and later.
48. See 'Japan's gangsters: Honourable mob', *The Economist*, 27.1.90, pp. 19–22.
49. See F. Robertson, *Triangle of Death: The Inside Story of the Triads – The Chinese Mafia* (Routledge and Kegan Paul, London, 1977); and F. Bresler, *The Trail of the Triads: An Investigation into International Crime* (Weidenfeld and Nicolson, London, 1980).
50. Hundreds of articles and books, both journalistic and academic, have been written on the Colombian cartels and their leaders. See G. Gugliotta, *Kings of Cocaine: Inside the Medellin Cartel* (Simon and Schuster, New York, 1989); G. Gugliotta, 'The Colombian cartels and how to stop them', Chapter 8 in Smith, *op. cit.*, pp. 111–29; R. Lee, 'Colombia's cocaine syndicates', Chapter 5 in McCoy and Block, *op. cit.*, pp. 93–125.
51. Mexican 'families' established links with Colombian cartels to use Mexico as a transhipment point for cocaine to the United States and Canada: 'Drug trafficking: Mexico and Colombia in comparative perspective', *Journal of International Affairs*, Vol. 35, No. 1, 1981, pp. 95–115. Now, Colombians have moved to Mexico to take over personally many of the cocaine operations there: 'Colombians take over "coke" trade in Mexico', *Christian Science Monitor*, 9.1.89, p. 11. Perhaps the most infamous Mexican organisation was the Caro Quintero Group. Caro Quintero is currently serving a 40-year jail sentence but has become an 'anti-hero' for Mexico's poor.
52. Despite the eradication of the Sicilian 'Pizza Connection' in 1984, the Sicilian mafia controls a world-wide network in the heroin market. See R. Blumenthal, *Last Days of the Sicilians* (Times Books, New York, 1988) on the 'Pizza Connection'; and W. Greenhaw, *Flying High: Inside Big Time Drug Smuggling* (Dodd, Mead, New York, 1984).
53. See 'Mafia and former Soviet gangs join forces in crime', *The Times*, 30.11.92.

208 *Notes*

54. *INCB Report 1990, op. cit.*, Overview, pp. 2–8.
55. *INCB Report 1992, op. cit.*, para. 108, p. 19. European and South American criminal organisations have predominantly been utilising couriers to smuggle cocaine into Europe by air via Ghana, Morocco and Nigeria, and more recently Cape Verde, the Ivory Coast and Senegal. In Africa as a whole in 1991, the total quantity of cocaine seized represented a six-fold increase on the 1990 figure.
56. United Nations Department of Public Information, January 1990, quoted in A. Jamieson, *Global Drug Trafficking* (Conflict Studies 234, Research Institute for the Study of Conflict and Terrorism, 1990), p. 3.
57. See 'US must save coffee deal to fight cocaine', *Independent*, 15.9.89.
58. See A. Salizar, *'Analysis economico de cultivos alternativos a la coca en la region del Alto Huallaga'*, Project AD/PER/86/459 OSP-PNUD (Lima, 1990), as quoted in Smith, *op. cit.*, p. 82.
59. MacDonald, *Mountain High, op. cit.*, p. 65.
60. See F. LaMond Tullis, 'Cocaine and food: Likely effects of a burgeoning transnational industry on food production in Bolivia and Peru', in W. Ladd Hollist and F. LaMond Tullis, *Pursuing Food Security. Strategies and Obstacles in Africa, Asia, Latin America and the Middle East* (Lynne Rienner Publishers, Boulder and London, 1987), Chapter 12, pp. 247–83.
61. *Ibid.*
62. See MacDonald, *op. cit.*; also McCoy and Block, *op. cit.*, p. 4.
63. 'The cocaine economies', *The Economist*, 8.10.88, p. 24.
64. See MacDonald, 'Venezuela, Ecuador, and Chile: Future Avalanches', in *Mountain High, White Avalanche, op. cit.*, pp. 83–97.
65. MacDonald, *op. cit.*, p. 133.
66. See *INCB Report 1992, op. cit.*, para. 95, p. 17.
67. *Ibid.*, paras 89–119, pp. 17–20.
68. *Report of the International Narcotics Control Board for 1991*, United Nations document E/INCB/1991/2, para. 12, p. 5.
69. For a more detailed consideration of the United Nations in this period, see Chapter 4.
70. E. A. Nadelmann, 'Drug prohibition in the United States: Costs, consequences, and alternatives', *Science*, Vol. 245, 1 September 1989, pp. 939–47.
71. *Report of the International Narcotics Control Board for 1993*, United Nations document E/INCB/1993/1, Overview.
72. 'U.S. anti-narcotics activities in the Andean Region', Home Committee on Government Operations, November 1990, as quoted in Hartman and Vilanova, *op. cit.*, p. 172.
73. *INCB Report 1992, op. cit.*, para. 238.
74. Smith, *op. cit.*, p. 8.
75. See *INCB Report 1990, op. cit.*, p. 3.
76. *INCB Report 1992, op. cit.*, para. 327. See also 'Drug lords turn attention to poppy triangle', *Financial Times*, 4.12.91; 'Colombia's barons switch to heroin', *Independent*, 27.2.92; 'Colombian heroin "heading this way"', *Guardian*, 1.5.92.

77. Head of the US Drug Enforcement Administration (DEA), as quoted in 'New kings of coke', *Time*, 1.7.91, p. 29.
78. See *INCB Report 1992*, *op. cit.*, para. 292, p. 41.
79. See 'The Nigerian Connection: The newest link in the growing heroin trade', *Newsweek*, 7.10.91, p. 43; also, 'Nigerian mafia nets millions in bank fraud and benefit rackets', *Sunday Times*, 10.10.93.
80. The Chemical Action Task Force was initiated by the United States and established by the Group of Seven major industrialised countries and the President of the CEC in 1990. However, the Task Force was disbanded in 1993 and follow-up tasks were assumed by the International Narcotics Control Board and by other United Nations bodies.
81. See G. L. Sternbach, MD, and J. Varon, MD, 'Designer drugs. Recognizing and managing their toxic effects', *Postgraduate Medicine*, Vol. 91, No. 8, June 1992.
82. *INCB Report 1992*, *op. cit.*, 'South and Central America and the Caribbean', pp. 42–8.
83. Andreas and Bertram, 'From Cold War to Drug War' in Hartman and Vilanova, *op. cit.*, p. 172.
84. *Enhancement of the Efficiency of the United Nations Structure for Drug Abuse Control. Report of the Secretary-General*. United Nations document A/45/652/Add. 1.
85. See 'It doesn't have to be like this', *The Economist*, 2.10.89.
86. US Drug Enforcement Administration, *Intelligence Trends*, Vol. 14 (USDEA, Washington DC, 1987), p. 6, as quoted in Smith, *op. cit.*, pp. 10–11.
87. For details on the 1909 Shanghai Conference and the International Opium Convention of 1912 that followed, see the next chapter.
88. R. O. Keohane and J. S. Nye (eds), *Transnational Relations and World Politics* (Harvard University Press, Cambridge, Mass., 1972), and *Power and Interdependence: World Politics in Transition* (Little, Brown, Boston, 1977). Although Keohane and Nye were not the first to use the concept of interdependence (Rosenau wrote about interdependence before Keohane and Nye) they have been credited with the concept.
89. P. Willetts, *Transnational Actors and Changing World Order* (Occasional Papers Series No. 17, PRIME, International Peace Research Institute, Meigaku, Japan, 1993), pp. 18–19.
90. See *Letter dated 20 February 1990 from the Permanent Representatives of Bolivia, Colombia, Peru and the United States of America to the United Nations addressed to the Secretary-General*. UN document A/S-17/8.
91. Willetts, *Transnational Actors and Changing World Order*, *op. cit.*, p. 19.
92. See 'Pre-theories and theories of foreign policy', first published in R. B. Farell (ed.), *Approaches to Comparative and International Politics* (Northwestern University Press, Evaston, 1966), pp. 27–92 and reprinted in J. N. Rosenau, *The Scientific Study of Foreign Policy* (New York, The Free Press, 1971), pp. 95–149.
93. Rosenau, *The Scientific Study of Foreign Policy*, *op. cit.*, p. 141.
94. R. Mansbach and J. A. Vasquez, *In Search of Theory. A New Para-*

digm for Global Politics (Columbia University Press, New York, 1981), p. 59.

95. R. O. Keohane and J. S. Nye, *Power and Interdependence* (Little, Brown and Company, Boston, 1977 and 1989), p. 65.

96. D. Easton, *A Framework for Political Analysis* (Prentice-Hall, Inc, Englewood Cliffs, NJ, 1965), p. 30.

97. Mansbach and Vasquez, *op. cit.*, pp. 56–7.

98. C. P. Kindleberger, 'Hierarchy versus inertial cooperation', *International Organization*, Vol. 40, No. 2, 1986, pp. 841–7.

99. Mansbach and Vasquez, *op. cit.*, Chapter 4, 'Agenda politics', p. 87. Mansbach and Vasquez refer to the work of Cobb and Elder as the best analysis of agenda-building in the literature, but say their work is incomplete.

100. Mansbach and Vasquez, *op. cit.*, p. 113.

101. *Ibid.*, p. 114.

3 A HISTORY OF DRUG USE: THE DYNAMICS OF CHANGE

1. Article 23(c) of the Covenant of the League of Nations empowered the League to control both licit and illicit manufacture of, and trade and traffic in, opium and other dangerous substances. See *A Guide to the International Drug Conventions* (Commonwealth Secretariat, London, 1988), p. 3. See Chapter 4 for an overview of international co-operation on drug control.

2. S. Strange, '*Cave! hic dragones*: A critique of regime analysis', in S. D. Krasner (ed.), *International Regimes* (Cornell University Press, Ithaca and London, 4th edn, 1986, first pub. 1983), pp. 337–54.

3. See A. Stein, 'Coordination and collaboration: regimes in an anarchic world', pp. 115–41 in Krasner, *op. cit.*

4. Krasner, *op. cit.*, p. 3.

5. For a fascinating history of early drug use see B. Whitaker, *The Global Connection. The Crisis of Drug Addiction* (Jonathan Cape, London, 1987), Part 1; B. Inglis, *The Forbidden Game. A Social History of Drugs* (Hodder and Stoughton, London, 1975); and K. Bruun, L. Pan and I. Rexed, *The Gentlemen's Club* (University of Chicago Press, Chicago, 1975).

6. As quoted in G. L. Henderson, 'Designer drugs: Past history and future prospects', *Journal of Forensic Sciences*, Vol. 33, No. 2, March 1988, pp. 569–75.

7. 'Cocaine "first used 2,000 years ago"', *Independent*, 16.6.91.

8. Whitaker, *op. cit.*, p. 7.

9. *Ibid.*

10. D. Aitken and T. Mikuriya, 'The forgotten medicine. A look at the medical uses of cannabis', *Ecologist*, Vol. 10, Nos. 8/9, Oct–Nov. 1980, p. 272.

11. Whitaker, *op. cit.*, p. 4.

12. See D. E. Owen, *British Opium Policy in China and India* (Yale University Press, New Haven, 1934), p. 52; and also J. Rowntree, *The*

Imperial Drug Trade (Methuen and Co., London, 1905), pp. 284–6.

13. See D. T. Courtwright, *Dark Paradise. Opiate Addiction in America before 1840* (Harvard University Press, London, 1982); and C. E. Terry and M. Pellens, *The Opium Problem* (Patterson Smith, London, 1970, first pub. 1928).

14. V. Berridge and G. Edwards, *Opium and the People. Opiate Use in Nineteenth-Century England* (Yale University Press, New Haven and London, 1987), p. 11.

15. E. M. Brecher, *Licit and Illicit Drugs* (Greenwood Press, Boston, 1972), p. 4, ref. 9.

16. See Whitaker, *op. cit.*, p. 25.

17. Berridge and Edwards, *op. cit.*, p. 259.

18. A. W. McCoy, *The Politics of Heroin. CIA Complicity in the Global Drug Trade* (Lawrence Hill Books, New York, 1991), p. 7.

19. Courtwright, *op. cit.*, p. 37.

20. For a detailed look at the impact of opium smoking in the United States, see Courtwright, *op. cit.*, Chapter 3, 'Addiction to opium smoking'.

21. T. M. Parssinen, *Secret Passions, Secret Remedies: Narcotic Drugs in British Society, 1820–1930* (Institute for the Study of Human Issues, Philadelphia, 1993), pp. 35–6.

22. 'Report of the Pharmacy Bill Committee to the General Medical Council', *British Medical Journal*, Vol. 2, 1868, p. 39, as quoted in Berridge and Edwards, *op. cit.*, p. 119.

23. For details concerning the politics of the Act see Berridge and Edwards, *op. cit.*, Chapter 10, 'The Pharmacy Act', pp. 113–22.

24. *Ibid.*, p. 125.

25. Berridge and Edwards, *op. cit.*, p. 149.

26. *Ibid.*, p. 150.

27. P. Eddy, H. Sabogal, S. Walden, *The Cocaine Wars* (Arrow Books, London, 1988), p. 46.

28. The Registrar General's Office was the forerunner for today's Home Office Advisory Council on the Misuse of Drugs.

29. For more detail about the role of Quakers see B. D. Johnson, 'Righteousness Before revenue: The forgotten moral crusade against the Indo-Chinese opium trade', *Journal of Drug Issues*, Fall 1975, pp. 304–26, and J. B. Brown, 'Politics of the poppy: The Society for the Suppression of the Opium Trade, 1974–1916, *Journal of Contemporary History*, Vol. 8, July 1973, pp. 97–111.

30. A. W. McCoy, *The Politics of Heroin, op. cit.*, p. 88.

31. Berridge and Edwards, *op. cit.*, p. 179.

32. A. H. Taylor, *American Diplomacy and the Narcotics Traffic, 1900–1939. A Study in International Humanitarian Reform* (Duke University Press, Durham, NC, 1969), p. 29.

33. T. Dennett, *Americans in Eastern Asia: A Critical Study of the Policy of the US with Reference to China, Japan and Korea in the Nineteenth Century* (Barnes and Noble, Inc, New York, 1941), p. 116.

34. For a discussion of the participation of Americans in the China opium trade, see Taylor, *op. cit.*, Chapter 1, 'The United States and the opium problem in the nineteenth century'.

35. Dennett, *op. cit.*, p. 117.
36. D. F. Musto, *The American Disease. Origins of Narcotic Control* (Yale University Press, New Haven and London, 1973), pp. 66–7.
37. Musto, *op. cit.*, p. 36.
38. H. J. Morgenthau, *Politics Among Nations: The Struggle for Power and Peace* (Knopf, New York, 2nd. edn 1954, first pub. 1948), p. 9.
39. *Ibid.*, p. 528.
40. *Ibid.*, p. 5.
41. R. O. Keohane and J. S. Nye (eds), *Transnational Relations and World Politics* (Cambridge, Mass., 1971).
42. H. J. Morgenthau and K. W. Thompson (eds), *Principles and Problems of International Politics* (Knopf, New York, 1950), Preface.
43. In the inaugural lecture by the first Stevenson Professor at the London School of Economics, a state-centred approach to international history was stressed. See C. K. Webster, 'The study of international history', *History*, Vol. 18, 1933, pp. 99–100.
44. See, for example, D. C. Watt et al., 'What is diplomatic history?', *History Today*, Vol. 18, 1985, pp. 33–41.
45. A. De Conde, 'On the Nature of International History', *International History Review*, Vol. 10, 1989, pp. 286–7 as quoted in J. A. Scholte, 'From power politics to social change', *Review of International Studies*, Vol. 19, No. 1, January 1993, pp. 3–21.
46. See P. B. Evans et al. (eds), *Bringing the State Back In* (Cambridge University Press, Cambridge, 1985).
47. For a brief overview of the concept of 'world society' see E. Luard, *Basic Texts in International Relations* (Macmillan, London, 1992), Chapter 34, 'The world society approach', pp. 559–74.
48. S. D. Krasner, 'Structural causes and regime consequences' in Krasner, *op. cit.*, pp. 3–4.
49. *Ibid.*, p. 11.
50. D. J. Puchala and R. F. Hopkins, Chapter 2, 'Grotian Perspectives', in Krasner, *op. cit.*, pp. 61–91.
51. R. O. Keohane, *After Hegemony. Cooperation and Discord in the World Political Economy* (Princeton University Press, Princeton, New Jersey, 1984), p. 32.
52. R. W. Mansbach and J. A. Vasquez, *In Search of Theory. A New Paradigm for Global Politics* (Columbia University Press, New York, 1981), p. 11.
53. *Ibid.*, p. 29.
54. D. Easton, *The Political System. An Enquiry into the State of Political Science* (Alfred A. Knopf, New York, 1953), Chapter 5, Section 2, 'The authoritative allocation of values for a society', p. 129.
55. Mansbach and Vasquez, *op. cit.*, p. 29.
56. K. Young, 'Values in the policy process', in C. Politt et al., *Public Policy in Theory and Practice* (Hodder and Stoughton, Open University Press, Sevenoaks, 1979), pp. 30–41.
57. See F. Parkinson, *The Philosophy of International Relations: A Study in the History of Thought* (Sage, London, 1977).
58. W. Landecker, 'The scope of a sociology of International Relations',

Social Forces, Vol. 17, 1938, p. 175, as quoted in Scholte, 'From power politics to social change', *op. cit.*, p. 10.

59. See T. Parsons, 'Order and Community in the International Social System', in J. N. Rosenau (ed.), *International Politics and Foreign Policy: A Reader in International Theory* (Free Press, New York, 1961), pp. 120–29.
60. Mansbach and Vasquez, *op. cit.*, p. 58.
61. *Ibid.*
62. *Ibid.*, p. 58.
63. See D. Easton, *A Framework for Political Analysis* (Prentice Hall, Inc, Englewood Cliffs, New Jersey, 1965), p. 50.
64. Mansbach and Vasquez, *op. cit.*, pp. 56–7.
65. *Ibid.*, pp. 61–2.
66. Mansbach and Vasquez, *op. cit.*, pp. 56–7.
67. Bruun et al., *op. cit.*, pp. 9–12.
68. *Report of the British Delegates to the International Opium Conference, Held at the Hague, Dec. 1911–Jan. 1912*, Miscellaneous No. 11 (1912), Cd. 6448. H.M. Stationery Office, London, 1912.
69. See Article 23(c) of the Covenant of the League of Nations, *op. cit.*
70. Mansbach and Vasquez, *op. cit.*, pp. 109–10.
71. Easton, *A Framework*, *op. cit.*, p. 50.
72. E. Adler and P. M. Haas, 'Conclusion: epistemic communities, world order, and the creation of a reflective research program', in *International Organization*, Vol. 46, No. 1, Winter 1992, quoting J. G. March and J. Olson, 'The new institutionalism: Organisational factors in political life', *American Political Science Review*, Vol. 78, September 1984, pp. 734–49.
73. J. G. Ruggie, 'International responses to technology: Concepts and trends', *International Organization*, Vol. 29, No. 3, Summer 1975, pp. 557–70.
74. *Ibid.*, p. 569.
75. *Ibid.*
76. See P. M. Haas, 'Knowledge, power and international policy coordination', *International Organization*, Special Issue, Vol. 46, No 1, Winter 1992.
77. P. M. Haas, 'Obtaining international environmental protection through epistemic consensus', *Millennium, Journal of International Studies*, Vol. 19, No. 3, Vol. p. 349.
78. Although Krasner acknowledges the importance of shared beliefs in regime creation, he never fully commits himself to a notion of change other than that determined by shifting state power.
79. P. M. Haas, 'Obtaining international environmental protection through epistemic consensus', *op. cit.*, Abstract.
80. *Ibid.*
81. Adler and Haas, *op. cit.*, p. 367.
82. Berridge and Edwards, *op. cit.*, p. 155.
83. E. B. Haas, 'Why collaborate? Issue-linkage and international regimes', *World Politics*, Vol. 32, No. 3, April 1980, p. 362.

4 THE UNITED NATIONS AND INTERNATIONAL DRUG CONTROL

1. The reasons and motivations for the inclusion of cocaine in international control were described in the previous chapter. For information on this and other Conventions of the period, see Dr S. K. Chatterjee, *A Guide to International Drug Conventions: Explanatory materials for the preparation of legislation in the implementation of the major international drug conventions* (Commonwealth Secretariat, London, 1988), Chapter 2.
2. Raw opium, according to the Convention, is the spontaneously coagulated juice obtained from the capsules of the *Papaver somniferum*, which has been submitted only to the necessary manipulations for packaging and transport. Prepared opium is the product of raw opium obtained by a series of special operations, by dissolving, boiling, heating and fermentation, which transforms the substance into an extract suitable for consumption. Developed countries were therefore far more willing to reach agreement on raw opium than on prepared opium, as they traded the latter.
3. See B. Inglis, *The Forbidden Game. A Social History of Drugs* (Hodder and Stoughton, London, 1975), pp. 174–5.
4. See J. G. Starke, 'The 1936 Convention for the Suppression of the Illicit Traffic in Dangerous Drugs', *American Journal of International Law*, Vol. 31, 1937, p. 3.
5. The six different drug-control treaties and three amending protocols are: the Hague Opium Convention of 1912; the '1925 Agreement'; the Geneva International Opium Convention, 1925; The Convention for Limiting the Manufacture and Regulating the Distribution of Narcotic Drugs, 1931; the '1931 Agreement'; The Convention for the Suppression of the Illicit Traffic in Dangerous Drugs, 1936; and the '1946 Protocol', the '1948 Protocol' and the '1953 Protocol' amending these Conventions and Agreements. For details see Chatterjee, *op. cit.*
6. See *The Single Convention on Narcotic Drugs, 1961, done at New York on 30 March 1961*, Appendix IV in Chatterjee, *op. cit.*, p. 108.
7. *Ibid.*, Preamble, p. 11.
8. *Ibid.*, Article 38, p. 125.
9. S. D. Stein, *International Diplomacy, State Administrators and Narcotics Control. The Origins of a Social Problem* (Gower, Aldershot, 1985), p. 5.
10. The International Narcotics Control Board was established by ECOSOC Resolution 1106 (XL) of 2 March 1968, pursuant to the Single Convention, Article 45(2).
11. Article 9(2)(3) of the Single Convention, *op. cit.*
12. Article 9(3) of the Single Convention, *op. cit.*
13. See General Assembly Resolution 40/122 of 13 December 1985. For details of the Conference participation see, *Report of the International Conference on Drug Abuse and Illicit Trafficking, Vienna, 17–26 June 1987*, United Nations document A/CONF.133/12, Chapter III, 'Attendance and organization of work', pp. 97–100.

14. The *Comprehensive Multidisciplinary Outline of Future Activities in Drug Abuse Control* is included as Part A of the report of the conference. See Report of the International Conference on Drug Abuse and Illicit Trafficking, *op. cit.*

15. See *Report of the International Conference on Drug Abuse and Illicit Trafficking, op. cit.*, Section 1, 'Prevention and Reduction of the Illicit Demand for Narcotic Drugs and Psychotropic Substances', para. 21, p. 12.

16. *Ibid.*, para. 225, p. 51, *Comprehensive Multidisciplinary Outline*, Chapter III, 'Suppression of illicit traffic'.

17. *Ibid.*, para. 1, p. 1, 'Introduction'.

18. See *United Nations Conference for the Adoption of a Convention Against the Illicit Traffic in Narcotic Drugs and Psychotropic Substances, Vienna, Austria, 25 November–20 December 1988*, United Nations document E/CONF.82/4.

19. *United Nations Convention Against Illicit Traffic in Narcotic Drugs and Psychotropic Substances*, United Nations Document E/CONF. 82/15 and Rev. 1, 19 December 1988.

20. See M. C. Bassiouni (ed.), talking about why states undertake international criminal law commitments in *International Criminal Law*, Vol. 1, Crimes, 507, 1986, as quoted in D. W. Sproule and P. St-Denis, 'The UN Drug Trafficking Convention: An Ambitious Step', *The Canadian Yearbook of International Law*, 1989, pp. 263–93, quote at p. 264.

21. D. Stewart, 'Internationalizing The War on Drugs: The UN Convention Against Illicit Traffic in Narcotic Drugs and Psychotropic Substances', *Denver Journal of International Law and Policy*, Vol. 18, No. 3, 1990, pp. 387–404, quote at p. 388.

22. See 18 U.S.C. 981 (a) (1) (B), as quoted in Stewart, *op. cit.*, p. 396.

23. See Articles 20 and 21, Vienna Convention, *op. cit.*

24. Article 1(b) Vienna Convention, *op. cit.*

25. *Report of the Second Interregional Meeting of Heads of National Drug Law Enforcement Agencies, Vienna, 11–15 September 1989*, United Nations document E/CN.7/1990/2.

26. See *Political Declaration and Global Programme of Action adopted by the General Assembly at its seventeenth special session, devoted to the question of international co-operation against illicit production, supply, demand, trafficking and distribution of narcotic drugs and psychotropic substances*, United Nations document A/RES/S-17/2.

27. See *Political Declaration, op. cit.*, para. 6, p. 5.

28. United Nations document A/S-17/PV.1, 27, as quoted in J. Donnelly, 'The United Nations and the Global Drug Control Regime', pp. 282–305 in P. H. Smith (ed.), *Drug Policy in the Americas* (Westview Press, Boulder, 1992), quote at p. 292.

29. See *Report of the Group of Experts to advise and assist the Secretary-General on the enhancement of the efficiency of the United Nations structure for drug abuse control: Drugs and the United Nations; Meeting the Challenge.* Annex to *International Action to Combat Drug Abuse and Illicit Trafficking. Programme for the Biennium 1990–1991: Enhancement of*

the efficiency of the United Nations structure for drug abuse control. Report of the Secretary-General. United Nations document A/45/652/Add.1., 23 October 1990, *op. cit.*

30. See, *Activities of the United Nations International Drug Control Programme. Report of the Executive Director.* United Nations document E/CN.7/1993/3, 8 February 1993.

31. *Report of the International Narcotics Control Board* for 1992, United Nations document E/INCB/1992/1, Overview, para., 2, p. 1.

32. World Bank, *Bolivia: agricultural sector review*, report No. 9882–BO, 6 April 1992; *Bolivia: updating economic memorandum*, report No. 11123–BO, 8 October 1992; and *Peru: agricultural policies for economic efficiency*, No. 10605–PE, 11 September 1992.

33. The Trevi Group was established following a United Kingdom initiative in 1975. Although primarily set up to deal with anti-terrorism matters, its working groups cover particular aspects such as police equipment, public order matters (such as football hooliganism) and serious crime, including drug trafficking.

34. Europol's role is by no means clear: some European countries, like Germany, want it to become a fully operational European-style FBI. For the present it is restricted to providing analysis to police narcotic squads.

35. See Title VI and Declaration 32 of the Final Act of the Maastricht Treaty, in *The Unseen Treaty on European Union. Maastricht 1992* (David Pollard Publishing, Oxford, 1992), p. 3.

36. M. Bertrand, 'Some reflections on reform of the United Nations', reproduced as Chapter 12 in P. Taylor and A. J. R. Groom (eds), *International Institutions at Work* (Pinter Publishers, London, 1988), p. 195.

37. Papers presented at the Moscow Roundtable are reproduced in J. P. Renninger, *The Future Role of the United Nations in an Interdependent World* (Martinus Nijhoff Publishers, London, 1989).

38. *Activities of the United Nations International Drug Control Programme*, *op. cit.*, para. 20, p. 5.

39. See I. Claude, *Swords into Ploughshares* (Random House, New York, 1959) as the landmark text which emphasised the actual and potential roles of international organisations in a more broadly conceived process of international governance.

40. F. Kratochwil and J. G. Ruggie, 'International organization: A state of the art on an art of the state', *International Organization,* Vol. 40, No. 4, Autumn 1986, pp. 753–75.

41. J. G. Ruggie, 'International responses to technology: Concepts and trends', *International Organization*, Vol. 29, No. 3, Summer 1975, p. 570.

42. See Chapter 1 for reference to the 1982 conference; 'The Study of Regimes in International Relations – State of the Art and Perspectives' held in Tübingen, Germany, 14–18 July 1991. Selected papers presented at the conference were published in the volume, *Regime Theory and International Relations*, edited by V. Rittberger, with the assistance of P. Mayer (Clarendon Press, Oxford, 1993).

43. K. Waltz, *Theory of International Relations* (Addison-Wesley, Reading, Mass., 1979), especially Chapters 5 and 6.

44. S. D. Krasner (ed.), 'Structural causes and regime consequences: regimes as intervening variables', in *International Regimes* (Cornell University Press, Ithaca, New York, 4th edn 1986, first pub. 1983), pp. 1–21.
45. D. J. Puchala and R. F. Hopkins, 'International regimes: Lessons from inductive analysis', pp. 61–91 in Krasner, *op. cit.*, quote from p. 63; and O. Young, 'Regime dynamics: The rise and fall of international regimes', pp. 93–113 in Krasner, *op. cit.*
46. O. Young, 'International regimes: Problems of concept formation', *World Politics,* Vol. 32, No. 3, April 1980, pp. 331–56.
47. Puchala and Hopkins, *op. cit.*, p. 63.
48. *Ibid.*, p. 62.
49. Stein, 'Coordination and collaboration: Regimes in an anarchic world', pp. 115–41 in Krasner, *op. cit.*
50. J. Donnelly, 'International human rights: A regime analysis', *International Organization,* Vol. 40, No. 3, Summer 1986, pp. 599–642, quote at p. 602.
51. Stein, *op. cit.*, pp. 312–13.
52. Puchala and Hopkins, *op. cit.*, p. 62, Footnote 2; D. Easton, 'An approach to the analysis of political systems', *World Politics*, April 1957, pp. 383–400.
53. D. Easton, *A Framework for Political Analysis* (Prentice Hall, Englewood Cliffs, 1965), p. 30.
54. D. Easton, *A Systems Analysis of Political Life* (The University of Chicago Press, Chicago and London, 1979, first pub. 1965), Chapter 12, 'Objects of support: The regime', pp. 190–212.
55. *Ibid.*, p. 193.
56. *Ibid.*
57. Krasner, *op. cit.*, p. 2.
58. Strange, '*Cave! hic dragones*: A critique of regime analysis', pp. 337–55 in Krasner, *op. cit.*, quote at p. 338. For a discussion of her criticisms see Chapter 1.
59. Report of the Group of Experts, *op. cit.*, p. 4.
60. See *Report of the International Conference on Drug Abuse and Illicit Trafficking*, *op. cit.*, para. 21, p. 12.
61. Bassiouni, *op. cit.*
62. Donnelly, 'International human rights', *op. cit.*, p. 603.

5 KEEP OFF THE GRASS: DRUG NORMS AND INTERNATIONAL RELATIONS

1. D. J. Puchala and R. F. Hopkins, 'International regimes: Lessons from inductive analysis', pp. 61–91 in S. D. Krasner, *International Regimes* (Cornell University Press, Ithaca and London, 4th edn 1986, first pub. 1983).
2. S. Haggard and B. A. Simmons, 'Theories of international regimes', *International Organization,* Vol. 41, No. 3, Summer 1987, pp. 491–517.
3. O. R. Young, *International Cooperation. Building Regimes for Natural*

Resources and the Environment (Cornell University Press, Ithaca and London, 1989), p. 207.

4. R. Keohane, 'Neoliberal institutionalism: A perspective on world politics', pp. 1–20 in *International Institutions and State Power: Essays in International Relations Theory* (Boulder, Colo., 1989), quote from p. 4.

5. E. Haas, 'Words can hurt you; or, who said what to whom about regimes', pp. 23–61 in Krasner, *International Regimes, op. cit.*, quote at p. 23.

6. Y. Ferguson and R. W. Mansbach, *The Elusive Quest: Theory and International Politics* (University of South Carolina Press, Columbia, SC, 1988), p. 37.

7. F. Kratochwil, 'The force of prescriptions', *International Organization*, Vol. 38, No. 4, Autumn 1984, p. 686.

8. *Ibid.*, p. 687.

9. E. Ullmann-Margalit, *The Emergence of Norms* (Oxford University Press, Oxford, 1977), p. 12.

10. J. Rosenau, *The Scientific Study of Foreign Policy* (The Free Press, New York, 1981), p. 105n.

11. M. Rokeach, *The Nature of Human Values* (Free Press, New York, 1973), p. 5.

12. R. M. Williams, 'The concept of values', *International Encyclopedia of the Social Sciences*, Vol. 16 (Free Press, New York, 1968), p. 284.

13. The cosmopolitan and communitarian debate centres around three points: a concept of the person, the morality of states and universalism versus particularism. For a recent elaboration of the debate see C. Brown, *International Relations Theory: New Normative Approaches* (Columbia University Press, New York, 1992).

14. F. Kratochwil, *Rules, Norms, and Decisions. On the conditions of practical and legal reasoning in international relations and domestic affairs* (Cambridge University Press, Cambridge, 1991) p. 253.

15. R. M. Williams, *American Society. A Sociological Interpretation* (Alfred A. Knopf, New York, 2nd edn, revised, 1968, first pub. 1960), p. 25.

16. T. Nardin, *Law, Morality, and the Relations of States* (Princeton University Press, Princeton, 1983), p. 4. 'Purposive association' consists of relations among those who get together to further particular ends and who, if they adopt rules, adopt them as instruments of that pursuit'.

17. F. Kratochwil, 'On the relevance of International Law', *Journal of International Affairs*, Vol. 37, Winter 1984, p. 344.

18. F. Kratochwil, 'Contract and regimes. Do issue specificity and variations of formality matter', pp. 73–93 in V. Rittberger (ed.), *Regime Theory and International Relations* (Clarendon Press, Oxford, 1993), p. 74.

19. Williams, *American Society, op. cit.*, p 24.

20. Ullmann-Margalit, *op. cit.*, p. 12.

21. *Ibid.*

22. H. L. A. Hart, *The Concept of Law* (Oxford University Press, Oxford, 1961).

23. Ullmann-Margalit, *op. cit.*, pp. 12–13.

24. *Ibid.*

25. P. Bean, *The Social Control of Drugs* (Martin Roberston, London, 1974), p. 15.
26. T. Hobbes, *Leviathan* (Oxford University Press, Oxford, 1962, first pub. 1651), p. 100.
27. E. H. Carr, *The Twenty-Years' Crisis, 1919–1939: An Introduction to the Study of International Relations* (Macmillan, London, 1981, first pub. 1939), pp. 87–8.
28. D. Hume, *Treatise on Human Nature* as quoted by A. Hurrell, 'International society and the study of regimes: A reflective approach', pp. 49–73 in V. Rittberger, *op. cit.*
29. Recent work on Hobbes has picked up on the work of Stanley Hoffman, writing 30 years earlier that Hobbes should be viewed as 'the founder of utilitarian theories of international law and relations'. See S. Hoffman, 'Rousseau on war and peace', *American Political Science Review*, Vol. 57, No. 2, June 1963.
30. T. Parsons, 'The distribution of power in American society', *World Politics*, Vol. X, No. 1, October 1957, as quoted in, S. Kim, *A Quest for a Just World Order* (Westview Special Studies in International Relations, Westview Press, Boulder, Colorado, 1984), p. 24.
31. J. Rawls, *A Theory of Justice* (Harvard University Press, Cambridge, Mass., 1971).
32. Kratochwil, *Rules, Norms and Decisions, op. cit.*, p. 10.
33. F. Kratochwil, 'Rules, norms, values and the limits of "Rationality"', *Archiv für Rechts- und Sozialphilosophie*, Vol. 73, 1987, p. 309.
34. See *Crime Prevention and Criminal Justice. The strengthening of international cooperation in combatting organized crime. Report of the Secretary General* (United Nations document A/47/381, 28 September 1992), p. 4.
35. *Ibid.*
36. See *Eighth United Nations Congress on the Prevention of Crime and the Treatment of Offenders, Havana, 27 August–7 September 1990* (United Nations publication, Sales No. E.91.IV.2), Chapter I, Section C.
37. J. Ruskin, *The Stones of Venice*, Vol. 3 (Smith, Elder, London, 2nd edn, 1858–1867, 3 volumes, first pub. 1851), p. 815.
38. T. E. Jordan, *Victorian Childhood: Themes and Variations* (State University of New York Press, 1987), p. xiii.
39. J. S. Mill, *On Liberty* (Penguin Books, Middlesex, 1986, first pub. 1859), p. 69.
40. See 'Drug liberalisation attacked', *Financial Times*, 20.5.94. A similar decision has recently been taken by a court in Germany. See 'German judge says legal ban on soft drug violates constitution', *Independent*, 29.2.92.
41. E. Haas, *op. cit.*, p. 51.
42. Strange, '*Cave! hic dragones*: A critique of regime analysis', pp. 337–55 in Krasner, *International Regimes, op. cit.*, p. 346.
43. S. Kim, *op. cit.*, pp. 23–4.

6 THE INTERNATIONAL MONEY-LAUNDERING CONTROL REGIME

1. See *United Nations Conference for the Adoption of a Convention Against the Illicit Traffic in Narcotic Drugs and Psychotropic Substances, Vienna, Austria, 25 November–20 December 1988*, United Nations document E/CONF.82/4.
2. See 'Declaration of the World Ministerial Summit to Reduce Demand for Drugs and to Combat the Cocaine Threat, London, 9–11 April 1990' in W. C. Gilmore (ed.), *International Efforts to Combat Money Laundering* (Cambridge International Documents Series, Volume 4, in association with The Commonwealth Secretariat, London, Grotius Publications Ltd., Cambridge, 1992) Chapter V, Document E, pp. 285–90.
3. See, *Ninth Conference of the Non-Aligned Countries, Belgrade, Yugoslavia, 1989*, United Nations document A/44/551.
4. See 'Commonwealth Heads of Government Meeting, Kuala Lumpur, Malaysia, 18–24 October 1989: Communiqué *(extracts)*', Chapter 3, Document B, in Gilmore, *op. cit.*, pp. 157–9.
5. See 'Commonwealth Heads of Government Meeting, Harare, Zimbabwe, 16–22 October 1991: Communiqué *(extracts)*', in Gilmore, *op. cit.*, p. 164.
6. See *Report of the Second Interregional Meeting of Heads of National Drug Law Enforcement Agencies (Interregional HONLEA), Vienna, 11–15 September, 1989.* United Nations document E/CN.7/1990/2.
7. The lower end of the estimates is reflected by *The Drugs Trade in Latin America Report*, the upper end by the Group of Seven anti-drugs committee. See *The Drugs Trade in Latin America Report* (Latin American Newsletters, London, 1990).
8. *Report of the Conference for the Adoption of a Convention Against the Illicit Traffic in Narcotic Drugs and Psychotropic Substances*, *op. cit.*, p. 3.
9. See V. Coleman, *Drugs: The Argument for Decriminalisation*, p. 4, as quoted in R. Stevenson, *Winning The War on Drugs: To Legalise Or Not?* (Hobart Paper 124, The Institute of Economic Affairs, London, 1994), p. 74.
10. Committee on Banking Regulations and Supervisory Practices, *Prevention of Criminal Use of the Banking System for the Purpose of Money-laundering. Statement of Principles*, December 1988, Preamble, para. 4, p. 2. Source: Bank of England. The Basle Committee on Banking Regulations and Supervisory Practices comprises the representatives of the central banks and supervisory authorities of the Group of Ten countries (Belgium, Canada, France, Germany, Italy, Japan, the Netherlands, Sweden, Switzerland, the United Kingdom, the United States) and Luxembourg. See Appendix B.
11. Council of the European Communities, *Council Directive of 10 June 1991 on Prevention of the Use of the Financial System for the Purpose of Money Laundering*, Brussels, Document number 91/308/EEC, Article 1, p. 9.
12. *International Narcotics Control Strategy Report*, 1 March 1988 (US Department of State, Washington, DC), p. 46.

13. *Money Laundering: Guidance Notes for Banks and Building Societies*, December 1990, p. 2. Source: Bank of England.
14. *Financial Action Task Force On Money Laundering. Report of 7 February 1990*, Paris, p. 5. Source: Bank of England.
15. See *National Health Service Drug Tariff*, (HMSO, London, 1993), as quoted in R. Stevenson, *op. cit.*, p. 37.
16. See R. J. Michaels, 'The market for heroin before and after legalisation', in R. Hamowy (ed.), *Dealing with Drugs* (D. C. Heath and Company, Lexington, Mass., 1987), pp. 289–326.
17. 'Bankers outfox police to profit from hot money', *The Times*, 13.10.93.
18. Financial Action Task Force, *op. cit.*, p. 6.
19. E. A. Nadelmann, 'Negotiations in criminal law assistance treaties', *American Journal of Comparative Law*, Vol. 33, 1985, p. 467, at p. 499.
20. See 'High-tech boost for war on global fraud', *Daily Telegraph*, 28.3.92.
21. W. C. Gilmore (ed.), *International Efforts to Combat Money Laundering* (Cambridge International Documents Series, Volume 4, in association with The Commonwealth Secretariat, London, Grotius Publications Ltd, Cambridge 1992): 'Commission of the European Communities: *Proposal for a Council Directive on Prevention of Use of the Financial System for the Purpose of Money Laundering*, Explanatory Memorandum, 23 March 1990', Document E, pp. 243–9, quote 1(1), p. 243.
22. S. H. Aronson, 'Bell's electrical toy: What's the use?' in I. de Sola Pool (ed.), *The Social Impact of the Telephone* (MIT Press, Cambridge, Mass., 1977), pp. 15–39.
23. R. H. Veith, *Multinational Computer Nets: The Case of International Banking* (Lexington Books, New York, 1981), pp. 35–55.
24. R. O'Brien, *Global Financial Integration: The End of Geography* (Royal Institute of International Affairs, Pinter, London, 1992), p. 97.
25. See, for example, Robert E. Jackson, 'The hidden issues: What kind of order,' *Journal of Communication* 29 (Summer 1979), 152–3, as referred to in Veith, *op. cit.*, p. 35.
26. O'Brien, *op. cit.*, p. 100.
27. Financial Action Task Force, *op. cit.*, p. 13.
28. R. E. Powis, *The Money Launderers* (Probus Publishing Company, Chicago & Cambridge, 1992), p. xi.
29. Operation Greenback was formed in Miami in 1980, staffed primarily by Customs and IRS agents, to investigate drug-money laundering links. Operation Greenback was viewed as very successful and established that a class of professional money-laundering specialists had emerged, working with the drug-trafficking organisations.
30. See *Measures Against the Transfer and Safekeeping of Funds of Criminal Origin: Recommendation No. R(80)10 adopted by the Committee of Ministers of the Council of Europe on 27 June 1980 and Explanatory Memorandum*, Council of Europe, Strasbourg, in Gilmore, *International Efforts, op. cit.*, Chapter IV: 'European developments', Document A, pp. 169–76.
31. 'Statement of Principles', *op. cit.*, p. 3.
32. Financial Action Task Force Report, *op. cit.*, p. 10.

33. *Ibid.*
34. *United Nations Convention Against Illicit Traffic in Narcotic Drugs and Psychotropic Substances*, United Nations document E/CONF.82/15 and Rev. 1, 19 December 1988.
35. *Explanatory Report on the Convention on Laundering, Search, Seizure and Confiscation of the Proceeds from Crime*, Council of Europe, Strasbourg, p. 193, in Gilmore, *International Efforts, op. cit.*, Chapter IV, Document C, pp. 192–237.
36. House of Lords, Select Committee on the European Communities, *Money Laundering*, House of Lords Paper No. 6, 1990–1991, note 39, p. 7.
37. See, e.g., Article 305(bis) of the Swiss Penal Code which came into effect on 1 August 1990 and renders money laundering in respect of all forms of crime a criminal offence.
38. M. Levi, 'Regulating money laundering: The death mark of bank secrecy in the UK', *British Journal of Criminology*, Vol. 31, 1991, p. 115.
39. The Council of the European Communities, *op. cit.*, p. 3.
40. See 'Commission of the European Communities' in Gilmore, International Efforts, *op. cit.*, p. 244.
41. House of Lords Select Committee, *op. cit.*, note 39, p. 5.
42. House of Lords, *op. cit.*, note 39, p. 15.
43. 'Money Laundering: A central banker's view'. A speech given by Brian Quinn, Executive Director of the Bank of England, at the Conference arranged by the Joint Working Group on the Financial System's role in Combating Money Laundering, 11 February 1991, London, p. 1. Source: Bank of England.
44. Basle Statement of Principles, *op. cit.*, p. 2.
45. *Financial Times*, 19.4.89.
46. Quinn, *op. cit.*, p. 5.
47. *Ibid.*, p. 7.
48. Quinn, *op. cit.*, p. 14.
49. O'Brien, *op. cit.*, p. 98.
50. *Group of Seven Economic Declaration of 16 July 1989*, as quoted in Gilmore, International Efforts, *op. cit.*, Chapter 1, Document A, p. 3.
51. See *Report of the Financial Action Task Force on Money Laundering, 13 May 1991, Paris*. Source: Bank of England. Introduction.
52. *Financial Action Task Force on Money Laundering. Report of the 25th June 1992, Paris*, p. 5. Source: Bank of England.
53. *Financial Action Task Force On Money Laundering. Report of 16th June 1994, Paris*, p. 9. Source: Bank of England.
54. S. D. Krasner, *International Regimes* (Cornell University Press, Ithaca, New York, 4th edn 1986, first pub. 1983), p. 2.

7 INTERNATIONAL REGIMES AND DRUG CONTROL IN THE 1990S

1. O. Young, 'The politics of international regime formation: Managing natural resources and the environment', *International Organization*, Vol. 43, No. 3, Summer 1989, pp. 349–75.

2. P. M. Haas, 'Do regimes matter? Epistemic communities and Mediterranean pollution', *International Organization*, Vol. 43, No. 3, Summer 1989, pp. 377–403.
3. P. M. Haas, 'Banning chlorofluorocarbons: Epistemic community efforts to protect stratospheric ozone', *International Organization*, Vol. 46, No. 1, Winter 1992, pp. 187–225.
4. See A. Fikkan, G. Osherenko and A. Arikainen, 'Polar bears: The importance of simplicity', in O. Young and G. Osherenko (eds), *Polar Politics. Creating International Environmental Regimes* (Cornell University Press, Ithaca and London, 1993), pp. 96–152.
5. R. Tooze, 'Regimes and international co-operation', pp. 210–15 in A. J. R. Groom and P. Taylor (eds), *Frameworks for International Cooperation* (Pinter Publishers, London, 1990), quote at p. 211.
6. See R. W. Cox, 'The crisis of world order and the problem of international organization in the 1980s', *International Journal*, Vol. XXXV, No. 2, Spring 1980, p. 377.
7. S. D. Krasner (ed.), *International Regimes* (Cornell University Press, Ithaca and London, 1983), Chapter 5, 'Regimes and the limits of Realism: Regimes as autonomous variables', p. 358.
8. *Ibid.*, p. 360.
9. See C. Jonsson, *International Aviation and the Politics of Regime Change* (Frances Pinter, London, 1987), Introduction.
10. R. W. Mansbach and J. A. Vasquez, *In Search of Theory. A New Paradigm for Global Politics* (Columbia University Press, New York, 1981), p. 62.
11. D. Easton, *A Systems Analysis of Political Life* (The University of Chicago Press, Chicago and London, 1979, first pub. 1965), p. 45.
12. *Ibid.*
13. Mansbach and Vasquez, *op. cit.*, p. 56.
14. J. Donnelly, 'The United Nations and the global drug control regime', pp. 282–304, quote at pp. 282–3, in P. H. Smith (ed.), *Drug Policy in the Americas* (Westview Press, Oxford, 1992).
15. J. Donnelly, 'International human rights: A regime analysis', *International Organization*, Vol. 40, No. 3, Summer 1986, pp. 599–642. Types of international regimes at pp. 603–4.
16. K. D. Wolf and M. Zurn, '"International Regimes" und Theorien der Internationalen Politik', *Politische Vierteljahresschrift*, Vol. 27, pp. 210–21, as quoted in V. Rittberger (ed.), *Regime Theory and International Relations* (Clarendon Press, Oxford, 1993), p. 9.
17. Rittberger, *op. cit.*, p. 9. See also M. Mendler, 'Working conditions of foreign journalists in East–West relations: Regulating a conflict about values without a regime', in Rittberger, *op. cit.*, pp. 216–49.
18. '£70m cocaine haul "marks end of territorial policing"', *Guardian*, 11.1.94.
19. See Declaration 32 of the Final Act of the Maastricht Treaty in *The Unseen Treaty. Treaty on European Union. Maastricht 1992* (David Pollard Publishing, Oxford, 1992), p. 63.
20. See, 'Pressure grows for an EC-wide detective force', *Independent*, 20.4.92. The UK National Criminal Intelligence System (NCIS) came

into being on 1 April 1990. Consisting of five regional offices and a London base, NCIS was a new departure for the British police.

21. R. Birch, 'Why Europe Needs Interpol', *Police Review*, 17.1.92, as quoted in B. Hebenton and T. Thomas, 'Rocky path to Europol. Europe's police see information-sharing as the key to controlling the traffickers, but who controls the controllers?' *Druglink*, Vol. 7, issue 6, November–December 1992, p. 9.

22. 'Drugs liberalisation attacked', *Financial Times*, 20.5.94.

23. 'German judge says legal ban of soft drugs violates constitution', *Guardian*, 29.2.92.

24. A series of articles by Nadelmann that appeared in the journals *Foreign Policy*, *The Public Interest* and *Science* were of particular significance. In 1987, Trebach, a university professor, established the Drug Policy Foundation in Washington, DC, which became the most significant American institutional voice against the drug war.

25. M. Friedman and T. Szasz, *On Liberty and Drugs: Essays on the Free Market and Prohibition*, ed. by A. S. Trebach and K. B. Zeese (The Drug Policy Foundation Press, Washington, DC, 1992).

26. E. Brecher, *Licit and Illicit Drugs,* Greenwood Press, Boston, 1972).

27. See, for example, the editorial of *The Independent* on 15.5.93, 'Thinking the unthinkable on drug-related crime', and 2.10.93, 'A drug law that promotes crime'; also, 'It doesn't have to be like this', *The Economist*, 2.10.89, and 'Bring drugs within the law', 15.5.93.

28. See E. A. Nadelmann, 'The case for legalisation' in J. A. Inciardi (ed.), *The Drug Legalization Debate* (Studies in Crime, Law and Justice, Vol. 7, Sage Publications, London, 2nd edn 1991), p. 19.

29. 'Drug law foes praise Schultz for new stand', *Santa Cruz Sentinel* (Associated Press), 11.13.89, as quoted in C. Reinarman and H. G. Levine, 'A peace movement has emerged against the War on Drugs', *The International Journal on Drug Policy*, Vol. 2, No 1, July/August 1990, pp. 10–12, quote at p. 11.

30. 'Judge advocates legalising drugs', *Independent*, 13.10.93 and 'Legalise all drugs says Judge Pickles', *Daily Mail*, 6.6.91.

31. See 'Depenalise drug use, says Interpol boss', *Independent*, 30.12.93; 'Legalise drugs now: it's the only answer', *Daily Telegraph*, 5.10.93; 'Police chief queries drug law', *Guardian*, 23.5.94.

32. *The Lancet*, Vol. 337, 16.2.91, p. 402.

33. It has been estimated that more than 50 per cent of all the people with AIDS in New York, and many other parts of the country, as well as the majority of AIDS-infected homosexuals, have contracted the disease directly or indirectly through illegal intravenous drug use. See Nadelmann in Inciardi, *op. cit.*, p. 34.

34. See 'Legalising drugs: Another look', *The Economist*, 22.1.94.

35. Coordinamento Radicale Antiproibizionista, *The Cost of Prohibition On Drugs. Papers of the International Anti-Prohibitionism Forum* (CORA, Italy, 1989) and A. S. Trebach and K. Zeese (eds), *Drug Policy 1989–1990. A Reformer's Catalogue* (Drug Policy Foundation, Washington, DC, 1989).

36. In the summer of 1992 the Bolivian government began an international

campaign to legalise coca leaf exports in the form of herbal tea. Coca and all its derivatives are currently classified as intoxicants by the Vienna Convention. The government emphasised the nutritional and medical uses of the drug at the 22nd Assembly of the Organization of American States in Nassau, calling for 'the legitimate industrialisation and commercialisation of the sub-products derived from the innocent coca leaf and its protein-rich and medicinal qualities'. Mr Ronald MacLean, Bolivian Foreign Minister, as reported in *The Financial Times*, 3.5.92.
37. 'Spanish judges campaign to legalise drugs', *Independent*, 16.2.91. Recently, however, the Spanish government has enacted legislation that strengthens measures to prevent drug use.
38. 'One in three backs legalising cannabis', *Independent*, 3.3.94.
39. 'Magistrates oppose rise in drug fines', *Guardian*, 15.2.94.

Bibliography

THEORETICAL SOURCES

E. Adler and P. M. Haas, 'Conclusion: epistemic communities, world order, and the creation of a reflective research program', *International Organization*, Vol. 46, No. 1, Winter 1992.

R. J. Barry Jones and P. Willetts (eds), *Interdependence on Trial. Studies in the Theory and Reality of Contemporary Interdependence* (Frances Pinter, London, 1984).

C. R. Beitz, *Political Theory and International Relations* (Princeton University Press, Princeton, New Jersey, 1979).

C. Brown, *International Relations Theory: New Normative Approaches* (Columbia University Press, New York, 1992).

A. Chetley, *The Politics of Baby Food: Successful Challenges to an International Marketing Strategy* (Frances Pinter, London, 1986).

R. W. Cox, 'The crisis of world order and the problem of international organization in the 1980s', *International Journal*, Vol. XXXV, No. 2, Spring 1980.

J. Donnelly, 'International human rights: A regime analysis', *International Organization* Vol. 40, No. 3, Summer 1986.

E. Durkheim, *The Rules of Sociological Method* (Free Press, New York, 1964).

D. Easton, *The Political System. An Enquiry Into the State of Political Science* (Alfred A. Knopf, New York, 1953).

D. Easton, *A Framework for Political Analysis* (Prentice-Hall, Inc, Cliffs, New Jersey, Englewood 1965).

D. Easton, *A Systems Analysis of Political Life* (The University of Chicago Press, Chicago and London, 1979, first pub. 1965).

P. B. Evans et al. (eds), *Bringing the State Back In* (Cambridge University Press, Cambridge, 1985).

R. B. Farell (ed.), *Approaches to Comparative and International Politics* (Northwestern University Press, Evaston, 1966).

Y. Ferguson and R. W. Mansbach, *The Elusive Quest: Theory and International Politics* (University of South Carolina Press, Columbia, SC, 1988).

M. Frost, *Towards a Normative Theory of International Relations* (Cambridge University Press, Cambridge, 1986).

R. Gilpin, *US Power and the Multinational Corporation* (Basic Books, New York, 1975).

A. J. R. Groom and P. Taylor (eds), *Frameworks for International Cooperation* (Pinter Publishers, London, 1990).

E. B. Haas, 'Is there a hole in the whole? Knowledge, technology, interdependence, and the construction of international regimes', *International Organization*, Vol. 29, No. 3, Summer 1975.

E. B. Haas, 'Why collaborate? Issue-linkage and international regimes', *World Politics*, Vol. 32, No. 3, April 1980.

P. M. Haas, 'Do regimes matter? Epistemic communities and Mediterranean pollution', *International Organization*, Vol. 43, No. 3, Summer 1989.

P. M. Haas, 'Obtaining international environmental protection through epistemic consensus', *Millennium: Journal of International Studies*, Vol. 19, No. 3, 1990.

P. M. Haas, 'Banning chlorofluorocarbons: Epistemic community efforts to protect stratospheric ozone', *International Organization*, Vol. 46, No. 1, Winter 1992.

P. M. Haas (ed.), 'Knowledge, power, and international policy coordination', *International Organization*, Special Issue, Vol. 46, No. 1, Winter 1992.

S. Haggard and B. A. Simmons, 'Theories of international regimes', *International Organization*, Vol. 41, No. 3, Summer 1987.

J. A. Hall (ed.), *States in History* (Basil Blackwell, Oxford, 1986).

H. L. A. Hart, *The Concept of Law* (Oxford University Press, Oxford, 1961).

C. Hartman and P. Vilanova (eds), *Paradigms Lost: The Post Cold War Era* (Pluto Press and TNI, London, 1992).

T. Hobbes, *Leviathan* (Oxford University Press, Oxford, 1962, first pub. 1651).

S. Hoffman, 'Rousseau on war and peace', *American Political Science Review*, Vol. 57, No. 2, June 1963.

C. Jonsson, *International Aviation and the Politics of Regime Change* (Frances Pinter, London, 1987).

R. O. Keohane, *After Hegemony. Cooperation and Discord in the World Political Economy* (Princeton University Press, Princeton, New Jersey, 1984).

R. O. Keohane, *Neorealism and its Critics* (Columbia University Press, New York, 1986).

R. O. Keohane, *International Institutions and State Power: Essays in International Relations Theory* (Boulder, Colo., 1989).

R. O. Keohane and J. S. Nye (eds), *Transnational Relations and World Politics* (Harvard University Press, Cambridge, Mass., 1971).

R. O. Keohane and J. S. Nye, *Power and Interdependence: World Politics in Transition* (Little, Brown, Boston, 1977).

S. Kim, *A Quest for a Just World Order* (Westview Special Studies in International Relations, Westview Press, Boulder, Colorado, 1984).

C. P. Kindleberger, *The World in Depression 1929–1939* (University of California Press, Berkeley, 1973).

C. P. Kindleberger, 'Hierarchy versus inertial cooperation', *International Organization*, Vol. 40, No. 2, Spring 1986.

S. D. Krasner, 'State power and the structure of international trade', *World Politics*, Vol. 28, No. 3, April 1976.

S. D. Krasner (ed.), *International Regimes* (Cornell University Press, Ithaca, New York and London 4th edn 1986, first pub. 1983).

F. Kratochwil, 'The force of prescriptions', *International Organization*, Vol. 38, No. 4, Autumn 1984.

F. Kratochwil, 'On the relevance of International Law', *Journal of International Affairs*, Vol. 37, Winter 1984.

F. Kratochwil, 'Rules, norms, values and the limits of "Rationality"', Archiv für Rechts- und Sozialphilosophie, Vol. 73, 1987.

F. Kratochwil, 'Regimes, interpretation and the "Science" of politics: A reappraisal', *Millennium: Journal of International Studies*, Vol. 17, No. 2, 1988.

F. Kratochwil, *Rules, Norms, and Decisions. On the conditions of practical and legal reasoning in international relations and domestic affairs* (Cambridge University Press, Cambridge, 1991).

F. Kratochwil and E. D. Mansfield, *International Organization. A Reader* (HarperCollins, New York, 1994).

F. Kratochwil and J. G. Ruggie, 'International organization: A state of the art or an art of the state', *International Organization*, Vol. 40, No. 4, Autumn 1986.

K. R. Leube, *The Essence of Friedman* (Hoover Institute Press, Stanford, CA, 1987).

A. Linklater, *Men and Citizens in the Theory of International Relations* (Macmillan, London, 1990, first pub. 1982).

A. Linklater, 'International Relations theory: A critical-theoretical point of view', *Millennium: Journal of International Studies*, Vol. 21, No. 1, 1992.

R. M. MacLean, 'The proper function of International Law in the determination of global behaviour', *The Canadian Yearbook of International Law*, 1989.

R. W. Mansbach and J. A. Vasquez, *In Search of Theory. A New Paradigm for Global Politics* (Columbia University Press, New York, 1981).

J. G. March and J. Olson, 'The new institutionalism: Organisational factors in political life', *American Political Science Review*, Vol. 78, September 1984.

J. S. Mill, *On Liberty* (Penguin Books, Middlesex, 1986, first pub. 1859).

H. J. Morgenthau, *Politics Among Nations: The Struggle for Power and Peace* (Alfred A. Knopf, New York, 2nd edn 1954, first pub. 1948).

H. J. Morgenthau and K. W. Thompson (eds), *Principles and Problems of International Politics* (Alfred A. Knopf, New York, 1950).

E. A. Nadelmann, 'Global prohibition regimes: the evolution of norms in international society', *International Organization*, Vol. 44, No. 4, Autumn 1990.

T. Nardin, *Law, Morality, and the Relations of States* (Princeton University Press, Princeton, 1983).

R. O'Brien, *Global Financial Integration: The End of Geography* (Royal Institute of International Affairs, Pinter, London, 1992).

F. Parkinson, *The Philosophy of International Relations: A Study in the History of Thought* (Sage, London, 1977).

T. Parsons, 'The distribution of power in American society', *World Politics*, Vol. X, No. 1, October 1957.

T. Parsons and E. Shils (eds), *Toward a General Theory of Action* (Harvard University Press, Cambridge, Mass., 1951).

C. Politt et al., *Public Policy in Theory and Practice* (Hodder and Stoughton, Open University Press, Sevenoaks, 1979).

J. Rawls, *A Theory of Justice* (Harvard University Press, Cambridge, Mass., 1971).

J. P. Renninger, *The Future Role of the United Nations in an Interdependent World* (Martinus Nijhoff Publishers, London, 1989).

V. Rittberger, *International Regimes in East–West Politics* (Pinter Publishers, London, 1990).

V. Rittberger (ed.), *Regime Theory and International Relations* (Clarendon Press, Oxford, 1993).

M. Rokeach, *The Nature of Human Values* (Free Press, New York, 1973).

J. N. Rosenau (ed.), *International Politics and Foreign Policy: A Reader in International Theory* (Free Press, New York, 1961).

J. N. Rosenau, *The Scientific Study of Foreign Policy* (The Free Press, New York, 1971).

J. N. Rosenau, *The Study of Global Interdependence: Essays on the Transnationalization of World Affairs* (Frances Pinter, London, 1980).

J. N. Rosenau and E. O. Czempiel (eds), *Governance without Government: Order and Change in World Politics* (Cambridge University Press, Cambridge, 1992).

P. Rosenau, 'Once again into the fray: International Relations confronts the Humanities', *Millennium: Journal of International Studies*, Vol. 19, No. 1, 1990.

J. G. Ruggie, 'International responses to technology: Concepts and trends', *International Organization*, Vol. 29, No. 3, Summer 1975.

J. A. Scholte, 'From power politics to social change', *Review of International Studies*, Vol. 19, No. 1, January 1993.

L. Sklair, *Sociology of the Global System* (Harvester Wheatsheaf, London, 1991).

T. Skocpol, *States and Social Revolutions: A Comparative Analysis of France, Russia and China* (Cambridge University Press, Cambridge, 1979).

P. Taylor, *International Organization in the Modern World* (Pinter Publishers, London and New York, 1993).

P. Taylor and A. J. R. Groom (eds), *International Institutions at Work* (Pinter Publishers, London, 1988).

E. Ullmann-Margalit, *The Emergence of Norms* (Oxford University Press, Oxford, 1977).

K. Waltz, *Theory of International Relations* (Addison-Wesley, Reading, Mass., 1979).

V. Ward, 'Regime norms as 'implicit' third parties: Explaining the Anglo-Argentine relationship', *Review of International Studies*, Vol. 17, 1991.

D. C. Watt et al., 'What is diplomatic history?' *History Today*, Vol. 18, 1985.

P. Willetts, *Pressure Groups in the Global System. The Transnational Relations of Issue-Orientated Non-Governmental Organizations* (Frances Pinter, London, 1982).

P. Willetts, *Transnational Actors and Changing World Order* (Occasional Papers Series No. 17, PRIME, International Peace Research Institute, Meigaku, Japan, 1993).

P. Willetts with M. Bentham, P. Hough and D. Humphreys, 'The issue of issues in Regime Theory: Use of the concepts of Issues, Issue-Linkages and Policy domains in the study of international organisations and international regimes'. Unpublished paper presented at the British International Studies Association, Global Environmental Change Group, City University, 17 July 1992.

R. M. Williams, *American Society. A Sociological Interpretation* (Alfred A. Knopf, New York, 2nd edn, revised, 1968, first pub. 1951).

O. R. Young, 'International regimes: Problems of concept formation', *World Politics*, Vol. 32, No. 3, April 1980.

O. R. Young, 'International regimes: Toward a new theory of institutions', *World Politics*, Vol. 29, October 1986.

O. R. Young, 'The politics of international regime formation: Managing natural resources and the environment', *International Organization*, Vol. 43, No. 3, Summer 1989.

O. R. Young, *International Cooperation. Building Regimes for Natural Resources and the Environment* (Cornell University Press, Ithaca and London, 1989).

O. R. Young, and G. Osherenko (eds), *Polar Politics Creating International Environmental Regimes* (Cornell University Press, Ithaca and London, 1993).

EMPIRICAL SOURCES

Books

R. Ashley, *Cocaine: Its History, Uses, and Effects* (St. Martin's Press, New York, 1975).

P. Bean, *The Social Control of Drugs* (Martin Robertson, London, 1974).

V. Berridge and G. Edwards, *Opium and the People. Opiate Use in Nineteenth-Century England* (Yale University Press, New Haven and London, 1987).

E. M. Brecher, *Licit and Illicit Drugs* (Greenwood Press, Boston, 1972).

F. Bresler, *The Trail of the Triads: An Investigation into International Crime* (Weidenfeld and Nicolson, London, 1980).

K. Bruun, L. Pan and I. Rexed, *The Gentlemens Club* (University of Chicago Press, Chicago, 1975).

P. Cohen, *Drugs as a Social Construct* (University of Amsterdam, Amsterdam, 1990).

D. T. Courtwright, *Dark Paradise. Opiate Addiction in America before 1840* (Harvard University Press, London, 1982).

T. Dennett, *Americans in Eastern Asia: A Critical Study of the Policy of the US with Reference to China, Japan and Korea in the Nineteenth Century* (Barnes and Noble, Inc, New York, 1941).

N. Dorn, K. Murji and N. South, *Traffickers. Drug Markets and Law Enforcement* (Routledge, London and New York, 1992).

T. Draper, *A Very Thin Line: The Iran–Contra Affairs* (Hill and Wang, New York, 1991).

P. Eddy, H. Sabogal, S. Walden, *The Cocaine Wars* (Arrow Books, London, 1988).

G. Edwards, *Alcohol Problems in the Developing Countries* (World Health Organization, Geneva, 1978).

R. Fagan, *Forging Peace: The Challenge of Central America* (Basil Blackwell, New York, 1987).

J. Fairbank, *Trade and Diplomacy on the China Coast* (Harvard University Press, Cambridge, Mass., 1953).

M. Friedman and T. Szasz, *On Liberty and Drugs: Essays on the Free Market and Prohibition*, ed. A. S. Trebach and K. B. Zeese (Drug Policy Foundation Press, Washington, DC, 1992).

W. Greenhaw, *Flying High: Inside Big Time Drug Smuggling* (Dodd, Mead, New York, 1984).

L. Grinspoon and J. Bakalar, *Cocaine: A Drug and Its Social Evolution* (Basic Books, New York, 1976).

G. Gugliotta, *Kings of Cocaine: Inside the Medellin Cartel* (Simon and Schuster, New York, 1989).

R. Hamowy (ed.), *Dealing with Drugs* (D. C. Heath and Company, Lexington, Mass., 1987).

B. Harrison, *Drink and the Victorians. The Temperance Question in England 1815–1872* (Faber and Faber, London, 1971).

E. J. Hobsbawm, *Industry and Empire: The Making of Modern English Society* (Pantheon, New York, 1968).

N. Hopkinson, *Fighting the Drug Problem* (Wilton Park Papers 15, HMSO, London, 1990).

M. H. Hunt, *The Making of a Special Relationship: The United States and China to 1914* (Columbia University Press, New York, 1983).

J. A. Inciardi, *The Drug–Crime Connection* (Sage, Beverly Hills, 1981).

J. A. Inciardi (ed.), *The Drug Legalization Debate* (Studies in Crime, Law and Justice, Vol. 7, Sage Publications, London, 2nd edn 1991).

B. Inglis, *The Forbidden Game. A Social History of Drugs* (Hodder and Stoughton, London, 1975).

R. G. A. Jackson, *A Study of the Capacity of the United Nations Development System*, United Nations document DP/5 1969 (Geneva, 1969).

A. Jamieson, *Global Drug Trafficking* (Conflict Studies 234, Research Institute for the Study of Conflict and Terrorism, 1990).

A. Jamieson, *Drug Trafficking After 1992. A Special Report* (Conflict Studies 250, Research Institute for the Study of Conflict and Terrorism, 1992).

C. J. Johns, *Power, Ideology, and the War on Drugs* (Praeger Series in Criminology and Crime Control Policy, Praeger, New York, 1992).

H. C. Jones and P. W. Lovinger, *The Marijuana Question* (Dodd, Mead, New York, 1985).

T. E. Jordan, *Victorian Childhood: Themes and Variations* (State University of New York Press, 1987).

J. Kaplan, *The Hardest Drug: Heroin and Public Policy* (University of Chicago Press, Chicago, 1983).

K. Kramer and J. Cameron (eds), *A Manual on Drug Dependence* (World Health Organization, Geneva, 1975).

W. Ladd Hollist and F. LaMond Tullis, *Pursuing Food Security. Strategies and Obstacles in Africa, Asia, Latin America and the Middle East* (Lynne Rienner Publishers, Boulder and London, 1987).

P. D. Lowes, *The Genesis of International Narcotics Control* (Droz, Geneva, 1966).

S. B. MacDonald, *Dancing on a Volcano: The Latin American Drug Trade* (Praeger, New York, 1988).

S. B. MacDonald, *Mountain High, White Avalanche. Cocaine and Power in the Andean States and Panama* (Washington Papers 137, Praeger, New York, 1989).

A. W. McCoy, *The Politics of Heroin. CIA Complicity in the Global Drug Trade* (Lawrence Hill Books, New York, 1991).

A. W. McCoy and A. Block (eds), *War on Drugs. Studies in the Failure of U.S. Narcotics Policy* (Westview Press, Oxford, 1992).

E. Morales, *Cocaine: White Gold Rush in Peru* (University of Arizona Press, Tucson, 1989).

D. F. Musto, *The American Disease. Origins of Narcotic Control* (Yale University Press, New Haven and London, 1973).

R. T. Naylor, *Hot Money and the Politics of Debt* (Simon and Schuster, New York, 1987).

R. O'Brien, *Global Financial Integration: The End of Geography* (Royal Institute of International Affairs, Pinter, London, 1992).

D. E. Owen, *British Opium Policy in China and India* (Yale University Press, New Haven, 1934).

T. M. Parssinen, *Secret Passions, Secret Remedies: Narcotic Drugs in British Society, 1820–1930* (Institute for the Study of Human Issues, Philadelphia, 1993).

J. L. Philips and R. W. Wynne, *Cocaine: The Mystique and the Reality* (Avon Books, New York, 1980).

R. E. Powis, *The Money Launderers* (Probus Publishing Company, Chicago and Cambridge, 1992).

F. Robertson, *Triangle of Death: The Inside Story of the Triads – The Chinese Mafia* (Routledge and Kegan Paul, London, 1977).

J. Rowntree, *The Imperial Drug Trade* (Methuen and Co., London, 1905).

R. Rudgley, *The Alchemy of Culture. Intoxicants in Society* (British Museum Press, London, 1993).

P. H. Smith (ed.), *Drug Policy in the Americas* (Westview Press, Oxford, 1992).

S. D. Stein, *International Diplomacy, State Administrators and Narcotics Control. The Origins of a Social Problem* (Gower, Aldershot, 1985).

R. Stevenson, *Winning The War on Drugs: To Legalise Or Not?* (Hobart Paper 124, The Institute of Economic Affairs, London, 1994).

M. Sutton and A. Maynard, *Trends in the Cost Effectiveness of Enforcement Activity in the Illicit Heroin Market, 1979–1990* (Centre for Health Economics, University of York, 1994).

A. H. Taylor, *American Diplomacy and the Narcotics Traffic, 1900–1939. A Study in International Humanitarian Reform* (Duke University Press, Durham, NC, 1969).

P. Taylor, *The Smoke Ring: Tobacco, Money and Multinational Politics* (Mentor, New York, 1985).

C. E. Terry and M. Pellens, *The Opium Problem* (Patterson Smith, London, 1970, first pub. 1928).

P. Thane (ed.), *The Origins of British Social Policy* (Croom Helm, London, 1978).

R. H. Veith, *Multinational Computer Net: The Case of International Banking* (Lexington Books, New York, 1981).

B. Webb and S. Webb, *The History of Liquor Licensing in England* (Longman Group, London, 1903).

Wen-tsao Wu, *The Chinese Opium Question in British Opinion and Action* (Academy Press, New York, 1928).

B. Whitaker, *The Global Connection. The Crisis of Drug Addiction* (Jonathan Cape, London, 1987).

S. Wisotsky, *Breaking the Impasse* (Greenwood Press, New York, 1986).

J. H. Young, *The Toadstool Millionaires: A Social History of Patent Medicines in America before Federal Regulation* (Princeton University Press, Princeton, 1961).

F. E. Zimring and G. Hawkins, *The Search for Rational Drug Control* (Cambridge University Press, Cambridge, 1992).

Journals

C. Abel, 'Columbia and the drug barons: Conflict and containment', *The World Today*, May 1993.

D. Aitken and T. Mikuriya, 'The forgotten medicine. A look at the medical uses of cannabis', *Ecologist*, Vol. 10, Nos. 8/9, Oct–Nov. 1980.

P. R. Andreas and K. E. Sharpe, 'Cocaine Politics in the Andes', *Current History*, 91, February 1992.

D. Anglin and G. Speckart, 'Narcotics use and crime: A multi-method analysis', *Criminology*, Vol. 26, No. 2, 1988.

G. Arnao, 'The Semantics of Prohibition', *The International Journal on Drug Policy*, Vol. 2, No. 1.

B. M. Bagley, 'Columbia and the War on Drugs', *Foreign Affairs*, Fall 1988, No. 67105.

R. Baratta, 'Political violence in Ecuador and the AVC', *Terrorism*, Vol. 10, 1987.

J. B. Brown, 'Politics of the poppy: The Society for the Suppression of the Opium Trade, 1974–1916', *Journal of Contemporary History*, Vol. 8, July 1973.

B. Bullington and A. A. Block, 'A Trojan horse: Anti-communism and the war on drugs', *Contemporary Crises*, Vol. 14, 1990, pp. 39–55.

D. Cheney, 'DOD and its role in the War against Drugs', *Defense*, Nov–Dec 1989.

J. Dillin, 'Nation's liberties at risk?', *Christian Science Monitor*, 2.2.90.

D. A. Eastwood and H. J. Pollard, 'The accelerating growth of coca and colonisation in Bolivia', *Geography*, Vol. 72, 1987.

W. C. Gilmore, 'International action against drug trafficking: Trends in United Kingdom law and practice', *The International Lawyer*, Vol. 24, No. 2, Summer 1990.

P. Grier, 'Pentagon's support role increases', *Christian Science Monitor*, 1.9.89.

B. Hebenton and T. Thomas, 'Rocky path to Europol. Europe's police see information-sharing as the key to controlling the traffickers, but who controls the controllers?' *Druglink. The Journal of Drug Misuse in Britain*, Vol. 7, issue 6, Nov–Dec 1992.

G. L. Henderson, 'Designer Drugs: Past History and Future Prospects', *Journal of Forensic Sciences*, Vol. 33, No. 2, March 1988, pp. 569–75.

E. S. Herman, 'U.S. sponsorship of international terrorism: An overview', *Crime and Social Justice*, Nos. 27–28, 1987.

J. A. Inciardi, 'Beyond cocaine: basuco, crack, and other coca products', *Contemporary Drug Problems*, Fall 1987.

B. D. Johnson, 'Righteousness before revenue: The forgotten moral crusade against the Indo-Chinese opium trade', *Journal of Drug Issues*, Fall 1975.

E. Josephson, 'Marijuana decriminalization: The process and prospects of change', *Contemporary Drug Problems*, Fall 1981.

J. Kaplan, 'Taking Drugs Seriously', *The Public Interest*, 92, Summer 1988, pp. 32–50.

D. P. Kumarasingha, 'Drugs: A growing problem in Sri Lanka', *Forensic Science International*, Vol. 36, 1988.

V. Kusevic, 'Drug abuse control and international treaties', *Journal of Drug Issues*, Vol. 7, No. 1, 1977.

R. W. Lee III, 'The Latin American Drug Connection', *Foreign Policy* 61, Winter 1985/86.

R. W. Lee III, 'Why the U.S. cannot stop South American cocaine', *ORBIS, Journal of World Affairs*, Vol. 32, Part 4, Fall 1988.

R. W. Lee III, 'Dimensions of the South American cocaine industry', *Journal of Interamerican Studies and World Affairs*, Vol. 30, Nos. 2–3, 1988.

M. Levi, 'Regulating money laundering: The death mark of bank secrecy in the UK', *British Journal of Criminology*, Vol. 31, 1991.

E. A. Nadelmann, 'Negotiations in criminal law assistance treaties', *American Journal of Comparative Law*, Vol. 33, 1985.

E. A. Nadelmann, 'Unlaundering dirty money abroad: US foreign policy and financial secrecy jurisdictions', *Inter-American Law Review*, Vol. 18, 1986.

E. A. Nadelmann, 'Drug prohibition in the United States: Costs, consequences, and alternatives', *Science*, Vol. 245, 1 September 1989.

R. del Olmo, 'Aerobiology and the war on drugs: a transnational crime', *Social Justice*, No. 30, 1987.

P. J. Rice, 'New laws and insights encircle the Posse Comitatus Act', *Military Law Review*, Vol. 104, Spring 1984.

G. Saltmarsh, 'Tracking dirty money down to the cleaners', *Police Review*, 8 June 1990.

D. W. Sproule and P. St-Denis, 'The UN Drug Trafficking Convention: An ambitious step', *The Canadian Yearbook of International Law*, 1989.

J. G. Starke, 'The 1936 Convention for the Suppression of the Illicit Traffic in Dangerous Drugs', *American Journal of International Law*, Vol. 31, 1937.

G. L. Sternbach, MD, and J. Varon, MD, 'Designer drugs. Recognizing and managing their toxic effects', *Postgraduate Medicine*, Vol 91, No. 8, June 1992.

D. Stewart, 'Internationalizing The War on Drugs: The UN Convention Against Illicit Traffic in Narcotic Drugs and Psychotropic Substances', *Denver Journal of International Law and Policy*, Vol. 18, No. 3, 1990.

V. P. Vatuk and S. J. Vatuk, 'Chatorpan: A culturally defined form of addiction in North India', *International Journal of the Addictions*, Vol. 2, No. 1, Spring 1967.

A. Wagstaff and A. Maynard, 'Economic aspects of the illicit drug market and drug enforcement policies in the United Kingdom: Summary of the report', *British Journal of Addiction*, Vol. 84, 1989.

United Nations documents

Report of the Group of High-Level Intergovernmental Experts to Review the Efficiency of the Administrative and Financial Functioning of the United Nations, General Assembly Official Records; Forty-First Session, Supplement No. 49 (A/41/49), New York, 1986.

Report of the International Conference on Drug Abuse and Illicit Trafficking, Vienna, 17–26 June 1987, United Nations document A/CONF.133/12.

United Nations Conference for the Adoption of a Convention Against the Illicit Traffic in Narcotic Drugs and Psychotropic Substances, Vienna, Austria, 25 November–20 December 1988, United Nations document E/CONF.82/4.

United Nations Convention Against Illicit Traffic in Narcotic Drugs and Psychotropic Substances, Vienna, 19 December 1988. United Nations Document E/CONF.82/15.

Report of the Second Interregional Meeting of Heads of National Drug Law Enforcement Agencies, Vienna, 11–15 September 1989, United Nations document E/CN.7/1990/2.

Ninth Conference of the Non-Aligned Countries, Belgrade, Yugoslavia, 1989, United Nations document A/44/551.

Letter dated 20 February 1990 from the Permanent Representatives of Bolivia, Colombia, Peru and the United States of America to the United Nations addressed to the Secretary-General. United Nations document A/S-17/8.

Declaration of the World Ministerial Summit to Reduce the Demand for Drugs and to Combat the Cocaine Threat, held in London from 9–11 April 1990, United Nations document A/45/262.

Report of the Third Meeting of Heads of National Drug Law Enforcement Agencies (HONLEA), Africa, held at Cairo from 4 to 8 June 1990. See United Nations document E/CN.7/1991/2.

Eighth United Nations Congress on the Prevention of Crime and the Treatment of Offenders, Havana, 27 August–7 September 1990 (United Nations publication, Sales No. E.91.IV.2).

Report of the Economic and Social Council, International Action to Combat Drug Abuse and Illicit Trafficking: International co-operation in drug abuse control. Report of the Secretary-General. United Nations document A/45/542, 23 October 1990.

Political Declaration and Global Programme of Action adopted by the General Assembly at its seventeenth special session, devoted to the question of international co-operation against illicit production, supply, demand, trafficking and distribution of narcotic drugs and psychotropic substances, 15 March 1990. United Nations document A/RES/S-17/2.

Enhancement of the Efficiency of the United Nations Structure for Drug Abuse

Control. Report of the Secretary-General, 23 October 1990. United Nations document A/45/652/Add.1.

Report of the International Narcotics Control Board for 1990, United Nations document E/INCB/1990/1.

Report of the International Narcotics Control Board for 1991, United Nations document E/INCB/1991/1.

Report of the Commission on Narcotic Drugs on its Thirty-Fifth Session, Vienna, 6–15 April 1992, United Nations document E/CN.7/1992/14.

Crime Prevention and Criminal Justice. The strengthening of international cooperation in combatting organized crime. Report of the Secretary General United Nations document A/47/381, 28 September 1992.

Report of the International Narcotics Control Board for 1992, United Nations document E/INCB/1992/1.

Report of the International Narcotics Control Board for 1993, United Nations document E/INCB/1993/1.

Commission on Narcotic Drugs, *Activities of the United Nations International Drug Control Programme. Report of the Executive Director*, 8 February 1993. United Nations document E/CN.7/1993/3.

Fund of the United Nations International Drug Control Programme: Proposed Revision of the Programme Budget for the Biennium 1992–1993 and Proposed Outline for the Biennium 1994–1995. Report of the Executive Director. United Nations document E/CN.7/1993/5.

Non-UN documents

Report of the British Delegates to the International Opium Conference, Held at the Hague, Dec. 1911–Jan. 1912, Miscellaneous No. 11 (1912), Cd. 6448. H.M. Stationery Office, London, 1912.

Measures Against the Transfer and Safekeeping of Funds of Criminal Origin: Recommendation No. R(80)10 adopted by the Committee of Ministers of the Council of Europe on 27 June 1980 and Explanatory Memorandum, Council of Europe, Strasbourg.

Home Affairs Committee, *Misuse of Hard Drugs* (Interim Report), House of Commons Paper No. 399, HMSO, 1985.

International Narcotics Control Strategy Report, 1 March 1988 (US Department of State, Washington, DC).

Dr. S. K. Chatterjee, *A Guide to the International Drug Conventions: Explanatory materials for the preparation of legislation in the implementation of the major international drug conventions* (Commonwealth Secretariat, London, 1988).

Basle Committee on Banking Regulations and Supervisory Practices, *Prevention of criminal use of the banking system for the purpose of money-laundering. Statement of Principles.* December 1988.

US Senate Committee on Foreign Relations. Subcommittee on Terrorism, Narcotics, and International Operations, *Drugs, Law Enforcement, and Foreign Policy*. US Government Printing Office, Washington, DC, 5 May 1989.

The United States Attorneys and Attorney General of the United States, *Drug Trafficking, A Report to the President of the United States*, 3 August

1989, US Department of Justice, Office of the Attorney General.

National Drug Control Strategy, Office of National Drug Control Policy, US Government Printing Office, Washington, DC, 1989.

Financial Action Task Force on Money Laundering. Report of 7 February 1990, Paris.

Report of the Caribbean Drug Money Laundering Conference, Oranjestad, Aruba, 8–10 June 1990, Foreign and Commonwealth Office, London.

The Drugs Trade in Latin America Report, Latin American Newsletters, London, 1990.

Commission of the European Communities: Proposal for a Council Directive on Prevention of Use of the Financial System for the Purpose of Money Laundering and Explanatory Memorandum, 23 March 1990.

Joint Money Laundering Working Group, *Money Laundering: Guidance Notes for Banks and Building Societies*, December 1990.

House of Lords, Select Committee on the European Communities, *Money Laundering* House of Lords Paper No. 6, 1990–91.

'Money laundering: A Central Banker's view'. A speech given by Brian Quinn, Executive Director of the Bank of England at the Conference arranged by the Joint Working Group on the Financial System's role in Combating Money Laundering, 11 February 1991, London.

Dr W. C. Gilmore, *Combatting International Drugs Trafficking: The 1988 United Nations Convention Against Illicit Traffic in Narcotic Drugs and Psychotropic Substances*, Explanatory Documentation (Commonwealth Secretariat, London, 1991).

F. LaMond Tullis, *Beneficiaries of the Illicit Drug Trade: Political Consequences and International Policy at the Intersection of Supply and Demand*, United Nations Research Institute for Social Development, Discussion Paper 19, Geneva, March 1991.

F. LaMond Tullis, *Illicit Drug Taking and Prohibition Laws: Public Consequences and the Reform of Public Policy in the United States*, Discussion Paper 21, United Nations Research Institute for Social Development, Geneva, April 1991.

Financial Action Task Force on Money Laundering. Report of 13 May 1991, Paris.

Council of the European Communities, *Council Directive of 10 June 1991 on Prevention of the Use of the Financial System for Purpose of Money Laundering*, Brussels, Document number 91/308/EEC.

Joint Money Laundering Working Group, *Money Laundering: Guidance Notes for Insurance Business*, July 1991.

Joint Money Laundering Working Group, *Guidance Notes for Investment Business*, September 1991.

The Unseen Treaty on European Union, Maastricht 1992 (David Pollard Publishing, Oxford, 1992).

International Efforts to Combat Money Laundering. Cambridge International Documents Series, Volume 4. Edited by Dr W. C. Gilmore in association with The Commonwealth Secretariat, London (Grotius Publications Ltd., Cambridge, 1992).

World Bank, *Bolivia: agricultural sector review*, Report No. 9882–BO, 6 April 1992.

Financial Action Task Force on Money Laundering. Report of 25 June 1992, Paris.

World Bank, *Peru: agricultural policies for economic efficiency*, Report No. 10605-PE, 11 September 1992.

World Bank, *Bolivia: updating economic memorandum*, Report No. 11123-BO, 8 October 1992.

Financial Action Task Force on Money Laundering. Report of 29 June 1993, Paris.

Financial Action Task Force On Money Laundering. Report of 16 June 1994, Paris.

Index